Out of Poverty

OUT OF POVERTY

COMPARATIVE POVERTY REDUCTION STRATEGIES IN EASTERN AND SOUTHERN AFRICA

Edited by
Flora L. Kessy & Arne Tostensen

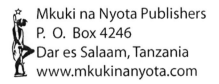 Mkuki na Nyota Publishers
P. O. Box 4246
Dar es Salaam, Tanzania
www.mkukinanyota.com

This book is published by:

Mkuki na Nyota Publishers Ltd
P. O. Box 4246
Dar es Salaam, Tanzania
Email: editorial.uhariri@mkukinanyota.com
Website: www.mkukinanyota.com

ISBN: 978-9987-08-006-9

TABLE OF CONTENTS

LISTS OF TABLES AND FIGURES

Chapter 8: Eastern & Southern Africa

LIST OF FIGURES

Chapter 2: Tanzania

Chapter 4: Zambia

Chapter 5: Botswana

LIST OF ABBREVIATIONS AND ACRONYMS

ABB	Activity-Based Budget
ACP	African Caribbean Pacific
AfDB	African Development Bank
AGOA	Africa Growth and Opportunity Act
AiA	Appropriation in Aid
AIDS	Acquired Immune Deficiency Syndrome
ALDEP	Arable Lands Development Programme
AMREF	African Medical and Research Foundation
ANC	Ante-natal Care
APEJ	Africa Policy E-Journal
APR	Annual Progress Report
ARVs	Anti-retroviral drugs
ASAL	Arid and Semi-Arid Lands
BAMB	Botswana Agricultural Marketing Board
BIDPA	Botswana Institute for Development Policy Analysis
BWP	Botswana Pula (currency)
CBI	Cross-Boarder Initiative
CBK	Coffee Board of Kenya
CBO	Community-Based Organisation
CBOH	Central Board of Health
CBS	Central Bureau of Statistics
CCM	Chama cha Mapinduzi
CEDA	Citizen Entrepreneurial Development Agency
CDF	Comprehensive Development Framework
COMESA	Common Market for Eastern and Southern Africa
CPI	Consumer Price Index
CSPR	Civil Society for Poverty Reduction
CSO	Civil Society Organisation
CSO	Central Statistical Office
DDCC	District Development Coordinating Committee
DDT	Dichloro-Diphenyl-Trichloroethane (pesticide)
DHS	Demographic and Health Survey
EAC	East African Community
EPR	Employment to Population Ratio
ERS	Economic Recovery Strategy for Wealth and Employment Creation
ESRF	Economic and Social Research Foundation
EU	European Union
FDI	Foreign Direct Investment
FHH	Female-Headed Household
FNDP	Fifth National Development Plan
FSP	Food Security Pack
G8	Group of Eight

GDP	Gross Domestic Product
GIDD	Gender in Development Division
GNP	Gross National Product
GOB	Government of Botswana
GRZ	Government of the Republic of Zambia
HDI	Human Development Index
HIPC	Highly Indebted Poor Countries
HIV	Human Immunodeficiency Virus
HPI	Human Poverty Index
IFI	International Financial Institution
IGAD	Inter-Governmental Authority on Development
ILO	International Labour Organization
IMCM	Improving Malaria Case Management
IMF	International Monetary Fund
IMG	Independent Monitoring Group
IOR-ARC	Indian Ocean Rim Association for Regional Cooperation
IPAR	Institute of Policy Analysis and Research
IP-ERS	Investment Programme for the Economic Recovery Strategy
I-PRSP	Interim Poverty Reduction Strategy Paper
IRHS	Integrated Rural Household Survey
IRS	Integrated Rural Survey
ITN	Insecticide-treated Net
JAST	Joint Assistance Strategy for Tanzania
JASZ	Joint Assistance Strategy for Zambia
KANU	Kenya African National Union
KENIFO	Kenya Information
KIPPRA	Kenya Institute for Public Policy Research and Analysis
KNBS	Kenya National Bureau of Statistics
KRDS	Kenya Rural Development Strategy
KTDA	Kenya Tea Development Authority
LCMS	Living Conditions Monitoring Survey
MAFF	Ministry of Agriculture, Food and Fisheries
MCDSS	Ministry of Community Development and Social Services
MDG	Millennium Development Goal
M&E	Monitoring and Evaluation
MED	Monitoring and Evaluation Directorate
MFDP	Ministry of Finance and Development Planning
MFI	Microfinance Institution
MFPED	Ministry of Finance, Planning and Economic Development
MKUKUTA	Mkakati wa Kukuza Uchumi na Kupunguza Umaskini Tanzania
MoE	Ministry of Education
MoFNP	Ministry of Finance and National Planning
MoH	Ministry of Health
MPER	Ministerial Public Expenditure Review

MSC	Microfinance Support Centre
MTCS	Medium-Term Competitive Strategy
MTCT	Mother-to-Child Transmission
MTEF	Medium Term Expenditure Framework
MW	Megawatt
NACA	National AIDS Coordinating Agency
NACC	National AIDS Control Council
NAD	Namibia Dollar
NAMPAADD	National Master Plan for Arable Agriculture and Dairy Development
NARC	National Rainbow Coalition
NCC	National Coordination Committee
NDP	National Development Plan
NEAP	National Environmental Action Plan
NEMA	National Environment Management Authority
NEPRU	Namibian Economic Policy Research Unit
NER	Net Enrolment Ratio
NESC	National Economic and Social Council
NGO	Non-Governmental Organisation
NHIES	National Household Income and Expenditure Survey
NIMES	National Integrated Monitoring and Evaluation System
Norad	Norwegian Agency for Development Cooperation
NPCS	National Planning Commission Secretariat
NPEP	National Poverty Eradication Plan
NPES	National Poverty Eradication Strategy
NPRAP	National Poverty Reduction Action Programme
NPRS	National Poverty Reduction Strategy
NPV	Net Present Value
NSGRP	National Strategy for Growth and Reduction of Poverty
NUSAF	Northern Uganda Social Action Fund
NWASCO	National Water Supply and Sanitation Council
ODA	Official Development Assistance
PAF	Poverty Action Fund
PAM	Programme against Malnutrition
PAP	Poverty Action Plan
PARMFOR	Participatory Methodologies Forum in Kenya
PARU	Poverty Analysis Research Unit
PDCC	Provincial Development Coordinating Committee
PEAP	Poverty Eradication Action Plan
PEM-AAP	Public Expenditure Management and Accountability Action Plan
PEMD	Planning and Economic Management Department
PER	Public Expenditure Review
PHC	Primary Health Care
PIP	Public Investment Programme
PLWHA	People Living With HIV and AIDS

PMA	Plan for Modernisation of Agriculture
PMMP	Poverty Monitoring Master Plan
PMES	Poverty Monitoring and Evaluation System
PMS	Poverty Monitoring System/Strategy
PMTCT	Prevention of Mother-to-Child Transmission
PPA	Participatory Poverty Assessment
PRGF	Poverty Reduction Growth Facility
PRS	Poverty Reduction Strategy
PRSP	Poverty Reduction Strategy Paper
PWAS	Public Welfare Assistance Scheme
RAD	Remote Area Dweller
RADP	Remote Area Development Programme
REPOA	Research on Poverty Alleviation
RSDP	Road Sector Development Programme
SACU	Southern African Customs Union
SADC	Southern African Development Community
SAG	Sector Advisory Group
SAP	Structural Adjustment Programme
SBAS	Strategic Budget Allocation System
SEAPREN	Southern and Eastern Africa Policy Research Network
SEP	Strategic Export Programme
SME	Small- and medium-sized enterprises
SMP	Staff Monitored Programme
STD	Sexually Transmitted Disease
TAS	Tanzania Assistance Strategy
TB	Tuberculosis
TCDD	Tanzania Coalition on Debt and Development
TDHS	Tanzania Demographic and Health Survey
THIS	Tanzania HIV and AIDS Indicators Survey
TNDP	Transitional National Development Plan
UBOS	Uganda Bureau of Statistics
UJAS	Uganda Joint Assistance Strategy
UN	United Nations
UNAIDS	Joint United Nations Programme on HIV/AIDS
UNDP	United Nations Development Programme
UPE	Universal Primary Education
URT	United Republic of Tanzania
USA	United States of America
USAID	United States Agency for International Development
USD	United States Dollar
VAT	Value Added Tax
VPO	Vice President's Office
WB	World Bank
WMS	Welfare Monitoring Survey

WRAP	Water Resources Action Programme
WSSD	World Summit for Social Development
WTO	World Trade Organization
ZAWA	Zambia Wildlife Authority
ZFAP	Zambia Forestry Action Plan
ZMK	Zambia Kwacha (currency)

ACKNOWLEDGEMENTS

This book has been produced under the auspices of the Southern and Eastern Africa Policy Research Network (SEAPREN) which comprises a number of policy research institutes in these two sub-regions of Africa. The book emanates from one of the sub-projects under the SEAPREN umbrella that was coordinated by the Economic and Social Research Foundation (ESRF) in Dar es Salaam. The activities of the network have been supported by the Norwegian Agency for Development Cooperation (Norad) through a generous financial grant. Notwithstanding financial sponsorship and overall direction, neither Norad nor the SEAPREN Steering Committee has in any way attempted to influence the analyses and assessments made in the various chapters. The usual disclaimer applies: no inference, viewpoint or assessment should be interpreted to reflect the views of the SEAPREN Steering Committee or the policies of Norad. The authors are themselves responsible for the substance of their contributions. It is hoped, however, that the book will feed into the ongoing debate regarding poverty reduction policies and practices in the sub-regions, as well as contribute to improving existing strategies to reduce poverty.

All contributors are grateful to the institutions to which they are affiliated for making research time available to write their chapters and to participate in successive workshops where their drafts were discussed and critiqued. Thanks are also owed to Richard Moorsom for competent language and copy-editing, to Inger Nygaard for formatting the chapters, and to Margaret Binns who compiled the index which vastly enhanced the usefulness of the book to the readers.

Finally, but not least, we would like to thank our publisher *Mkuki na Nyota* and its staff, Deogratias Simba and Fraternus Lyimo, whose forthcoming attitude and patience in the face of delays were highly appreciated.

Flora L. Kessy
Arne Tostensen
Dar es Salaam and Bergen,
May 2008

Aiko, Rose is a macroeconomist with the Swiss Cooperation Office in Tanzania. She holds a Master degree in economics from the University of Dar es Salaam, Tanzania. Ms. Aiko has researched and published on macroeconomic policy issues, with a particular focus on economic reforms and anti-poverty policies. She has also been involved in a number of consultancy assignments on the socio-economic impacts of HIV and AIDS. Before joining the Swiss Cooperation Office, Ms. Aiko worked with the Bank of Tanzania (2004–2007) and the Economic and Social Research Foundation (ESRF) (2002–2004). E-mail: rose.aiko@gmail.com or lisa2002tz@yahoo.com

Elepu, Gabriel is a Lecturer in the Department of Agricultural Economics and Agribusiness, Makerere University, Kampala, Uganda. He holds a PhD degree in Agricultural and Consumer Economics with an emphasis in agribusiness management from University of Illinois at Urbana-Champaign, USA. His research and consultancy work include regoverning markets, farm-agribusiness linkages, producer and consumer behaviour, value chain analysis, and poverty. Email: elepu@agric.mak.ac.ug

Kalinda, Thomson is a Lecturer and currently serves as Head of Department of the Department of Agricultural Economics & Extension Education at the University of Zambia (UNZA), Lusaka. He obtained his PhD in Rural Studies from the University of Guelph in Canada. Prior to joining UNZA, Dr. Kalinda worked as an agricultural economist in the Planning Division of the Ministry of Agriculture. He has wide experience as a researcher and consultant both for the Zambian government and international organisations in a wide range of studies related to project planning; project impact assessments; poverty and food security. He has published numerous refereed journal articles and commissioned studies. His current research interests include rural livelihood strategies and poverty assessments; local indigenous knowledge systems; technology adoption; and the impact of HIV and AIDS on rural communities in Zambia. E-mail: htkalinda@yahoo.com

Kerapeletswe, Charity K. is the Managing Director of the National Food Technology Research Centre (NFTRC) in Kanye, Botswana and holds a PhD in environmental economics from the University of York, United Kingdom. Her work experience spans policy research on economic and social issues such as poverty and livelihoods, agricultural development, environmental management and biodiversity conservation, property rights, gender, impact assessment, and the socio-economic effects of HIV and AIDS. Dr. Kerapeletswe has published in the Journal of Sustainable Development in Africa; International Affairs Journal; Environment and Development Economics Journal. Prior to joining NFTRC, Dr. Kerapeletswe worked for Botswana Institute for Development Policy Analysis (BIDPA) as a Senior Research Fellow. Previously, she worked for the Rural Industries Innovation Centre as Chief Extension Officer and between 1990 and 1996 for the Ministry of Agriculture as an agricultural economist where she was responsible for monitoring and evaluation of development programmes, some of which geared towards poverty reduction. She started her career working for the Botswana National Development Bank as a project officer. Dr. Kerapeletswe also serves as an advisor in various national committees and boards. Email: charike@naftec.org

Kessy, Flora Lucas is a Senior Social Research Scientist at the Ifakara Health Research and Development Centre (IHRDC), holds a PhD in Agricultural and Consumer Economics with a major in Household and Consumer Economics and a minor in Women and Gender in Global Perspective from University of Illinois at Urbana Champaign, USA. She has researched and published on issues related to poverty, gender and development, and reproductive health in particular family planning and HIV and AIDS. Dr. Kessy has also been involved in several consultancy activities related to poverty, HIV and AIDS, resource tracking and budget analysis, and project evaluation. She has published articles in *Tanzania Journal of Development Studies, American Behavioral Scientist Journal, Uongozi Journal, Tanzania Journal of Population Studies and Development,* and *Journal of Biosocial Science.* Prior to joining IHRDC, Dr. Kessy was a Senior Research Fellow at the Economic and Social Research Foundation (ESRF) (2002–2006), and a Lecturer at Sokoine University of Agriculture, Development Studies Institute (1992–2001). Email: fkessy@gmail.com or fkessy@ihrdc.or.tz

Oyugi, Lineth Nyaboke is an Assistant Research Fellow in the macroeconomics programme at the Institute of Policy Analysis and Research (IPAR), Nairobi, Kenya. She holds MA (Economics) and BA (Hons) degrees from the University of Nairobi. Prior to her current appointment at IPAR, Ms. Oyugi worked as an economist/statistician in the Ministry of Planning and National Development, Macroeconomics Department and in the Ministry of Finance, Economic Secretary's Office. Ms. Oyugi has researched and published on poverty; planning and budgeting; policy and the role of institutions, and fiscal decentralisation. Her areas of interest include poverty and vulnerability, public policy, economic reforms, planning and budgeting, debt, and monitoring and evaluation. Email: loyugi@ipar.or.ke or nyabokemoraa@yahoo.co.uk

Schade, Klaus is Acting Director at the Namibian Economic Policy Research Unit (NEPRU) in Windhoek, Namibia. He has specialised on macroeconomic and fiscal issues, but has also worked on regional integration and trade as well as poverty and HIV and AIDS. He is currently leading a project on the construction of a Social Accounting Matrix for Namibia. Major recently completed projects include a Public Expenditure Tracking Survey for the health and education sectors in Namibia; a study on domestic revenue mobilisation in the context of regional integration; deepening integration in SADC; macroeconomic policies and their impacts; as well as a survey on perceptions about regional integration. He has been co-editor of the *Monitoring Regional Integration in Southern Africa Yearbook since 2006 and of Regional Integration in Southern Africa – Vol. 12: Macroeconomic policies and social impacts – A comparative analysis of 10 country studies and surveys.* Email: Klaus.Schade@nepru.org.na

Tostensen, Arne is a Senior Researcher at the Chr. Michelsen Institute, Bergen, Norway, where he has been employed since 1985 – between 1988 and 1994 as director. He holds a PhD in sociology from the University of Bergen and has been involved in research on governance and political institutions in Eastern and Southern Africa, particularly in Kenya, Malawi, Tanzania and Uganda. Poverty and poverty reduction strategies, labour migration, and human rights are among his other research interests. Furthermore, he has conducted research on regional organisations such as the Southern African Development Community (SADC) and the East African Community (EAC). He has published and edited several books on the above topics and published widely in journals and anthologies. Apart from his research, Dr. Tostensen has taken part in a large number of consultancies. E-mail: arne.tostensen@cmi.no

CHAPTER 1

POVERTY REDUCTION IN EASTERN AND SOUTHERN AFRICA: AN INTRODUCTION

Arne Tostensen and Flora Kessy

1.1 INTRODUCTION

Although poverty reduction has been a long-standing concern of most African countries since independence, it has gradually moved up the priority order to assume the top place since the turn of the millennium. This focus has not only been evident at national levels in the countries concerned but also in the policies of the international donor community. On the strength of their size, research capacity, and financial muscle the twin International Finance Institutions (IFIs) – the World Bank and the International Monetary Fund (IMF), also referred to as the Bretton Woods institutions – have been near hegemonic in designing policies and setting the stage for the international development community at large.

From their establishment in the mid-1940s, the mandates of the two Bretton Woods institutions were different, though complementary. The IMF was designed to regulate an international monetary order based on the members' commitment to freely convertible currency transaction and orderly exchange arrangements. This meant involvement in monetary management and short-term stabilisation of the macro-economic balances of its members' economies. The Bank's remit, on the other hand, was to contribute to long-term economic growth and sustainable development, mainly through financing large-scale infrastructure projects. This strict division of labour was maintained by and large until the mid-1980s. Since then, there has been a trend towards a convergence of mandates, albeit not yet a complete one.

In the early 1970s, the then World Bank President, Robert S. McNamara, put poverty reduction firmly on the Bank's agenda: 'We should strive to eradicate absolute poverty by the end of this century. That means in practice the elimination of malnutrition and illiteracy, the reduction of infant mortality, and the raising of life-expectancy standards to those of the developed nations' (McNamara 1973: 27).

At least at the rhetorical level the Bank's commitment to poverty reduction culminated more than two decades later in *World Development Report 2000/2001: Attacking Poverty*. In the preface to this report former World Bank President, James D. Wolfensohn, made the following all-out statement: 'We at the Bank have made it our mission to fight poverty with passion and professionalism, putting it at the centre of all the work we do' (World Bank 2000: v). The same report goes some way towards conceptualising poverty. Attention is drawn to three basic dimensions: deprivation, vulnerability, and powerlessness. Being poor means being deprived of basic needs such as food, shelter, education, and health. Living at the margin also makes the poor particularly vulnerable to adverse shocks, both natural disasters and human-made calamities. A third dimension of being poor is powerlessness: the poor are ill equipped to alter the social relations that made them poor in the first instance.

How poverty is conceptualised bears decisively on the formulation of poverty-reducing strategies. Above all, analyses of causality are critical inputs to policies designed to help the poor out of their predicament. Since it is recognised that poverty is complex and multi-faceted, it follows that strategies pointing the way out of poverty must be comprehensive and multi-pronged. At a general level, the World Bank (2000: 37–41) has formulated a three-pronged strategy:

- promoting opportunity,
- facilitating empowerment,
- enhancing security.

Promoting opportunity is associated with economic growth and involves creating new jobs, establishing credit facilities and expanding markets; and building physical and social infrastructure in terms of roads, electricity, water supply, sanitation, schools and health facilities. This is in itself banal and totally unsurprising coming from a banking institution. It is more surprising that the Bank is also concerned with the pattern and quality of economic growth, especially its distributive effects. In fact, the Bank asserts that greater equity is necessary and that action by the state is required to support the build-up of human, land and infrastructural assets that poor people can own or have access to.

Facilitating empowerment implicitly recognises that poverty reflects unequal social and power relations. Powerlessness is the hallmark of poverty. Although pointing to the intrinsically political nature of empowerment, the Bank shies away from its full implication: political struggle. Instead, the Bank speaks of collaboration among poor people, the middle class and other groups in society. It is not acknowledged that empowerment of the poor must mean the disempowerment of the non-poor – in relative terms – since the power concept is a relational one. Thus, poverty reduction entails changing social and power relations – often in fundamental ways. Glossing over this fact is perhaps attributable to the constraints imposed by the Articles of Agreement, and makes the strategy flawed.

Enhancing security requires national action to mitigate the consequences of adverse shocks for the poor. This can be done through various social security schemes, specific emergency programmes, building up buffer stocks, and diversifying household income sources.

As always, the proof of the pudding is in the eating. In assessing the resultant poverty reduction strategies it might be useful to apply the hierarchy of interventions suggested by Green (1994):

- *Primary redistribution*, that is, enabling poor households to produce and earn more, in order for them to be able to fend for themselves on a sustainable basis rather than being dependent perpetually on relief and hand-outs. This is considered the core of an effective poverty-reducing strategy whose ultimate objective is the eradication of poverty altogether, however distant the achievement of that objective may seem.
- *Secondary redistribution*, that is, providing basic health services, safe water, nutrition, education, and extension services to poor households to raise their present and future productive capacities.
- *Tertiary redistribution*, that is, building and reinforcing safety nets of cash or kind (particularly food) transfers to alleviate consumption shortfalls due to conjunctural shocks such as droughts, floods or other natural or man-made calamities (e.g. civil strife and war).

In the above schema primary redistribution is akin to the World Bank's notions about opportunities, and especially empowerment. Secondary redistribution, on the other hand, is coupled primarily to opportunities but less to empowerment. Finally, tertiary redistribution is almost synonymous with enhancing security. In the past, the donor community has been criticised for restricting itself to secondary and tertiary redistribution. Since then, there has been a development, however, in the donors' mode of thinking. To include empowerment as a key element in poverty reduction strategies is a step forward towards addressing primary redistribution. Likewise, the World Bank is talking about 'negotiated land reform', which potentially could alter rural power relations dramatically in favour of the poor and contribute substantially towards reducing poverty. And the pendulum seems to have swung from the erstwhile extreme liberalism towards state intervention in selected fields.

Although a broad consensus of sorts has been arrived at regarding the general precepts of anti-poverty policies, it is acknowledged that there is no 'quick fix' to the poverty problem, or a universal blueprint that will fit all situations. At the national and local levels, each country needs to design its own package of anti-poverty policies, tailored to the circumstances at hand and reflecting national priorities. A major step towards that end was the Heavily Indebted Poor Countries (HIPC) Initiative.

1.2 The HIPC Initiative

The first HIPC Initiative was launched in 1996, and its successor, the Enhanced HIPC Initiative, in 1999 (see, for details, Birdsall et al. 2002; Teunissen and Akkerman 2004). They form laudable attempts at large-scale debt cancellation rather than palliatives such as debt rescheduling and interest rate reduction. They are focused on the cancellation of debts owed to the IFIs and the regional development banks because a large proportion of the HIPC's debts are owed to these multilateral institutions. But bilateral and commercial creditors also provide debt relief through this scheme.

The technical design of the original HIPC Initiative as conceived by IMF and World Bank staff made eligibility conditional on the maintenance of macro-economic stability under IMF-approved programmes for at least 6 years – referred to as the 'decision point' – and receipt of a permanent reduction in their official debt stocks only after another 3 years of a satisfactory policy environment to reach the 'completion point'. These conditions proved too stringent for most HIPCs. The eligibility criteria under the enhanced HIPC scheme were more lenient, therefore, and included the following:

- low per capita income;
- demonstrated good reform performance;
- ratio of net present value of debt to exports exceeding 150%;
- ratio of net present value of debt to tax revenue exceeding 250% for open economies (i.e. minimum 30% exports to GNP ratio) with substantial tax revenue (i.e. minimum 15% of GNP).

Its broader coverage and softer conditions were, however, not the only entirely new elements in the enhanced HIPC concept. Equally important was the linkage of debt cancellation to poverty reduction. To qualify for debt relief under the Enhanced HIPC Initiative, a country is required to prepare a wide-ranging Poverty Reduction Strategy Paper (PRSP) that demonstrates its intention to use the freed resources for poverty-reducing purposes. Not only must the PRSP document chart the course towards poverty reduction, its preparation should also involve broad participation by civil society and other domestic stakeholders. Such an inclusive process is meant to create 'national ownership' of the strategy and promote political legitimacy among the citizenry. The participatory preparation of the PRSP is also intended to add instrumentality and facilitate its effective implementation.

Eligible countries begin receiving debt service relief once the decision point has been reached, that is, once the *ex ante* conditions are fulfilled in terms of macro-economic track record and the approval of the PRSP by the boards of the IMF and the World Bank. The permanent debt stock reductions are delayed until the completion point once the *ex post* conditions have been met in terms of process, performance benchmarks and the use of HIPC resources.

Most African states are poor and heavily indebted, the majority of which have embarked on PRSPs as an avenue towards poverty reduction with financial assistance from the Bank and the IMF. However, not all African countries are both poor and heavily indebted. Some have graduated to middle-income status owing to windfall revenue or consistently sound policies over many years. As a result, they are not eligible for debt relief under the HIPC Initiative. Even so, having a comparatively high GDP per capita on average does not mean that poverty is non-existent within the borders of non-HIPC countries. In most African countries a sizable section of their populations can be classified as poor or extremely poor. Therefore, almost without exception all African countries have designed strategies to address their respective poverty problems. But they have not all done it in the same way. How are they different or similar? Before delving into that question, some space must be devoted to the PRSP design template.

1.3 DESIGNING A PRSP

The World Bank has published a two-volume *Sourcebook on Poverty Reduction Strategies* of altogether 1252 pages, prepared mainly by Bank staff. The preface to these volumes states that they reflect the thinking and practices associated with the Comprehensive Development Framework, the *World Development Report 2000/2001: Attacking Poverty*, as well as experiences and best practices from elsewhere. It asserts that the *Sourcebook* is not prescriptive and should not be taken as a recipe for a blueprint. Notwithstanding these disclaimers, the *Sourcebook* can be considered as the terms of reference for the preparation of PRSPs. It is replete with such phrases as 'a PRSP is expected to', which certainly suggest a prescriptive streak. The fact that the *Sourcebook* is extremely detailed reinforces its prescriptive nature. The conditionality inherent in the PRSP exercise under the HIPC facility is underscored by the fact that the respective boards of the Bank and the IMF must approve the resultant PRSP before funds can be released. It is justified, therefore, that we consider the *Sourcebook* as the effective terms of reference for the PRSPs.

Simply put, a PRSP is a recipe for reducing poverty in heavily indebted low-income countries that are eligible for debt relief under the HIPC Initiative. The PRSPs are meant to show how the funds released or freed will be spent with a view to reducing poverty in the countries concerned. Some 70 low-income countries are at various stages of a PRSP process, the great majority of them in Africa.

Certain principles underlie the PRSP processes, which should be (Klugman 2002: 3 in vol. 1):

- country-driven and -owned, predicated on broad-based participatory processes for formulation, and on outcome-based progress monitoring;
- results-orientated, focusing on outcomes that would benefit the poor;
- comprehensive in scope, recognising the multi-dimensional nature of the causes of poverty and measures to redress it;
- partnership-orientated, providing a basis for the active and co-ordinated participation of development partners (bilateral, multilateral and non-governmental);
- based on a medium- and long-term perspective for poverty reduction, recognising that sustained poverty reduction cannot be achieved overnight.

The *Sourcebook* devotes an entire chapter to participation in an operational sense (Klugman 2002: Chapter 7 in vol. 1). The participatory process is seen as a method for stakeholders to influence and share control over priority setting, policy-making, resource allocation, implementation, and monitoring. The stakeholders include civil society organisations, ministries and parliaments. The mass media play a special role in contributing to the transparency of the process by way of websites, newspapers, radio and TV programmes, etc. The role of Bank and IMF staff, on the other hand, is neither to drive the participation process nor to co-ordinate it, but rather to facilitate it.

Similar to participation, an entire chapter is devoted to governance (Klugman 2002: Chapter 8 in vol. 1). Governance is broadly defined as the exercise of power through a country's economic, social, and political institutions. Organisational rules and routines, formal laws and informal practices inform these institutions and, in turn, they shape the incentive structure for policy-makers, overseers and providers of public services. Key elements of good governance are transparency and accountability at all levels. It is asserted that the poor are likely to suffer most from bad governance. Hence, empowering the poor through participation is a means of enhancing governance.

Macroeconomic and trade issues are given prominence in Chapters 12–13 in the second volume (Klugman 2002). Separate chapters (21–22 and 24–25 in vol. 2) are also devoted to energy; transport; information and communication technologies; and mining. Real sectors such as agriculture and manufacturing are subsumed under other chapters. The social sectors that impinge directly on the plight of the poor are dealt with in separate chapters: health, nutrition and population; social protection; water and sanitation; and education (Klugman 2002: Chapters 17–19 and 23 in vol. 2). Cross-cutting issues such as community-driven development, gender, and the environment are addressed in Chapters 9–11 of volume 1. Key issues related to measurement, monitoring, and evaluation are treated in several introductory chapters. In sum, it is evident that the *Sourcebook* is comprehensive and leaves little to chance. The PRSP approach to poverty reduction has stimulated much debate and controversy. Some scholars have provided assessments of PRS experiences in Africa to date that are both hopeful and realistic (see Booth 2003; Wangwe 2001).

Although the precepts contained in the *Sourcebook* do not apply to non-HIPC strategies, the question arises as to whether they nevertheless have exerted some influence on home-grown variants, and, if so, to what extent.

1.4 POVERTY REDUCTION STRATEGIES IN EASTERN AND SOUTHERN AFRICA

This book covers both HIPCs and non-HIPCs in Eastern and Southern Africa. The former have charted PRSPs under the HIPC terms of reference as set out in the *Sourcebook*, whereas the latter have produced home-grown strategies independently of the HIPC regime. How have they differently or similarly gone about the task of charting their respective strategies? Interesting research issues emerge as to their comparison. Notwithstanding the fact that all of these strategies are aimed at reducing poverty, they may be based on different principles, have different implementation plans, and may hence result in different outcomes. What concepts and analyses have underpinned their efforts? Is the PRSP concept so pervasive by now that it informs all poverty reduction endeavours? Or have the countries that have not been subjected to HIPC conditionality found alternative ways of redressing poverty through home-grown policy designs?

This book aims at tracing and mapping the poverty reduction policies adopted by six countries since the mid-1990s with a view to highlighting differences and similarities. The first three are HIPCs, comprising Tanzania, Uganda, and Zambia, while the last three are non-HIPCs, comprising Botswana, Kenya, and Namibia. It is of particular interest to compare these two categories to ascertain whether they differ substantially or largely converge. However, there may turn out to be differences even within each of the two groups of countries. Such an evaluative comparison yields valuable insights and helps to identify 'best practices' in poverty reduction policies. In addition, the role of regional groupings in creating policy environments conducive for poverty reduction efforts at the country level is explored.

Specifically, the study attempts to review the different anti-poverty strategies adopted by the selected HIPCs and non-HIPCs; to assess the implementation arrangements in terms of priority, linkages to budgets, and monitoring and evaluation systems; to document the main economic, social and political factors influencing poverty generation or reduction since the mid-1990s; and finally, to review the poverty indicators and changes in the state of poverty over the same period.

Thus, to produce a comparative foundation the research has sought to answer the following research questions:

- Do the PRSPs differ in orientation and substance from the home-grown strategies adopted by the countries not eligible under the HIPC initiative?
- If the PRSPs differ from home-grown strategies, how can that be explained and what social forces have asserted themselves to produce those differences?
- If the PRSPs and the home-grown strategies are largely the same in orientation and substance, can that be explained in terms of the emergence of a broad international consensus on the precepts of poverty reduction efforts, regardless of country-specific circumstances?
- Do key policy-makers and technocrats have a full appreciation of the issues involved and how do they prioritise?
- Has the poverty situation in these countries deteriorated in terms of depth and prevalence (i.e. trends in the state of poverty in these countries over time)?
- What are the implementation arrangements in terms of time schedules, milestones, linkages to budgets, monitoring and evaluation?
- What role do regional groupings play in creating policy environments conducive to

poverty reduction efforts at the country level, for example, the East Africa Community, the Southern Africa Development Community and others?

1.5 APPROACH, METHODOLOGY AND IMPLEMENTATION

This study draws on the available literature and secondary sources of data, supplemented by primary data collected through semi-structured qualitative interviews with key policy-makers and other stakeholders. The project has been implemented in seven phases:

Phase 1: Literature survey and analysis

During this phase a compilation was made of empirical material relating to poverty policies in the six countries. In addition, general literature of a theoretical or conceptual nature reflecting the 'state of the art' on poverty and economic development was collected for the purpose of underpinning the empirical comparative analyses.

Phase 2: Analysis of economic and social trends affecting the poverty situation

A brief account of emerging economic and social trends was made for each of the countries. This was done on the basis of the countries' development plans and visions, statistical data, monitoring reports, etc. and on macroeconomic projections, taking into account relevant external economic factors.

Phase 3: Impact assessment of different poverty reduction strategies

Although not undertaking comprehensive impact studies, the country case studies attempted to gauge the impact of different strategies on reducing poverty by drawing on available Household Budget Surveys, Poverty Monitoring Reports and Participatory Poverty Assessment Reports, wherever available. Using these secondary data sources, the current state of poverty and trends over time were assessed using income and non-income poverty indicators such as education, health and water.

Phase 4: Interviews with key policy-makers and other stakeholders

An interview round was conducted aiming at soliciting policy-makers' views of achievements in poverty reduction to date and the challenges ahead. The researchers undertook in-depth interviews based on a semi-structured interview guide. Interviewees comprised the political and administrative heads of ministries of finance and planning as well as the larger line ministries, parliamentarians and leading politicians in general, representatives of important civil society organisations, members of academia, and donors, including the IFIs.

Phase 5: Country case reports

The analyses undertaken in phases 1–3 together with the results of the interviews with policy-makers formed the basis of six country case study reports. Each report contains a poverty profile as it has evolved over time, the evolution of poverty reduction strategies, an assessment of achievements, and a review of future problems and prospects.

Phase 6: Comparative synthesis report

Based on the six country case studies a comparative synthesis report was compiled. Differences and similarities between the above-mentioned groups of HIPC and non-HIPC countries are highlighted. Differences within those categories are also distinguished. In conclusion, some policy recommendations are made.

Phase 7: Dissemination of findings

The findings were presented to policy-makers at a dissemination conference in Windhoek on 5–6 July 2007. On that occasion the researchers met with policy-makers from Eastern and Southern Africa to exchange views and insights. The publication of this book is also an important means of dissemination.

Project implementation

The project was implemented under the auspices of the Southern and Eastern African Policy Research Network (SEAPREN). This endeavour has been funded by the Norwegian Agency for Development Cooperation. Within the SEAPREN network the Economic and Social Research Foundation (ESRF) in Dar es Salaam was designated the lead institution for this sub-project on Comparative Poverty Reduction Strategies and its general coordinator. Flora Kessy of the ESRF (currently at Ifakara Health Research and Development Centre) has acted as coordinator for the SEAPREN institutes and Arne Tostensen on behalf of the Chr. Michelsen Institute.

A regional methodological workshop was held in Dar es Salaam in June 2004 by the SEAPREN researchers to decide on a common approach and interview guides for the in-depth interviews with policy-makers and other stakeholders. A second workshop was organised in Dar es Salaam in October 2006 to review and critique the country case studies with a view to improving them, and to plan the remainder of the project period. Finally, the six country case studies and a preliminary version of the comparative conclusion were presented at a workshop in Windhoek on 5 July 2007. This book is the tangible output of the project.

1.6 STRUCTURE OF THE BOOK

The subsequent chapters of the book cover the HIPC and non-HIPC categories. The HIPC category comprises Tanzania, Uganda, and Zambia, whereas the non-HIPC group covers Botswana, Kenya, and Namibia. All these country case studies can be read independently of each other. However, they form the prelude and foundation of the concluding chapter, which compares the two categories of PRSPs and home-grown strategies. The comparative chapter also fleshes out differences and similarities within the two categories.

REFERENCES

Birdsall, N., J. Williamson and B. Deese (2002), *Delivering on Debt Relief: From IMF Gold to a New Aid Architecture*, Washington D.C.: Institute for International Economics.

Booth, D. (ed.) (2003), *Fighting Poverty in Africa: Are PRSPs Making a Difference?* London: Overseas Development Institute.

Green, R. H. (1984), 'Production by Poor People', *IDS Bulletin*, Vol. 25, No. 3, pp. 40–50.

Klugman, J. (ed.) (2002), *A Sourcebook for Poverty Reduction Strategies. Volume 1: Core Techniques and Cross-Cutting Issues; Volume 2: Macroeconomic and Sectoral Approaches*, Washington D.C.: World Bank.

McNamara, R. S. (1973), *Address to the Board of Governors*, Nairobi: International Bank for Reconstruction and Development.

Teunissen, J. J. and A. Akkerman (eds.) (2004), *HIPC Debt Relief: Myths and Reality*, The Hague: Forum on Debt and Development (FONDAD).

Wangwe, S. (2001), 'Poverty Reduction Strategy Paper: Experiences and Lessons from Tanzania', Paper Presented at the Meeting of the ECA-Sponsored PRSP Learning Group for African Countries, Addis Ababa, 5–6 November 2001.

World Bank (2000), *World Development Report 2000/2001: Attacking Poverty*, Oxford: Oxford University Press.

CHAPTER 2

THE EVOLUTION OF POVERTY REDUCTION STRATEGIES IN TANZANIA

Flora Kessy and Rose Aiko

2.1 INTRODUCTION

Tanzania is located in East Africa with a total area of 945,000 km^2 and comprises a union between Tanganyika (Tanzania mainland) and Zanzibar. Administratively, Tanzania mainland is divided into 21 administrative regions with 124 administrative councils. According to the Tanzania Population and Housing Census of 2002, the country's population is estimated at 34.5 million, of whom about half are youth and children. The population of mainland Tanzania is mainly rural (77%), with slight variations in gender composition (United Republic of Tanzania [URT] 2003a).

Poverty reduction has been at the centre stage of development policy in Tanzania since the early 1960s. The first major commitment to poverty reduction was expressed in the first 5-year plan launched in 1964. In the following years, the government adopted a number of initiatives to ensure an all-inclusive development process through various social policies, including the Arusha Declaration of 1967. A key objective was to ensure that basic social services were available equitably to all members of society. Great strides were made in some sectors, such as education and health. However, with time, a gap emerged between policy and implementation due to resource shortfalls which constrained further progress in social indicators. Structural rigidities in the economy compounded the problem that towards the late 1970s Tanzania was in the midst of economic crisis and stagnation. Hence, the government encountered difficulties in financing existing social services while declining incomes further undermined the living standards of the poor.

Various efforts to revamp the economy through home-grown programmes continued throughout the early 1980s but with limited overall impact either on relieving the declining trend in social indicators or on achieving macroeconomic stability (Bigsten et al. 2000; Msambichaka et al. 1995). With the adoption of structural adjustment programmes (SAPs) under the aegis of the World Bank and the International Monetary Fund in 1985, Tanzania became preoccupied with the urgent need to restore macroeconomic stability (low and stable inflation rate, a realistic exchange rate, reducing fiscal deficit, improving growth performance, and improving aid effectiveness). In the process, public expenditures were slashed, causing the quality of most social services to deteriorate further due to lack of funding. Thus, while macroeconomic stability improved, similar achievements were not registered in social services and the well-being of the people. The quality of life continued to deteriorate and concerns mounted over the downward trend in social indicators.

As economic conditions and macroeconomic stability started improving in the mid-1990s, the government was once again able to deepen its focus on poverty reduction by articulating this priority in various national policy and strategy documents that would form the basis for future efforts to promote broad-based growth as a contribution to poverty reduction. The policy documents included the National Poverty Eradication Strategy (NPES 1998), the Joint (Government and Development Partners) Tanzania Assistance Strategy (TAS), and the country development Vision 2025 (1999). In 2000, the government developed the first generation Poverty Reduction Strategy Paper (PRSP) as its medium-term strategy for poverty reduction, building on the longer-term strategies outlined in the NPES and Vision 2025. The PRSP also underpinned Tanzania's qualification for Highly Indebted Poor Countries (HIPC) debt relief.

The implementation of the first generation PRSP was concluded in 2003/04, after which the government prepared a second generation PRS: the National Strategy for Growth and Reduction of Poverty (NSGRP), popularly known by its Kiswahili acronym MKUKUTA, which runs for the 2005–2010 period (URT 2005a). The major difference between the first generation PRSP and the NSGRP is that while the former focused on priority sectors likely to have strong impacts and contributions to poverty reduction, the latter adopts an outcome-based approach. The idea is that for broad-based success, linkages across sectors have to be fostered to ensure improvement of sectoral contributions to a common outcome: poverty reduction. The three main outcomes in the NSGRP are growth and reduction of income poverty; improvement in the quality of life and social well-being; and good governance and accountability. Both strategies, however, give considerable weight to cross-cutting issues such as HIV and AIDS, gender, environmental protection and conservation, and the role of good governance and accountability in fast progress towards poverty reduction.

This chapter traces the underpinnings of the poverty reduction strategy in Tanzania and assesses progress so far. The remaining part of the chapter is organised as follows. Section 2.2 explores the determinants of poverty in Tanzania, while Section 2.3 examines progress in poverty reduction. Section 2.4 looks at the guiding principles of the PRS by examining the policy formulation process; the appreciation of issues in the PRSP by policy-makers and technocrats; the implementation arrangements, including monitoring framework and linkage to the budget; and regional arrangements in shaping the path of poverty reduction efforts. The last section concludes the chapter.

2.2 Determinants of Poverty

Poverty is acknowledged to be a multidimensional phenomenon and for this reason effective measures to address it require conceptualising it not only as a lack of income or shortfall in the expenditure required to achieve a certain minimally acceptable living standard, but also as a lack of capabilities that individuals require in order to live meaningful and valued lives in their societies. Effective measures are thus those which are geared at reducing human poverty so as to create a society with people who are well physically, psychologically and in other ways, and who live in an accepting society, that is, without fear of social exclusion.

Such a society is predicated on access to food and other basic amenities, on access to essential services, such as basic health and education, and on access to care and protection from abuse, especially for children, young women and men as well as other particularly vulnerable people (UNDP 2002). Underlying these is access to income and assets, access to information, knowledge and development of skills, and participation in decision-making, which can be treated as means to the end – reduction of poverty.

Poverty in Tanzania is characterised by low income and expenditure, high mortality and morbidity, poor nutritional status, low-educational attainment, vulnerability to external shocks, and exclusion from economic, social and political processes. Though poverty is particularly widespread in the rural areas, there are significant regional differences in levels of poverty and in the relative importance of different aspects of poverty. Those particularly at risk are young children and youth, the very old, women, those in large households and those involved in subsistence agriculture, livestock production and small-scale fishing. While some progress has been made in the fight against poverty since independence, poverty remains a persistent problem in Tanzania.

Widespread poverty in rural areas is largely explained by low productivity, which is exacerbated by recurring drought, as agriculture is mostly rain-fed. In addition, post-harvest losses are considerable. Other contributing factors include inadequate access to inputs and the low level of technology used in agricultural production, where most farmers rely on hand hoe cultivation. Access to credit for smallholders and small-scale fishermen is also limited. Another important underlying cause is the low level of education and skill among the youth, which limits their potential. The formal education system does not sufficiently equip young people with skills that respond to market requirements and does not prepare them for self-employment. The poor road infrastructure also continues to be a major obstacle to agricultural growth as it limits the access of farmers and fishermen to markets and therefore acts as a disincentive for investment in higher productivity.

Poverty is also caused by high levels of unemployment and underemployment, which limit people's ability to acquire an adequate income. The rate of growth of the national economy has not been high enough to generate the number of jobs required. The economy is heavily dependent on agriculture, which provides employment for nearly 80% of the national labour force. However, the sector is highly labour-intensive, and is made up predominantly of small-scale farmers. A high rate of rural-to-urban migration also prevails, with most migrants falling under the age of 30 years. The number of new entrants to the labour force is estimated at around 650,000 annually, which compares unfavourably with the less than 40,000 new jobs that are created in the formal sector each year. The 2003 Poverty and Human Development Report estimates the unemployment rate at 12.9% but with underemployment in both rural and urban areas the unemployment situation may be more serious than the figures reveal (URT 2003b).

Lack of a comprehensive social security system to protect incomes represents another threat of vulnerability and reduces the effectiveness of efforts to reduce poverty. Formal sector coverage is very small and although there have been various reforms to improve the social security arrangements in the country, there is to date no organised social security system to take care of those working in the informal sector. With various socio-economic and demographic changes in the economy, traditional systems of social protection have also been greatly weakened.

2.3 ECONOMIC GROWTH AND POVERTY

Sound economic management, promotion of sustainable and broad-based growth, improving food availability and access, reducing income poverty of both men and women in rural and urban areas, and provision of reliable and affordable energy to consumers are specific goals, the attainment of which is being monitored under the NSGRP to assess progress in achievement of the government objective of achieving broad-based growth and a reduction of income poverty. Tanzania's record in sustaining macroeconomic stability has been impressive over the last decade, although significant challenges still remain with respect to exchange rate stability and a persistently growing current account deficit in the last 5 years. GDP growth performance has been impressive save for the anticipated decline in the growth rate in 2006 caused by protracted drought, leading to a food shortage and partly fuelling an energy supply crisis that has been exacerbated by surging world market prices of oil. Thus, after steadily rising from an average of 4.1% in the period 1996–2000 to 6.8% in 2005, GDP growth slowed down to 5.9% in 2006. The effects of drought also pushed the inflation rate up again to an average of 6.3% after having been kept below 5% since 2002 after averaging 12.5% in the period 1996–2000 (Table 2.1).

Table 2.1: Tanzania: Selected Macroeconomic Indicators, 2001–2007

	2001	2002	2003	2004	2005	2006	2007 (Forecast)
Real GDP growth (%)	5.7	6.2	5.7	6.7	6.9	5.9	7.0
Inflation (period average)	5.2	4.5	3.5	4.1	4.4	6.3	5.0
Current account (% of GDP)	-2.5	0.2	-1.1	-3.9	-7.9	12.7	

Sources: URT, Economic Survey (various issues); Macroeconomic Policy Framework 2006/07–2008/09.

Poverty and welfare indicators compiled by the Household Budget Survey 2000/01 showed modest progress in reducing poverty since 1990. There has been no comprehensive survey for tracking progress in income poverty since the turn of the millennium. The closest proxies for income poverty have been routine data collected annually by the Bureau of Statistics on changes in GDP and GDP per capita and sectoral changes in output, including their contribution to the national cake. These proxy indicators show that Tanzania still is one of the poorest countries in the world. At a GDP per capita of USD 336 in 2005, the implication is that if the national cake were divided equally to the population, all Tanzanians would still be living on less than a dollar a day, showing that poverty is generalised. Apart from a situation of generalised poverty, there also continues to be considerable spatial disparity in terms of poverty status. The rural areas are at a particular disadvantage, not only because more of the poor and deprived in the population live there, but also because the rural areas continue to have limited access to quality social services and other economic infrastructure required to help them take advantage of various opportunities arising in the liberalised environment to develop themselves.

Nationally, the Household Budget Survey (2000/01) estimated that the poverty headcount declined from 38.6% to 35.7% in the 10-year spell from 1990/91, while the food poverty headcount declined from 21.6% to 18.7%. In rural areas, however, the poverty headcount for both food and basic needs continued to be higher than in other areas. The Household Budget Survey estimated that the food poverty headcount ratio for rural areas declined from 21.1% to 20.4% whereas the basic needs poverty headcount declined from 40.8% to 38.7% (Figures 2.1 and 2.2). Notwithstanding these trends in headcount indicators, since the population has been growing year after year, so has the absolute number of the poor in both urban and rural areas. Moreover, the country also experienced a slight growth in income inequality as measured by the Gini-coefficient, which rose from 0.34 in 1991/92 to 0.35 in 2000/01 (URT 2002).

Figure 2.1: Food Poverty Status and Targets

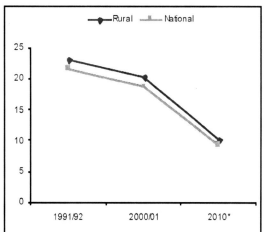
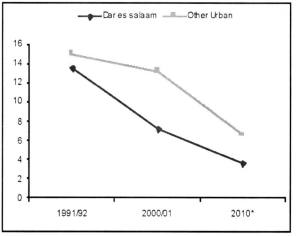

* National Target for 2010

Figure 2.2: Tanzania Basic Needs Poverty Status and National Target

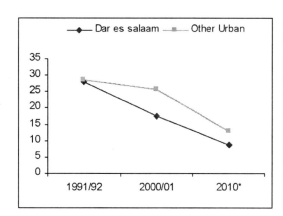
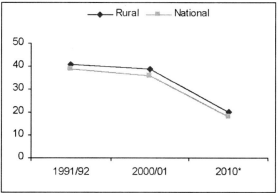

* National Target for 2010

An assessment of progress in reducing poverty since 2000 is made difficult by a lack of timely data on household income and expenditure because such information has not been compiled since the last survey in 2000/01. But although the last 3 years have recorded relatively higher rates of economic growth, it is unlikely that the national target of reaching a headcount ratio of

30% for basic needs poverty and 16% for food poverty in 2003 was actually met. The average rate of economic growth in Tanzania for the last 3 years has been around 6%. But despite the good growth performance the country has, during the same period, been affected by drought that led to food shortages as well as by fluctuations in the world market prices of its major exports which have continued to affect its export earnings.

Growth in formal employment opportunities has also been sluggish. In 2003 it was estimated that the unemployment rate in the country stood at around 12.9% with almost 50% of the unemployed living in rural areas. Each year it is estimated that about 650,000 job seekers enter the labour market in search of jobs but only about 6.5% of them are able to secure formal employment (in the private sector or in the public institutions). The rest are compelled to seek self-employment in either agriculture or informal activities, including employment as lowly paid domestic service. Since informal and agricultural self-employment is fraught with insecurity, the vulnerability of this category of individuals tends to be high, thus increasing the likelihood of falling into transient poverty over time.

Given this trend, the challenge of reducing income poverty for Tanzania is still a major one. The NPES target of halving poverty by 2010 and eradicating it altogether by 2025, when looked at in the context of recent economic trends, seems very ambitious. While the PRS emphasises high economic growth as a precondition for the reduction of extreme poverty and vulnerability, the average per capita GDP growth in the 1990s was too low and the recovery in the 2000s has so far been too modest to make a significant dent. Between 2000 and 2005, GDP grew at an average rate of 6.2% per year, compared to an average growth rate of 4.1% per year recorded between 1995 and 2000, but still fell short of the estimated growth rate of more than 7% over the medium term required for significant reduction in income poverty to be achieved. Furthermore, the persistence of institutional and structural impediments for a better trickle-down effect from growth to be felt also continues to limit the pace with which broad-based outcomes in income growth can be obtained.

This is not to say that there is no potential. On the contrary, the potential exists but the achievability of the targets depends on the extent to which current efforts can help to make growth pro-poor. The promotion of fast agricultural sector output growth is seen as part of the solution for broad-based growth, given that it employs a significant proportion of the population (more than 70%), and contributes about 45% of GDP and about one-third of export earnings. So far, however, its performance has been erratic and has remained prone to adverse weather conditions. Major efforts have been underway since 2001 to improve agricultural sector output, but their impact on the economy has remained modest. Agricultural sector output growth averaged 5.1% in the period 2001–2005, and though that is an improvement compared to the average rate of growth of 3.6% recorded between 1995 and 2000, it still is a far cry from the growth in mining and quarrying activities, which averaged 15.4% between 2001 and 2005. Mining has experienced a significant growth trend and is the sector into which major investment – especially Foreign Direct Investment – has been directed in the last decade, notwithstanding its small contribution to GDP.

The government targets the agricultural sector to grow by at least 10% by 2010, for broad-based rural income growth to be achieved. Major breakthroughs are still needed, therefore, to facilitate the growth of economic activities in this sector and others that are pro-poor to boost employment and income-raising opportunities as well as to increase productivity.

Improvement of infrastructure and market access for agricultural producers nationally and beyond will be an important element in achieving this goal.

2.4 QUALITY OF LIFE AND SOCIAL WELL-BEING

The NSGRP has five specific goals for improving the quality of life and social well-being. These relate to ensuring access to quality education (including improvement of gender parity) at all levels and improving literacy rates; improved survival, health, and well-being of children and women; improved access to clean water and sanitation services as well as a sustainable environment; achievement of adequate social protection and protection of the rights of the needy (vulnerable categories); and improved access to quality and affordable public services. The first three goals were being monitored in the course of implementation of the first PRS and indicators for assessing their progress are available, although some limitations continue to be reported and improvements are underway. In this section, therefore, reported progress is based only on indicators for which data are available.

2.4.1 Education and literacy achievements

During the 1990s, progress in education and literacy attainments was slow. In 1999 it was estimated that net enrolment in primary schools was 57.1%, just a slight improvement from 54.2% in 1992. During the same period the gross primary school enrolment rate had only showed a slight improvement by increasing to 77.1% in 1999 from 73.5% in 1990. Geographical disparities in enrolment indicators, however, continued to be wide with as much as 50% of all districts in the country recording enrolment rates below 50%. Completion rates in primary schools during this period remained stagnant at around 70% (URT 2003b).

With the implementation of various reforms and development programmes in the education sector, there has been considerable improvement in enrolment rates, school completion rates and in gender parity in education as reported in various Basic Statistics in Education reports. In 2006 the net enrolment rate in primary schools was estimated at 96.1%, up from 59% in 2000. Gross enrolment in primary schools in 2006 stood at 112.7%,[1] having gone up from the 77% recorded in 1999. The 2002 census results provide the most recent estimates of literacy rates: 69% among the population aged 15 years or more (62% for the male and 78% for the female population) (URT 2003a).

Considerable progress has also been made in improving gender parity in primary education but more remains to be done for secondary and higher learning institutions. In 2001 the ratio of girls to boys in primary schools was estimated at 0.97. However, many girls do not progress to secondary schools and higher learning institutions. In secondary schools in 2001 it was estimated that the girl/boy ratio in Form VI was only 0.51. This means that in the highest class in secondary education boys outnumber girls by a ratio of 2 to 1. The lower girl/boy ratio in higher education is related to low-transition rates for girls as well as a higher drop-out rate amongst girls compared to boys.

---

[1] Primary school gross enrolment ratios are calculated with the total number of pupils/students enrolled as a numerator and pupils in age group 7–13 as denominator. Where the enrolled pupils include children outside this age range ratios can exceed 100%.

Addressing existing barriers to accessing health care and increasing access to high quality health services, particularly for women and children in the rural and marginalised areas, have been given high priority in both the PRSP and MKUKUTA. Indicators for measuring progress on health and well-being have been included in the Poverty Monitoring System (PMS). Performance on some of these indicators and challenges in meeting the expected outcomes are discussed in the following sections.

Nutritional status of children

Undernutrition places children at a higher risk of morbidity and mortality and may cause impaired mental development. Indicators of children's nutritional status have been routinely measured by the Tanzania Demographic and Health Surveys (TDHS), which provide estimates for Tanzania between 1991/92, 1996 and 1999 and 2004. Three key indicators are used to measure the nutritional status of children over time: height for age (stunting), weight for height (wasting), and weight for age (underweight). While progress in reducing the proportion of children below the age of five who are underweight and stunted was very slow during the 1990s, preliminary results from the 2004 TDHS show that considerable achievements had been made since 1999. In 1999, it was estimated that 44% of below-five children were stunted, while 29% were underweight, which shows not much progress from the 1991/92 and 1996 TDHS reported values (Table 2.2). The proportion of underweight children actually rose slightly from 29% in 1991/92 to 31% in 1996. Preliminary results from the TDHS 2004, however, show that during the period from 1999 to 2004 the proportion of children below the age of five who are underweight fell to 22% while the proportion of stunted children went down to 38%. Further improvement was also recorded with respect to wasting in children. With continued efforts on improving the health and nutritional status of children, the prospects for achieving the national nutritional targets in 2010 seem good.

Table 2.2: Tanzania: Nutritional Status among Children

Variable	1991/92	1996	1999	2003 (PRS Targets)	2004	2010 (NSGRP Targets)
Underweight children below 5 years (%)	29	31	29	–	22	-
Stunting in under 5s (%)	43	43	44	–	38	20
Wasting in Under 5s (%)	6	7	5	–	3	2

Source: URT (2005b); National Bureau of Statistics and ORC Macro (2005).

Infant and child mortality

The 2004 TDHS indicates a recent rapid decline in mortality rates for both infants and under-five children compared to the stagnation in the same indicators during the 1990s. The TDHS estimates show that during the 1990s the mortality rate for under-fives increased from 137 deaths per 1000 live births in 1996 to 147 deaths in 1999. The census survey of 2001/02 showed a high figure (162 deaths per 1000 live births) for under-five mortality in 2002. The infant mortality rate also increased in the second half of 1990s from an average of 88 per 1000 live births recorded between 1991 and 1996 to 99 deaths per 1000 live births between 1994 and 1999, thus implying a reversion of the improvement recorded from the rate of 92 reached between 1987 and 1992 (National Bureau of Statistics and Macro Int. 2000; URT 2005b).

The above deterioration was attributed to increasing HIV infection rates in the 1990s, the declining quality of health services, and a decline in the ability of the population to afford health services following the implementation of cost-sharing measures in the health sector. Results from the 2004 TDHS, however, show that the infant mortality rate over the period 2000–2004 was about 68 per 1000 live births, which is a considerable decline from the rate during 1994 and 1999. Similarly, the report shows a considerable decline in under-five mortality from 147 per 1000 live births in the period 1995–1999 to 112 per 1000 live births in the last 5 years.

Maternal health

Problems related to pregnancy and birth continue to be a serious health problem for women and newborn children in the country. The TDHS 1996 estimated the maternal mortality rate at 529 per 100,000 live births in 1996. However, this rate went up in the subsequent 9 years to 578 per 100,000 live births in 2004, which implies that for every 1000 live births in Tanzania about 6 women die of pregnancy-related complications (National Bureau of Statistics and ORC Macro 2005). Among the immediate causes of poor survival and health status is the lack of access to quality health services, especially in rural areas.

The reliability of the estimates of maternal mortality in Tanzania is compromised, however, by the small numbers of deaths of pregnant women that are recorded as well as random fluctuations in mortality related to both pregnancy and childbirth (URT 2005). For this reason, proxy indicators on the proportion of deliveries that are assisted by health professionals and the percentage of births taking place at a health facility are being monitored. The proportion of births attended by skilled health workers was estimated in the TDHS (2005) to have gone up to 46% in 2004, from 41% in 1999, indicating that access to quality reproductive health services in Tanzania is still problematic. The accepted international standard by 2015 is to have 90% of births attended by skilled health personnel, and the NSGRP target for 2010 is 80% of births attended by skilled health professionals, which signifies a need for concerted efforts in the coming years if these targets are to be attained. As for births taking place in health facilities, survey data for 1990s showed a decline from 53% in 1991/92 to 44% in 1999, but there was a slight improvement thereafter with the figure rising to 47% in 2004 (National Bureau of Statistics and ORC Macro 2005).

Urban/rural and regional disparity in maternal health indicators is considerable: rural women are less likely than urban women to be in a health facility during childbirth or to have a skilled professional in attendance (National Bureau of Statistics and ORC Macro 2005; URT 2005b). Health facilities, especially in rural areas, continue to face challenges that include poor maintenance, lack of equipment, and inadequate staffing (number and quality). These inadequacies are largely attributed to poor planning and management systems in the health sector, and to healthcare charges and other unofficial costs for drugs and supplies as well as unofficial payments for services. Long distances, inadequate and costly transport systems, poor governance and accountability mechanisms, and poorly administered exemption and waiver schemes meant to protect the most vulnerable and poor people also contribute to exclusion from access to health services. Other contributing factors to the poor survival and health status in Tanzania include limited access to food and basic amenities, in particular clean water and adequate sanitation. Malnutrition is a major contributing factor to the high levels of mortality among pregnant women and lactating mothers.

Combating malaria, HIV and AIDS, and other infectious diseases

Malaria is one of the main causes of morbidity and mortality in Tanzania, resulting in about 30% of reported diseases and deaths. Malaria is highly endemic in about 80% of the country. There have been major endeavours to combat malaria (Malaria Control Programme) since the mid-1990s, which have included measures such as Improving Malaria Case Management with effective anti-malaria drugs, and the promotion of insecticide-treated nets (ITNs). Replacement of chloroquine with Sulphadoxine Pyrimethamine as an anti-malarial therapy was also undertaken in recent years with the hope of reducing malaria fatalities. The development of the 'dip-it-yourself' kit for home treatment, together with the government's elimination of sales tax on ready-made nets in Tanzania, resulted in an increase in the sale of ITNs, which are being hailed as the most promising available method for controlling malaria in tropical countries.

Comprehensive national data to facilitate an assessment of progress in malaria control nationally are unavailable, however. The only information that is currently available with reference to malaria control concerns a few sentinel surveillance sites. It shows that except for Dar es Salaam, where progress in reducing malaria has been more or less stagnant, malaria death rates in other sentinel sites have declined, indicating possibilities of improvement where the programmes are applied (URT 2005b). The national decline in child and infant mortality reported in the 2005 TDHS is partly attributed to more effective prevention and management of malaria cases, though precise estimates of percentage changes in mortality that are attributable to malaria control could not be made. The NSGRP proposes measurement of this variable (change in infant mortality attributed to reduction in malaria incidence) in the future as an indicator of improvement in the survival, health and well-being of children.

HIV and AIDS

Until 2004, estimates of HIV prevalence depended on blood donor data and on antenatal care attendees in surveillance sites. Since the surveillance estimates are generated annually they have been instrumental in facilitating analyses of trends over time. The estimates, however, have several caveats: they are not based on national or geographically representative samples. Rather, information is obtained from very specific sub-population samples and, furthermore, the sub-population samples are not representative of the Tanzanian population currently at risk (URT 2005b). The first nationally representative data were generated by the 2003/04 Tanzania HIV and AIDS indicators survey (THIS). Estimates from THIS show a national HIV prevalence rate of 7% (7.7% for women and 6.3% for men). Based on these prevalence rates, roughly 1.1 million people (0.6 million females and 0.5 million males) between ages 15 and 59 had been infected with HIV as of 2003. THIS also estimated the prevalence rate among pregnant women to be 6.8% in 2003. Surveillance data from 2003 generated a higher prevalence rate estimated at 9.6% among antenatal clinic attendees.[2] The overall prevalence rate among blood donors in 2003 was estimated at 8.8% (8.2% for male blood donors and 11.9% for female blood donors) (URT 2004).

Women of child-bearing age continue to be more vulnerable to new infections, compared to men. Furthermore, marked variations also exist across regions and across socio-economic groups. Some regions have very low-prevalence rates (e.g. Manyara and Kigoma with a prevalence rate of 2%), while others have considerably higher prevalence rates (e.g. Iringa and Mbeya at 13%). Urban residents also appear to be at a higher risk of contacting HIV with an overall prevalence rate of 12%, compared to rural area residents with a prevalence rate of 5.8%.

The burden of AIDS morbidity and mortality is already quite heavy and is expected to increase further over the next decade. The threat to the livelihoods of many people in the country continue to be daunting as it affects more the most productive and reproductive groups that comprise the workforce, and increasingly children who are the workforce of the future. The government has thus been facilitating the availability of anti-retroviral drugs to people living with AIDS as part of efforts to mitigate the impact of the pandemic. The national target is to provide life-extending drugs to 100,000 people with an advanced stage of the disease by 2006, and estimates as of August 2006 showed that 48% of the target had been achieved. New HIV infections continue to be reported, however, which signifies the need to keep coherent initiatives to combat HIV and AIDS at the centre stage of the national development agenda.

Tuberculosis treatment

The growth of HIV infection has partly been blamed for contributing to a continuing increase in the number of TB patients, notwithstanding progress recorded in TB treatment completion rates between 1998 and 2002. The government's response through Direct Observed Treatment Start Course treatment is showing some improvement, although comprehensive national information is still unavailable. Between 1998 and 2001 it was estimated that the treatment completion rate increased from 76% to 80.7%, and increased again slightly to 80.9% in 2003. The national average data, however, conceal significant variations in treatment completion rates among different regions of the country (some regions have completion rates below 70% while others have gone up above 90%). Smithson (2005) estimates that more than 50% of TB patients are also HIV positive, which is a marked increase when compared to the co-infection rate of 44% in 1998. Although precise data do not exist, anecdotal evidence suggests that the number of TB cases has been on the rise from 1998.

Recent national data on TB infection rates, treatment completion rates and death rates are not available, however, due to constraints facing the Information Management System of the Ministry of Health in collecting reliable national information. A specific national target for a treatment completion rate for TB is not mentioned in the NSGRP but it is an important indicator that will continue to be monitored in the future.

---

[2] From 24 antenatal clinics across six regions (out of Tanzania's 21 regions).

Both survey (collected by the National Bureau of Statistics) and routine data (from the Ministry of Water) suggest that access to clean and safe water sources has improved over the 1990 levels. In 1990, the proportion of the rural population with access to clean and safe water was below 45% but due to implementation by the government and the donor community of various national water initiatives this proportion grew to 49% in 2000. There have been further modest improvements in recent years and the most recent estimate (2003) shows that about 53.5% of the rural population have access to safe water, not far from the target of 55%. In urban areas, access to piped and protected water sources is currently estimated at 73%. The government is currently implementing the National Water Policy of 2002, building on important principles such as the sustainable management of water resources, gender equity in allocation, environmental sustainability and effective community participation.

Indicators of access to clean and safe water also include a composite consideration of distance to the water source, which was not included in earlier PRS indicative targets. Furthermore, the current NSGRP has specific national targets with respect to sanitation in Tanzania, which were lacking in past policy documents. These targets include the percentage of households with basic sanitation services (target 95% by 2010); the percentage of schools with adequate sanitary facilities (100% by 2010); the number of reported cholera cases per year (expected to be cut by 50% by 2010) (see Table 2.3); and the total area under community-based natural resource management.

Table 2.3: Water and Sanitation Progress

Indicator	Baseline		2001	2002	2003	2004	2005	NSGRP Targets
	Estimate	Year						*2010*
Proportion of population with access to piped or protected water as main drinking water source (%)*	Urban 73	2000/01	-	-	73	73	74	*90*
	Rural 53				53	53.5	53.7	*65*
Percent of households with basic sanitation facilities	91	2002		91	-	-	-	*95*
Percent of schools with adequate sanitation facilities			35.7	36.2	32.8	36.7		*100 (with a ratio of 1:20 for girls and 1:25 for boys)*
Number of reported cholera cases (per 100,000 people)			69	28.5	35	20.9		*Reduce outbreaks by half*

* Based on routine data collected by the Ministry of Water.

Sources: URT (2005c, 2006).

2.5 Tackling vulnerability

While vulnerability to socio-economic shocks is recognised as needing concerted attention in the ongoing efforts to reduce poverty, data to help gauge vulnerability trends and progress are limited. The 2003 PRS progress report noted that apart from a lack of trend data (time series), the indicators covered a disparate set of areas that were most likely not selected on the basis of a common conceptual policy framework. The course of implementation of the NSGRP would be the best opportunity to establish a coherent set of indicators but so far this has not been achieved. Consequently, specific targets to meet by 2010 are not clear.

The 2002 housing and population census nonetheless sheds light on categories of individuals that could be included in vulnerable population groups and who would thus require social protection. These are identified as children, people with disability, orphans, children from child-headed households, the elderly and children living with them, and children from households headed by disabled persons. The housing and population census revealed that these groups are at high risk of being excluded from access to social services such as education and health. Furthermore, even in cases where targeted programmes exist to assist them, some may still be excluded due to lack of information or the failure of the programmes to reach them. For a meaningful assessment of status to be made, efforts are required to define a comprehensive set of indicators within a reliable framework to help gauge the extent of the problem and what should/can be done to address the challenges of improving access to social protection in the coming years.

2.6 Enhancing governance and accountability

Good governance is recognised as having a direct bearing on the effectiveness of efforts undertaken to reduce poverty. In Tanzania, efforts to improve governance have been geared towards improving the legal and judicial system, enhancing service delivery and the efficiency of public expenditure management systems, checking corruption, and facilitating the role of local government in economic development through local government reforms, as well as through various initiatives to encourage the role of civil society in policy-making processes.

The NSGRP for the first time made an attempt to develop a comprehensive set of governance indicators based on NSGRP's stated outcomes, namely good governance and the rule of law; accountability of leaders and public servants; democracy; political and social tolerance; and peace, political stability, national unity and deepened social cohesion. From the limited set of indicators that could be gathered in the preparation of the NSGRP status report (2006), modest progress could be observed. Nonetheless, more efforts are needed to sustain what has been achieved so far and to address weaknesses that still remain, especially in relation to improving public financial accountability, fighting petty and grand corruption and enhancing the role and efficiency of the government in service delivery at all levels, especially for local government through the ongoing process of decentralisation by devolution. Further advancement of women's representation in leadership positions and in the civil service and ensuring equity in educational achievement in higher learning institutions is also called for. Building capacity for effective community participation in the implementation of development is paramount.

2.7 THE TANZANIA POVERTY REDUCTION STRATEGY

Since the early 1960s Tanzania has made various efforts to revamp the economy through home-grown programmes that continued to be implemented through to the early 1980s but with limited overall impact, both in terms of halting the declining trend in social indicators and in terms of achieving macroeconomic stability. In the mid-1990s, Tanzania started articulating once again its commitment to poverty reduction through the preparation of various policy and strategy documents, notably Vision 2025 and the National Poverty Eradication Strategy. The 2000s witnessed another thrust in that endeavour with the preparation and implementation of the PRSP under the HIPC initiative. This section describes the PRSP processes in Tanzania, focusing mainly on formulation and implementation arrangements.

2.7.1 The policy formulation process

The PRSP was produced originally as a requirement of consideration for debt relief under the HIPC Initiative. Thus, like the previous SAPs the PRSP could be looked at as a funding arrangement with the donor community, but this time around with a focus on tackling poverty. Tandari (2002) describes Tanzania's PRSP as essentially another 'medium-term funding mechanism for funding priority areas and sectors that have highest impact on poverty reduction'.

The guiding principle for the PRSP's formulation was the need to enhance local participation, ownership, and commitment to policy. These ingredients, particularly the ownership aspect, were perceived to be lacking in the SAPs and the lack was blamed for their limited success. With the publication of the Helleiner Report in 1995 and the subsequent establishment of the TAS in 1999 to guide donor government relations in the policy process, there was a growing perception that ownership and commitment to policy was improving considerably. To stimulate participation and mobilise support for policy beyond the government, the PRSP formulation exercise remains the most concrete manifestation of IMF/WB efforts to increase country ownership as it explicitly incorporates participation into the IMF/WB lending framework for poor countries (Stewart and Wang 2003).

However, starting at a stage where participation of local non-state actors in the policy formulation process was virtually absent, progress in securing local participation was initially very slow. Whereas the tradition of preparing policy documents has a long history – dating back to the day of independence – the policy formulation processes in Tanzania were mostly fragmented and took a closed technocratic nature (Booth 2005; Gould and Ojanen 2003). Participation of local non-state actors in policy processes in the country was limited to information sharing. The socio-political landscape preceding the introduction of the participatory conditionality attached to the PRSP significantly shaped the trajectory of participation in the formulation of the PRS. Though civil society organisations had started to voice their concerns actively in various fora in the second half of the 1990s, the closed technocratic nature of policy formulation dominated the formulation process of the Interim PRS for Tanzania such that participation was limited to consultations among a small group that Booth (2005) and Gould and Ojanen (2003) termed an 'iron triangle' of donors, internationally linked NGOs, and government technocrats. Outside this sphere, consultations were utterly absent.

The picture was somewhat different in the preparation of the full PRSP in the sense that representatives of civil society actors – most notably at national level – were consulted in the process. But even at this stage the process was still assessed as being compressed. Not only were the consultations rushed, there was also a deliberate move to block the participation of some civil society organisations, thus leading to the exclusion of some sections of the local non-state actors (Evans and Ngalewa 2003). For instance, facing a critical report by the Tanzania Coalition on Debt and Development (TCDD) on the macroeconomic framework of the strategy, the government refused to acknowledge the existence of the TCDD/PRSP Committee and blocked the leading role of the coalition in zonal workshops (Whitehead 2003). At regional level smaller NGOs (such as local women and youth networks) and representatives from some community-based organisations were invited to participate in consultative workshops, but owing to limited knowledge many spent more time trying to understand the PRSP than to contribute constructively to policy formulation. In the end, due to the hurried nature of consultations it became difficult to ascertain to what extent the views and concerns of the people consulted outside the 'iron triangle' were included in the final PRSP document. Whitehead (2003: 29) observed that 'the subsequent final draft hardly included any input from the civil society'.

The formulation of the second generation PRSP, the NSGRP, signalled considerable improvement in the model of participation of non-state actors in policy formulation, stemming from the cumulative learning gained from the pitfalls encountered in the formulation of the first PRSP. The strategy formulation exercise sought to deepen participation in and ownership of the strategy by actors at different levels of the government, the local non-state actors (civil society, community-based organisations, etc.) and development partners. It was undertaken as part and parcel of the PRSP review process as the PRSP wound up its third year of implementation. This time around, the consultations involved more participants with diverse backgrounds and also involved broader consultations within different levels of government. Furthermore, more time was allocated to ensure that there was adequate room for negotiating with a diversity of views so as to come up with a policy document that presented a common commitment of the country to improvement of living conditions (URT 2005a).

2.7.2 Policy-makers' and technocrats' appreciation of issues in the PRS

This section draws heavily on work by Evans and Ngalewa (2003), Gould and Ojanen (2003), and the Communication Strategy for MKUKUTA drawn up by the Vice President's Office (VPO) in 2005 (URT 2005d). Looking at the level of understanding of issues in the PRS in the early years, one finds that knowledge and understanding of policy issues in the first PRSP was limited and varied significantly within the government machinery. Evans and Ngalewa (2003) observe, for instance, that the understanding of issues surrounding the PRSP was more prevalent among senior government officials, and among staff from planning departments who were likely to have participated directly in the preparatory process. Outside these realms, however, engagement was virtually absent and, as a result, the understanding of the PRS and various policy issues involved was limited.

Knowledge and awareness of the PRS across the central and local governments as well as the depth of understanding about the PRS and its targets remained modest in the 3 years during which the PRSP was under implementation. It was observed that even though there was a gradual improvement in the process of engagement in policy-making as well as in knowledge and information sharing since the first PRS in 2000, such knowledge continued to be confined to a few middle- and senior-level officials in the central government, line ministries, some local governments, major NGOs in the country and prominent researchers and academicians (URT 2005a). This was largely due to limited communication in early years of PRSP implementation between the VPO and other sections of the government on issues related to the PRSP. There are also views that the limited awareness and knowledge about PRS in various government circles emanated from the legacy of a highly centralised system of policy-making in which information was not readily shared and the responsibility for taking and delivering decisions was severely disjointed (Evans and Ngalewa 2003; Gould and Ojanen 2003).

Limited understanding of the PRS was also apparent among the parliamentarians because of their scant involvement in defining the contents of the PRSP. Gould and Ojanen (2003) note that participation by parliamentarians in the preparation of the first PRS was limited to a 2-hour workshop on a Saturday in June 2000, and some training seminars on particular aspects of the PRSP organised by local NGOs. In effect, though many seemed to know much about the HIPC debt initiative due to the *Chama cha Mapinduzi* election campaign preceding the 2000 national election, very few had a clear grasp of the PRSP and even fewer could unpack the acronyms used in the policy document. The limited understanding of the PRSP among the parliamentarians was compounded by the legal framework governing their involvement in policy-making processes in the country. While parliament is expected to be at the centre stage of representative democracy and participatory policy-making processes, in Tanzania the parliament has been conditioned by the legal framework (a political system with strong presidential powers) to be on the receiving end – approving policy documents and enacting them into legislation and to give them public approval, without necessarily participating effectively in preparing them (Gould and Ojanen 2003).

Notwithstanding this caveat, the PRS initiative was well received both within and outside the government. It was viewed as an important step underpinning the commitment of both the government and the donor community to improving the living conditions of the population. Thus, following the establishment of the first full PRSP in 2000, officials, including the president himself, the minister of finance and several other members of the cabinet, promoted it in their speeches to the public. The government also set up a Steering Committee that included senior officials from all key ministries, representatives from civil society, the donor community and the private sector with a responsibility to monitor the PRSP implementation process. The work of this committee was to be supported by a Technical Committee responsible for organising consultations on the PRSP, for working with various ministries to review action plans and costings, and for overseeing the drafting of the PRSP. Outside the government, various NGOs undertook to educate Tanzanians, including government officials, about the PRSP. To build upon progress made since the first PRSP in enhancing knowledge about the PRSP, the VPO adopted a Communication Strategy in 2005 for the NSGRP. The objective of the communication strategy was to ensure that apart from extensive dissemination of information to various parts of the government and civil society, there was more sensitisation and advocacy with a view to enabling effective participation in the ensuing public debate and contribution to policy formulation and implementation.

Concerns were raised, however, with regard to the adequacy of funding for implementing the objectives set out in the PRSP and the realism of the time period (2 years) set for achieving the various poverty indicators. On the financing aspect, implementation of the PRSP is heavily dependent on donor funding, which besides being an unsustainable source of finance in the long term had also tended to be intermittent in the past. As for the realism of milestones set in the PRSP – notwithstanding a strong consensus about the need to have a clear focus of what is to be achieved in the lifespan of the PRSP – there was concern that given the short time frame set for its implementation and the capacity limitations in many government ministries to undertake significant strategic changes in such a short period of time, there could be an incentive to dub some of the already existing social programmes as 'poverty' programmes (Evans and Ngalewa 2003) without adequate analytical work just to ensure there were some measurable targets. With the ongoing reforms and capacity-building initiatives in the public sector, however, ministries are gradually enhancing their capacity for restructuring their priorities and developing implementable strategies to contribute more effectively towards poverty reduction. The government is also taking initiatives towards tapping domestic sources of revenue so as to reduce reliance on donor finance, although it is recognised that in the medium term the country will continue to rely on donor financing for the implementation of various programmes.

A long-standing problem of disjuncture between policy/strategy formulation and implementation persists. Furthermore, until the establishment of the NSGRP in 2005, the implementation of social policies (priority sector objectives and cross-cutting issues) and of macroeconomic policies tended to be treated as discrete undertakings with limited coherence to the effect that social policies took a residual position in the realm of policy implementation. The NSGRP improves upon the previous PRSP through the adoption of an outcome-based approach focusing on three clusters: (a) growth and reduction of poverty; (b) improvement of quality of life and social well-being; and (c) good governance and accountability in the public sector. Under the NSGRP, policy design and government initiatives are to be organised with respect to their contribution to the achievement of these and other related objectives, thus giving social policies added impetus compared to how they fared under the PRSP.

2.7.3 Implementation arrangements

Formulating a coherent and credible poverty reduction strategy is important but only part of the task. Linking the strategy to the budget as the main source of domestic funding and putting in place arrangements for monitoring progress towards the targeted outcomes are equally important so as to prevent the emergence of a policy implementation gap.

Milestones and linkages with the budget

Apart form putting emphasis on maintaining macroeconomic stability for fast growth as a prerequisite for poverty reduction, the first PRSP also identified a number of priority sectors to facilitate a faster achievement of the objective of poverty reduction. These sectors included primary education, rural roads, water, the legal and judicial system, primary health care and agriculture. The PRSP also delineated a set of cross-cutting issues to be included for funding along with the priority sectors in the government budget. The cross-cutting issues were HIV and AIDS, gender, governance, local government reform, human capital development and the environment.

Measurement of progress in these priority areas and the cross-cutting issues depends on routine data collection systems in the responsible priority sector ministries and departments, and in the ministries and departments overseeing the implementation of programmes covering cross-cutting issues. Progress in the PRSP has been monitored annually since its adoption in 2000/01. The Poverty Eradication Department in the VPO has produced and disseminated annual progress reports. Apart from the PRSP progress report, the Research and Analysis Technical Working Group in the Poverty Monitoring System (PMS) also publishes an annual Poverty and Human Development Report.

The priority sectors and cross-cutting issues became the cornerstones of the government effort to tackle non-income poverty. In some areas the government set clear and measurable targets to be achieved over the duration of the strategy period. For others, however, there were no clear targets and measurement of progress annually has therefore been impossible. The difficulty of measuring progress annually also emanated from heavy reliance on routine data collection arrangements within priority sector and cross-cutting issues ministries and departments where data collection and analysis exercises often do not coincide with the periods set for reviewing progress in the implementation of the PRS. For example, while the PMS insists on measuring progress annually, the demographic health survey conducted by the Ministry of Health is done only once in every 4 years, subject to the availability of funds. Similarly, while the PRS set targets on income poverty – for both food and basic needs poverty over its lifespan – measurement of annual progress towards these targets has been difficult because it is contingent upon the availability of the household budget survey, labour force surveys and census data, which in Tanzania are collected only once in every 10 years due to financial constraints.

Nevertheless, with the adoption of cluster-based implementation of the NSGRP the government budget has been realigned so that it is consistent with the NSGRP clusters. This is being done through cluster-based expenditure programming and a Strategic Budget Allocation System (SBAS) to the local government level in addition to government ministries, departments and agencies. Under this arrangement, direct interventions for NSGRP implementation are assured a given amount of resources in the budget, which for 2006 was estimated at 48% of the annual budget, slightly (only 1%) higher than the 2005 allocation. Within the budget allotted for direct NSGRP interventions, the shares for each cluster are: growth and reduction of income poverty (46%); improvement of the quality of life and social well-being (36%); and governance and accountability (18%). While this is being done and the linkage of the poverty reduction strategy to the budget is thus strengthened, allocation for NSGRP implementation needs to be guided by a comprehensive medium-term costing analysis. This would ensure that funding is adequate for achieving the set targets. Furthermore, expenditure tracking exercises are essential to establish whether the resources allocated are used for the intended purposes.

The PRS monitoring framework

The full PRSP (2000) contained little on the appropriate set-up for monitoring its implementation, which was probably attributable to the hurried preparation of the document. After its approval in 2000, however, a core group of government staff, donor representatives and researchers/ academics was formed to prepare a comprehensive poverty-monitoring framework – the Poverty Monitoring Master Plan (PMMP) – which was endorsed by the government and published in 2001, in time for the HIPC completion point. The PMMP drew heavily on work already initiated in the VPO with the support of the UNDP to design an integrated monitoring system based on a set of poverty and welfare indicators for monitoring the National Poverty Eradication Strategy of 1998 (Evans and Ngalewa 2003; Booth 2003).

The poverty monitoring system focused on the measurement of impacts, outcomes and proxy indicators. Priority sector programmes, for instance in health, education and water, focused on tracking output indicators with adequate monitoring mechanisms in place. In the process the Public Expenditure Review/Medium-Term Expenditure Frameworks, which had been in place since 1997, focused on inputs, with the emphasis on budget allocation and budget execution to ensure that priority areas are adequately funded. Institutional arrangements were also made to facilitate analytical work to establish the linkages between, on the one hand, impacts, outcomes and outputs and, on the other, inputs and outputs. The institutional design included a National Poverty Monitoring Steering Committee (with membership from relevant parts of the government, civil society, academia, and the private sector), a Technical Committee – the PRSP Technical Committee – and a number of smaller technical working groups to oversee the specific information and data needs of the system.[3] In 2001, poverty monitoring was also included in the budget guidelines, thus creating a clear institutional commitment to funding the activities under the PMMP. A significant percentage of resources, however, still needed to be mobilised from external sources to finance activities delineated in the PMMP.

While it has been described as impressive, ambitious, and involving thorough preparation informed by a good understanding of international best practice in the monitoring of strategic plans, the PMMP was faced by a number of limitations (Evans and Ngalewa 2003). First, its full implementation depended heavily on donor contributions, which in the long run may prove unsustainable. Second, it was a complex system that required considerable support from the VPO, which unfortunately also has very limited capacity. Third, the Tanzanian PMS refrains from creating an institutional home for the PMMP, which has raised concern over where the ultimate responsibility lies for ensuring that the relevant monitoring data are collected, analysed, reported to the parties concerned and used to chart progress and take corrective actions as and when required. It relies heavily on survey data and routine data-gathering arrangements and instruments that already exist in various government institutions, but these are unfortunately slow in generating data. Another limitation, not specific to Tanzania alone, is that the minimum set of indicators for poverty monitoring focuses heavily on poverty and social outcomes that require medium- to long-term monitoring and tends to ignore intermediate indicators that can generate information on trends and correlates in the short- to medium-term and on progress with institutional change (Evans and Ngalewa 2003; Booth 2005). Furthermore, with the routine data collection systems functioning very slowly and unevenly, coupled with limited capacity to reconcile data and information across administrative departments, the data required for measuring progress in poverty reduction are often unavailable when needed.

Other arrangements exist for monitoring the PRS implementation process outside the framework of the national PMMP. These include the regular Poverty Reduction Grant Facility (PRGF) review missions by the IMF and the Public Expenditure Review (PER) process, which is the performance-linking framework related to the Poverty Reduction Budget Support;

---

[3] The working groups are: (i) Routine Data Group under the President's Office – Regional Administration and Local Governments; (ii) Survey and Census Groups under the National Bureau of Statistics; (iii) Research and Analysis Working Group – overseen by the President's Office – Planning and Privatization in collaboration with Research on Poverty Alleviation (REPOA); and (iv) Dissemination Group under the Vice President's Office.

individual sector development programme reviews; and an Independent Monitoring Group formed to monitor implementation of the TAS. While these monitoring processes should ideally be substantially linked to the PMS, they run parallel to one another and have at times been cited to justify conflicting demands on the government. They are also to a large extent externally driven, for instance in the case of the regular PRGF reviews (Evans and Ngalewa, 2003).

Building on progress in periodic assessments of poverty trends since 2003, the NSGRP has come up with a more detailed set of indicators for poverty monitoring. This commendable improvement notwithstanding, some weaknesses remain, such as a continued lack of indicative targets for some goals to be achieved against which progress should be assessed. Moreover, data shortcomings arise from a lack of well-established information systems in some agencies charged with the responsibility of collecting and publishing routine data. Financial and human resource capacity constraints, especially at the local government level, are also a reason for the data inadequacies for some micro-level indicators.

In the course of implementation of the NSGRP, therefore, further improvement is imperative in terms of a comprehensive and optimal set of indicators to be used for assessing progress and establishing specific targets to be met. Furthermore, strengthening the institutional capacity (financial and human) of government ministries, departments and executive agencies responsible for collecting and publishing data for monitoring progress needs to be accorded higher priority.

2.7.4 The role of regional communities in creating an environment conducive for poverty reduction

The formulation and implementation of poverty reduction strategies are primarily the responsibility of individual countries. Nonetheless, the existence of and participation in regional trade arrangements and regional cooperative ventures are viewed as necessary to facilitate income improvement. Consequently, regional collaboration and trade facilitation may have a beneficial impact on poverty reduction. For Tanzania as in the rest of the world, openness to trade is at the centre stage of current economic policies. The ability of the country to benefit from free trade, however, has been hampered by inequality in the terms of trade with its developed trade partners. As a result, joining various regional trade arrangements within Africa has become a refuge, promising more favourable terms of trade and increasing market shares in countries that are at comparable levels of development and/or stand to offer better terms.

Tanzania is thus a member of several regional trading blocs that also act as coalitions in bargaining for better terms of trade with the rest of the world (e.g. SADC, EAC, Cross Border Trade Initiative, and Indian Ocean Rim Association for Regional Cooperation) (Musonda and Madete 2002). Membership in global trade arrangements such as the World Trade Organization and the signing of various protocols governing trade in goods and services are also viewed as essential to avoid being excluded from the global trading system. Yet, while Tanzania seems to be in a position to gain from preferential treatment accorded goods from poor countries entering developed country markets (e.g. arrangements under the ACP-EU and AGOA), structural and institutional limitations within the country remain to be addressed for the benefits to accrue to more local exporters and thus contribute to economic growth which, in turn, may trickle down to the poor.

2.8 CONCLUSION

While efforts to fight poverty and deprivation continue, poor linkages between macroeconomic achievements and poverty reduction remain a challenge that limits faster progress. Until the latest Household Budget Survey in 2001, progress in raising incomes and/or expenditures, as reflected in the developments in poverty headcount, had been only modest since the 1991/92 level. Poor macro–micro linkages and an uneven distribution of the benefits of growth in the rural and urban areas also persist, signifying a need to identify the missing links for a more broad-based and equitable growth to be achieved.

With respect to non-income poverty indicators, progress has been mixed. Although the country has made strides in improving enrolment rates and gender parity in primary schools, the quality of education offered has remained a major challenge. At the same time, for secondary and higher learning institutions there are still challenges in improving access (especially for girls/ women), and in ensuring that the education offered meets the needs of the labour market. With respect to health indicators, progress has been mixed and the challenges emanating from HIV and AIDS for achieving improvements in health and the economy continue to be great. While there has been some improvement in the nutritional and health status of children, the maternal mortality rate has continued to grow. Water and sanitation indicators also continue to be low despite ongoing initiatives with government and donor support. And the extent of improvement in social protection for vulnerable groups is unclear. This implies that concerted efforts are needed towards improving the well-being and quality of life of the population. Measures to empower communities and reduce vulnerability are also critical to ensure faster progress in poverty reduction.

Modest progress has been achieved in enhancing governance and accountability. Noting the relevance of good governance to ensuring the effectiveness of poverty reduction initiatives, more needs to be done in this area. Further improvement is also need in linking the budget and the poverty reduction strategy to the poverty monitoring system, especially with respect to defining and establishing indicators and assuring the quality of data. As exemplified by the 2006 NSGRP status report, considerable improvements have taken place. However, there is scope for further improvement to ensure that a comprehensive and optimal set of quality indicators are in place to facilitate reliable assessments of progress.

Tanzania also continues to record improvement in the degree of participation by various stakeholders in the policy formulation process. Capacity improvement among local non-state actors as well as within the government machinery is also leading to better linkage between policy formulation and implementation. Policy awareness is growing both within and outside the state machinery as the consultative imperative and information sharing take root with governance reforms. The challenge of reducing poverty, however, remains daunting for Tanzania. Moreover, the country continues to rely heavily on external donor finance for the implementation of programmes for the improvement of peoples' livelihoods. Even though the NSGRP recognises this external dependence, and notwithstanding the government's commitment to expanding its domestic revenues, in the medium term external reliance is likely to persist.

REFERENCES

Bigsten, A., D. Mutalemwa, Y. Tsikata, and S. Wangwe (2000), 'Tanzania', in Devarajan, S., D.R. Dollar and T. Holmgren (eds.), *Aid and Reform in Africa: Lessons from Ten Case Studies*, Washington D.C.: World Bank, pp. 287–360.

Booth, D. (2005), *Poverty Monitoring Systems: An Analysis of Institutional Arrangements in Tanzania*, Overseas Development Institute Working Paper No. 247.

Evans, A. and E. Ngalewa (2003), "Tanzania", in Booth, D. (ed.), *Fighting Poverty in Africa: Are PRSPs Making a Difference?* London: Overseas Development Institute.

Gould, J. and J. Ojanen (2003), *Merging in the Circle: The Politics of Poverty Reduction Strategy*, Helsinki: Institute of Development Studies, University of Helsinki.

Msambichaka, L.A, A.A. Kilindo, and G. Mjema (1995), *Beyond Structural Adjustment Programmes in Tanzania: Successes and Failures*, Dar es Salaam: Economic Research Bureau.

Musonda, F. and L. Madete (2002), *Tanzania Investment Policy and Performance – Report A*, prepared for Consumer Units and Trust Society (CUTS), India Investment for Development Project.

Stewart, F. and M. Wang (2003), *Do PRSPs Empower Poor Countries and Dis-empower the World Bank, or is it the Other Way Round?* Queen Elizabeth House Working Paper Series No. 108.

National Bureau of Statistics (NBS) [Tanzania] and Macro International Inc. (2000), *Tanzania Reproductive and Child Health Survey 1999*, Dar es Salaam and Calverton, MD: National Bureau of Statistics and Macro International Inc.

National Bureau of Statistics (NBS) [Tanzania] and ORC Macro. (2005), *Tanzania Demographic and Health Survey 2004–05*, Dar es Salaam: National Bureau of Statistics and ORC Macro.

Tandari, C.K. (2002), 'Poverty Reduction Strategy in Africa: a New Imposed Conditionality or a Chance for a New and Meaningful Development Policy?', paper presented at an International Conference in Lusaka, Zambia, 17–18 June 2002.

UNDP (2002), *Human Development Report: Deepening Democracy in a Fragmented World*, New York: Oxford University Press.

United Republic of Tanzania [URT] (2002), *Household Budget Survey*, Dar es Salaam: National Bureau of Statistics.

United Republic of Tanzania (2003a), *2002 Population and Housing Census*, Dar es Salaam: National Bureau of Statistics.

United Republic of Tanzania (Research and Analysis Working Group) (2003b), *Poverty and Human Development Report*, Dar es Salaam: Mkuki na Nyota Publishers.

United Republic of Tanzania (2004), *National AIDS Surveillance Report Number 18*, Dar es Salaam: National AIDS Control Programme (NACP).

United Republic of Tanzania (2005a), *The National Strategy for Growth and Reduction of Poverty (NSGRP)*, Dar es Salaam: Vice President's Office.

United Republic of Tanzania (Research and Analysis Working Group) (2005b), *Poverty and Human Development Report*, Dar es Salaam: Mkuki na Nyota Publishers.

United Republic of Tanzania (2005c), *Ministry of Water and Livestock Budget Speech 2005/06*, Dodoma: Ministry of Water and Livestock Development.

United Republic of Tanzania (2005d), *Communication Strategy for the National Strategy for Growth and Reduction of Poverty (NSGRP)*, Dar es Salaam: Vice President's Office.

United Republic of Tanzania (Research and Analysis Working Group) (2006), *NSGRP Status Report 2006: Progress towards the Goals for Growth*, Dar es Salaam: Ministry of Planning, Economy and Empowerment.

United Republic of Tanzania (various years), *The Economic Survey*, Dar es Salaam: President's Office, Planning and Privatization.

United Republic of Tanzania (various years), *Basic Statistics in Education*, Dar es Salaam: Ministry of Education and Culture.

Whitehead, A. (2003), *Failing Women, Sustaining Poverty: Gender in Poverty Reduction Strategy Papers*, Report for the UK Gender and Development Network, London: Christian Aid.

CHAPTER 3

POVERTY AND ITS REDUCTION IN UGANDA

Gabriel Elepu

3.1 INTRODUCTION

This chapter is divided into four main sections. The first section gives background information about Uganda and highlights key issues such as economic growth, poverty trends, education, employment, health, and community services. The second section provides the genesis, development, implementation, successes, and challenges of the poverty reduction strategy in Uganda. In the third section, conclusions are drawn while in the last section, areas for further research are identified.

3.2 ECONOMIC GROWTH

Uganda's economy has been registering positive growth rates averaging slightly over 5.5% since 2000. This is comparatively lower than the growth recorded in the 1990s when the economy was growing at an average annual rate of 6.5%. According to the Ministry of Finance, Planning and Economic Development (MFPED 2006), the real gross domestic product (GDP) at market prices is projected to grow by 5.9% in 2006/07. This will be slightly higher than the 5.3% increase recorded in 2005/06. Furthermore, the improved economic growth in 2006/07 is expected to come from the strong recovery of both agriculture and industry, in addition to a continued strong growth in services. Meanwhile, per capita GDP has continued to increase over time despite rapid population growth at about 3.4% per annum. Per capita income (in constant 2000 USD) rose slightly from USD 244 in 2000/01 to USD 262 in 2004/05 (see Table 3.1).

Table 3.1: Real GDP Growth Rates by Sector, Total Population and Per Capita GDP

Real GDP growth	2000/01	2001/02	2002/03	2003/04	2004/05	2005/06	2006/07
Agriculture	4.6%	3.9%	2.3%	0.8%	1.5%	0.4%	3.6%
Industry	6.0%	8.2%	6.7%	8.2%	10.8%	4.5%	7.6%
Services	5.2%	8.1%	5.7%	8.4%	8.7%	9.2%	7.0%
GDP at market prices	5.0%	6.4%	4.7%	5.5%	6.6%	5.3%	5.9%
GDP (USD Billion)	5.9	6.2	6.6	6.9	7.3	–	–
Population (Million)	23.3	24.1	24.9	25.7	26.5	27.2	–
Per capita GDP (USD)	244	248	255	257	262	–	–

Source: UBOS (2003, 2006), MFPED (various years), and the World Bank.

Table 3.2 shows the contribution to GDP by sector at basic prices. Though still large, the contribution of the agricultural sector to total GDP decreased from 41% in 2000/01 to 34% in 2005/06. The observed decline in the share of agriculture in GDP has been attributed partly to a slower growth of this sector relative to other sectors and partly to the process of structural transformation. Generally, the growth rate of agricultural output in 2005/06 was estimated to be 0.4%, the lowest since 1991/92. This minute growth was brought about by prolonged drought. As the second largest contributor to GDP after services and the largest contributor to rural employment and incomes, this low agricultural growth rate had adverse effects on poverty reduction.

Although it is anticipated that the real GDP growth rate of the agricultural sector will increase by 3.6% in 2006/07, representing a recovery from a declining trend since 1998/99, this is still a much lower growth rate compared to other sectors, which are expected to grow at a rate of at least 7%. For such an important sector of the economy, whose contribution is still important, this comparatively low rate of growth slows the overall real GDP growth rate, per capita income growth and poverty reduction.

Growth in industry declined from 10.8% in 2004/05 to 4.5% in 2005/06, the lowest since 2000/01. This was attributed to reduced electricity supply, which hampered the formal manufacturing sub-sector. However, it is anticipated that industry will grow by 7.6% in 2006/07, although the manufacturing sub-sector is expected to recover strongly only in the second half of the year when the generation of thermal energy is expected to commence. Real monetary construction growth has been in double digits for the last few years. In terms of its contribution to GDP, the industry sector is the smallest (20%), although on the rise.

Growth in services increased slightly from 8.7% in 2004/05 to 9.2% in 2005/06, making it the fastest growing sector of the economy. In 2006/07, it is expected that growth in services will remain strong at 7.0%. Transport and communications are the fastest growing sub-sectors at more than 15% since 2002/03. The rest of the sub-sectors (hotels and restaurants, wholesale and retail trade, community services, banking, real estate, etc.) have also been growing modestly and some even strongly. The contribution of the service sector to the overall economy has been increasing over time. Since 2001/02, this sector has been contributing most (over 40%) to overall GDP as compared to the other sectors.

Table 3.2: Sector Contribution to GDP, 2000/01–2005/06 (Percentages)

	2000/01	2001/02	2002/03	2003/04	2004/05	2005/06
Agriculture	40.8	39.9	39.0	37.4	35.6	34.0
Industry	18.6	18.9	19.3	19.8	20.6	20.5
Services	40.6	41.2	41.7	42.8	43.8	45.5

Source: UBOS (2003; 2006).

3.3 POVERTY TRENDS

Table 3.3 shows poverty trends in Uganda from 1992/93 until 2005/06. Three poverty indicators are used: P0[4], P1[5] and P2[6]. While P0 measures how widespread poverty is, P1 shows how poor the poor are, and P2 gives an indication of how severe poverty is. In general, Uganda has experienced a marked reduction in poverty since 1992/93. The poverty headcount dropped from 56% in 1992/93 to 31% in 2005/06. Similarly, the poverty gap (squared gap) declined from 21% (10%) in 1992/93 to 9% (4%) in 2005/06. However, there was a slight rise in poverty levels between 1999/00 and 2002/03. For example, the poverty headcount increased from 34% in 1999/00 to 38% in 2002/03. On the other hand, the Gini coefficient, a measure of income inequality, rose from 0.365 in 1992/93 to 0.395 in 1999/00 and further to 0.428 in 2002/03, depicting that there was an increase in income inequality at the national level in this period. This suggests that poverty reduction was attained through economic growth and not income redistribution. It is more surprising, however, that in the 1990s, when there was a general improvement in living standards, the poorest 20% became even poorer and so did not benefit from the economic growth during this period.

Table 3.3: Poverty Trends in Uganda, 1992/93–2005/06

Residence	Pop.	1992/93			1999/00			2002/03			2005/06		
	Share[a]	P0	P1	P2	P0	P1	P2	P0	P1	P2	P0	P1	P2
Rural/ Urban													
Rural	84.6	60.3	22.6	11.2	37.4	11.2	4.8	42.7	13.1	5.7	34.2	9.7	3.9
Urban	15.4	28.8	8.7	3.7	9.6	2.1	0.7	14.4	3.9	1.6	13.7	3.5	1.4
Region													
Central	29.2	45.6	15.3	7.0	19.7	4.4	1.5	22.3	5.5	1.9	16.4	3.6	1.3
Eastern	25.2	58.8	22.0	10.9	35.0	9.3	3.6	46.0	14.1	6.0	35.9	9.1	3.4
Northern	19.7	73.5	30.3	15.8	63.7	24.6	12.3	63.0	23.4	11.5	60.7	20.7	9.2
Western	25.9	52.7	18.7	9.0	26.2	6.1	2.1	32.9	8.5	3.3	20.5	5.1	1.8
Poverty	100.0	56.4	20.9	10.3	33.8	10.0	4.3	38.8	11.9	5.1	31.1	8.7	3.5
Gini coefficient		0.365			0.395			0.428			0.408		

A Population share of location/region during the 2005/06 UNHS.

Source: UBOS (2003; 2006).

The reduction in poverty in the 1990s has been attributed to the growth of consumption. It is estimated that per capita consumption grew by 5.3% per annum during the 1990s. The high rate of growth of consumption was a direct result of the impressive growth in GDP that occurred in all the sectors of the economy during this period. The key factor that has been pinpointed as the determinant of the increased consumption was the higher commodity prices resulting from the liberalisation of the economy. For example, after the liberalisation

---

[4] The P0 indicator is the 'headcount' or the percentage of individuals estimated to be living in households with real private consumption per adult equivalent below the poverty line for their rural or urban sub-region.

[5] The P1 indicator is the 'poverty gap' or the sum over all individuals of the shortfall of their real private consumption per adult equivalent from the poverty line, divided by the poverty line.

[6] The P2 indicator is the 'squared poverty gap' or the sum over all individuals of the *square* of the shortfall of their real private consumption per adult equivalent and the poverty line divided by the poverty line.

of the coffee industry farmers were able to obtain higher prices for their produce, which significantly reduced their poverty in the mid-1990s. The growth in cash crop production was a more important contributor to poverty reduction than increased food crop production over the 1992–1996 period, accounting for 48% of the reduction in poverty as compared to 14% for food crops (Appleton 2001).

Between 1997 and 2000, although economic growth slowed down poverty continued to fall owing to two major factors: strong agricultural growth and an increase in public expenditure. The proportional contributions were reversed over 1997–2000, with increased food crop production accounting for 43% of the reduction in poverty and cash crops for 27% (Appleton 2001). Both agricultural growth and increasing public expenditure impacted positively on the consumption of farmers and government workers. However, income inequality started to increase at this time.

After 2000, there was a general increase in poverty as well as income inequality. This has been attributed to numerous factors: slower growth in agriculture, a decline in commodity prices, income diversification, insecurity, high fertility and mortality, inequitable allocation of public funds, skewed distribution of assets, and social and cultural practices (MFPED 2004). Between 2000 and 2003, there was a general decline in growth in the agricultural sector, apart from the livestock sub-sector. This aggravated the poverty situation since agriculture is the main occupation of rural people. Moreover, the slow growth of the agricultural sector was coupled with falling prices for major export crops, such as coffee and cotton. During the same period, households began diversifying their incomes but faced stiff competition. The insecurity in the northern and eastern regions limited investment and economic growth. High fertility rates and the death of productive adults due to HIV and AIDS meant subdivision of productive assets or loss of income. The funding for social services increased but their effect on the poor remained minimal. Inequality in terms of asset ownership and income increased over the period. Lastly, some social and cultural practices, such as alcohol consumption, were blamed for the increased poverty.

Between 2002/03 and 2005/06, a strong growth in consumption among the rural population partly led to significant poverty reduction, but no significant changes were observed in urban areas. However, the incidence of poverty remained higher in rural than in urban areas. The slight improvement is attributed to improved security, aid, and trade with South Sudan. Ugandans also spend more today than a few years ago. In absolute terms, private expenditure on education and health more than doubled across all sections of society. Spending on cellphone airtime also went up, especially for the poorest (20%), for whom it more than doubled. Nationwide, the gap between the poor and the rich narrowed. At the national level, income inequality dropped by 4.5% (UBOS 2006).

In general, Ssewanyana et al. (2004) found that the three most important factors that explained changes in income inequality between 1992/93 and 1999/00 were geographical location, sector of employment, and education of the head of the household. But between 1999/00 and 2002/03, lack of access to community services, education and type of occupation of household head were found to be the most important factors. These findings seem to concur with those obtained from earlier studies (Deininger and Okidi 2002; Okurut et al. 2002; Mijumbi and Okidi 2001; Okwi 1999). Other factors affecting income inequality included household size, age, and sex of household head. Therefore, before examining the poverty reduction strategy in

Uganda, one must look at the situation and/or trends in terms of education, employment, health, and access to community services.

3.3.1 Education

In general, the literacy rate in Uganda in 2005/06 was 69%, showing a significant increment from 65% in 2002/03. However, literacy varies by gender; male literacy rates are generally higher than those for females. In 2005/06, the male literacy rate was estimated at 76% whereas the female literacy rate was estimated at 63%. There is also a considerable rural–urban and regional divide in literacy that has persisted over the years. There was a higher literacy rate in urban (86%) than rural areas (66%). Kampala, for example, had the highest literacy rate, exceeding 90% for each of the gender groups. The Central region had the highest literacy rate (80%) followed by the Western region (67%), Eastern region (63%), and last by the Northern region (59%), as shown in Table 3.4.

Table 3.4: Literacy Rates for Population Aged 10 Years and Above (Percentages)

Residence	1999/00			2002/03			2005/06		
	Male	Female	Both sexes	Male	Female	Both sexes	Male	Female	Both sexes
Rural/Urban									
Urban	92	82	86	90	84	87	89	83	86
Rural	72	54	62	74	60	67	74	58	66
Region									
Kampala	-	-	-	94	91	92	92	90	91
Central	81	74	77	82	74	79	78	82	80
Eastern	72	52	62	72	54	63	56	71	64
Northern	64	33	47	72	42	56	45	74	59
Western	74	61	67	79	69	74	60	74	67
Uganda	74	57	65	77	63	70	76	63	69

Source: UBOS (2003; 2006).

One of the key indicators of access to primary education selected for the Poverty Eradication Action Plan (PEAP) is the Primary School Net Enrolment Ratio (NER), which is the ratio of pupils in the official primary school age range (6–12 years) attending primary school to the total number of children in the same age range in the population. The Millennium Development Goal (MDG) on education is to achieve 100% enrolment of children 6–12 years by 2015. Table 3.5 shows that the Primary School NER in Uganda has basically remained unchanged for the last 5 years. Although it has been revealed that a sizeable number of children attending primary school are outside the official school age range, a lower NER could have resulted from children boycotting or dropping out of school due to economic, education system, socio-cultural, political and physical reasons. For example, almost 40% of the pupils who dropped out of school thought it was too expensive.

Table 3.5: Primary School Net Enrolment Ratio

Survey Year	Male	Female	Uganda
1999/00	85	84	84
2001	87	87	87
2002/03	85	86	86
2005/06	84	85	84

Source: UBOS (2003; 2006).

3.3.2 Employment

The employment situation in Uganda can be assessed by looking at the Employment to Population Ratio (EPR). EPR is defined as 'total employment of the population aged 14–64 years as a percentage of the total population in the same age group' (UBOS 2006). This ratio indicates the extent to which the population is involved in productive labour market activities. It also presents an indication of how the economy generates work. Generally, the EPR has increased from nearly 78% in 2002/03 to about 80% in 2005/06. The annualised employment growth rate varied by gender as it was higher for males (4.7%) than females (3.6%). Moreover, the employment growth rate was higher in urban areas (5.2%) than rural areas (4.0%). Regional disparities in the employment growth rate were reflected in the gap between the highest figure, for the Western region (7.4%), and the lowest, in the Eastern region (1.4%). At the same time, it was shown that the EPR had declined in Kampala and Northern regions compared to elsewhere (Table 3.6).

Table 3.6: Employment to Population Ratio for Persons 14–64 Years

	2002/03		2005/06		Employment growth rate
	%	Employment to population	%	Employment to population	
Sex					
Male	47.8	78.4	48.7	82.0	4.7
Female	52.2	76.7	51.3	79.0	3.6
Rural/Urban					
Urban	13.9	65.3	14.3	65.1	5.2
Rural	86.1	79.9	85.7	83.7	4.0
Region					
Kampala	5.6	63.5	5.3	60.1	2.3
Central	23.7	76.0	24.1	82.9	4.8
Eastern	27.0	79.5	24.9	83.5	1.4
Northern	18.6	83.0	17.9	77.4	2.9
Western	25.2	76.9	27.8	83.0	7.4
Uganda	100.0	77.5	100.0	80.4	4.1

Source: UBOS (2003; 2006).

The sectoral distribution of the economically active population shows that agriculture remains the major sector of employment in Uganda. The proportion of the population employed in agriculture increased from 66% in 2002/03 to 73% in 2005/06 (Table 3.7). Given the declining contribution of agriculture to the economy as shown in Table 3.2, the above employment situation presents a challenge to the government.

Table 3.7: Employment of Working Population 14–64 Years by Industry (Percentages)

Industry/sector of employment	2002/03	2005/06
Industry		
Agriculture, Hunting	65.5	73.3
Sales	12.5	8.1
Manufacturing	6.5	4.2
Education	2.8	2.6
Transport, Storage	2.1	2.0
Others	4.7	9.8
Sector of employment		
Primary	65.5	73.3
Manufacturing	7.7	4.2
Service	26.8	22.5
Total	100.0	100.0

Source: UBOS (2003; 2006).

3.3.3 Health

Malaria is the major killer disease in Uganda, especially among children. In 2005/06, its prevalence rate was approximately 50%. There was a higher-than-average incidence of malaria in Western, Kampala, Eastern, and Central regions. For unknown reasons, the Northern region was the least malaria-affected region with a prevalence rate of only 36%. Other diseases prevalent in Uganda were respiratory infections (14%) and diarrhoea (9%), as shown in Table 3.8. Due to the economic importance of malaria, attempts have been made by the government to reduce its incidence through the promotion of wider use of insecticide-treated mosquito nets. In 2005, taxes on mosquito nets were abolished to make protection against malaria more affordable. This apparently led to the increase in the use of mosquito nets from 13% in 2002/03 to 17% in 2005/06. The use of DDT to eradicate malaria vectors has also been proposed, although it is still a controversial issue among the public. Therefore, at the moment Uganda relies mostly on anti-malarial drugs such as fansidar, chloroquine, quinine and others to control malaria. However, the current challenges are the poor access to health facilities due to long distances and the ill-equipped or ill-managed health facilities.

Table 3.8: Population by Type of Illness, Region and Age Group in 2005/06 (Percentages)

	Malaria	Respiratory infections	Diarrhoea	Injury	Skin infections	Others	Total
Region							
Kampala	53.2	18.6	5.6	4.2	2.1	16.1	100.0
Central	50.9	15.9	5.9	9.7	3.1	14.6	100.0
Eastern	51.4	11.2	9.7	6.6	3.8	17.1	100.0
Northern	35.9	17.6	13.8	6.1	3.8	22.6	100.0
Western	57.4	12.3	9.6	4.8	2.2	13.9	100.0
Age							
Under 5	60.0	14.7	11.0	4.6	4.2	5.3	100.0
5–17	50.3	15.9	6.9	6.8	3.3	16.8	100.0
18–30	47.3	12.0	9.2	6.7	2.2	22.8	100.0
31–59	42.9	12.3	10.5	7.7	2.7	23.8	100.0
60+	33.7	14.2	12.1	11.6	3.2	25.0	100.0
Uganda	49.6	14.1	9.4	6.8	3.2	16.9	100.0

Source: UBOS (2003; 2006).

3.3.4 HIV prevalence

HIV and AIDS is another disease that has affected the economic development of Uganda by trimming down the productive labour force, reducing labour availability through sickness or care of the sick, and increasing the number of widows/widowers and orphans. In general, the prevalence rate of HIV and AIDS in adults aged 15–59 was 6.3% in 2004/05. The HIV and AIDS prevalence rate was higher among men aged 15–59 than women in the same age group, that is 5.2% versus 7.3%, suggesting differences in vulnerability to the disease by sex (Table 3.9). Realising the disastrous effects of HIV and AIDS, Uganda has devoted much effort and resources to combating it through mass education campaigns, the provision of condoms and anti-retroviral drugs. However, more effort and resources are required if HIV and AIDS is to be wiped out.

Table 3.9: HIV Prevalence by Age and Sex, 2004/05

Age	Percentage HIV positive		
	Male	Female	Both Sexes
15–19	0.3	2.6	1.5
20–24	2.4	6.3	4.7
25–29	5.9	8.7	7.6
30–34	8.1	12.1	10.3
35–39	9.2	9.9	9.6
40–44	9.3	8.4	8.8
45–49	6.9	8.2	7.6
50–54	6.9	5.4	6.1
55–59	5.8	4.9	5.4
15–59	5.2	7.3	6.3

Source: UBOS (2003; 2006).

3.3.5 Community services

Access to community services such as safe drinking water and electricity is one of the measures of community welfare (MFPED 2000; 2003). There was a slight improvement in access to safe drinking water between 2001 and 2005/06. Fifty-nine percent of the communities had access to safe drinking water in 2005/06 as compared to 56% in 2001. However, safe drinking water is more accessible in urban than rural communities. In 2005/06, 95% of people in urban communities had access to safe drinking water but only 54% for rural communities. The Central region had better access to safe drinking water (66%) than all other regions while the Northern region had the lowest proportion (51%). It is also worth noting that the availability of safe drinking water for all regions increased between 2001 and 2005/06 with the exception of the Northern region. By contrast, only 20% of the communities had access to electricity, up from 18% in 2001. Again, urban communities were more privileged (87%) than rural communities (51%), as shown in Table 3.10. The availability of electricity has far-reaching implications for the environment as wood fuel is the commonly used source of energy, particularly in rural areas.

Table 3.10: Access to Safe Drinking Water and Electricity by Residence (Percentages)

Residence	Safe drinking water		Electricity	
	2001	2005/06	2001	2005/06
Rural/Urban				
Urban	87	95	84	86.5
Rural	51	54	7.7	9.3
Region				
Central	62	66	–	–
Eastern	58	63	–	–
Northern	51	51	–	–
Western	52	55	–	–
National	56	59	17.8	19.5

Source: UBOS (2003; 2006).

3.4 THE POVERTY REDUCTION STRATEGY

Historically, Uganda has adopted a number of both popular and unpopular strategies since independence to fight poverty. In the late 1960s, the Obote I government drafted the 'Common Man's Charter', which was one of the steps taken under the 'move to the Left' when Uganda was pursuing a socialist line. However, this strategy did not materialise as there was a coup d'etat in 1971. One year later, the military government declared 'economic war', which saw the expulsion of Indians, who were managing most of the economy, and the transfer of the economy into the hands of indigenous people. Consequently, the once vibrant economy of the 1960s was shattered and the production of major cash crops (coffee and cotton) declined. In 1974, the government started a campaign, with little success, known as 'double production' in which farmers were forced to increase their output of coffee and cotton. The Amin government came to an end in 1979.

In the early 1980s, the Obote II government embarked on a post-conflict reconstruction and rehabilitation programme with the assistance of international donors and agencies such as the World Bank, the International Monetary Fund (IMF), the United States Agency for International Development (USAID) and the European Union (EU). However, not much success was registered due to the civil war and the short tenure of the government.

In 1986, the present (Museveni) government came to power. Under this government, various programmes aimed at tackling poverty have been instituted since 1987. These programmes include: post-conflict reconstruction and rehabilitation (e.g. economic recovery, structural adjustment, and disaster programmes), decentralisation, the PEAP, and the poverty action fund (PAF). These programmes are discussed in the following sections and it is worth noting that the new programmes built on the old ones rather than replacing them.

3.4.1 Post-conflict reconstruction and rehabilitation programmes

In the first decade after the internal conflict (1987–1997), the government focused on reconstruction and rehabilitation programmes, including economic, social, human, and physical infrastructure. In 1987, with assistance from the World Bank, Uganda embarked on economic recovery and structural adjustment programmes with an emphasis on privatisation and economic liberalisation. It is argued that some of the economic reforms have had a positive impact on the livelihoods of smallholders, many of whom were later able to move out of poverty (Balihuta and Sen 2001). The agricultural sector, for instance, benefited in a broad-based manner as there was increased production of food and cash crops, especially coffee and cotton. In addition, the growth in the agricultural sector in turn stimulated the rapid growth of non-farm activities in the rural economy, which provided households with greater choice in their livelihood strategies. As to why other economic reforms did not positively impact on the livelihoods of smallholder farmers, Balihuta and Sen identified three constraints: poor design and implementation of fiscal decentralisation programme, unavailability of agricultural finance, and agricultural advisory services.

The programmes directly addressing the reconstruction of social, human, and physical infrastructure included the Emergency Relief and Rehabilitation Programme, Luwero Triangle Rehabilitation, the Pacification and Development of Northern Uganda and Karamoja, and the Programme for the Alleviation of Poverty and Social Costs of Adjustment. Although some of the above programmes are still ongoing, their impact on poverty reduction appears to be minimal.

3.4.2 Decentralisation

Decentralisation can be defined as the 'devolution of power downwards so as to promote both popular participation and more appropriate and effective service delivery' (James et al. 2001). In the early 1960s, Uganda had experimented with a decentralised system of local governance but it was quickly abolished. However, with support from USAID this system was reintroduced in the 1990s. Decentralisation was first piloted in a few districts and focused on capacity building for the elected and appointed officials and representatives of civil society. The aim was to increase the capacity of local government to deliver services and to expand the involvement of civil society in decision-making and governmental oversight. Once there were significant improvements in their capacities in planning, budgeting, and financial management, the decentralised districts then qualified for the Local Government Development Programme Grant.

Currently, the decentralisation process is complete and local authorities are responsible for delivering most of the basic services that the government provides. Hence, each district is allocated conditional grants by the central government plus the unconditional and equalisation transfers. Districts are also expected to raise revenue from local sources to supplement the above funds.

Decentralisation has somewhat improved the delivery of services in Uganda. For example, it has been noted that decentralised primary school classroom construction has shown substantially reduced unit costs and faster construction rates than the previous centralised programmes (MFPED 2004). While improvements in fiscal mechanisms and the publication of fiscal transfers have led to a dramatic improvement in the passage of funds to their intended destinations, local autonomy in fiscal allocation has been slower to develop. The unconditional transfers and revenues are small relative to conditional grants, and they are often used mainly to defray administrative costs, including councillors' allowances, rather than to deliver services tailored to local needs.

3.4.3 The Poverty Eradication Action Plan

The PEAP forms the national vision to eradicate poverty and aims at wiping out absolute poverty by 2017. The evolution of PEAP can be traced back to 1995 when the national poverty forum was organised. This culminated in the formation of the committee that drafted the PEAP in 1997. The drafting of PEAP in 1997 involved extensive use of the existing data and literature on poverty in Uganda. The exercise also involved the participation of major stakeholders such as central and local governments, the donor community, and academicians. When PEAP was first prepared, strong emphasis was put on the provision of health and education services and support for the agriculture sector. However, since its formation in 1997, PEAP has been revised twice to update it in line with changing circumstances and emerging priorities (MFPED 2004).

In 2000, PEAP was first modified to include new information and ideas that had been obtained through further consultations with communities under the first Participatory Poverty Assessments (PPAs). This revised PEAP also echoed improvements in various sectors regarding their policies, investment plans, outcomes and performance indicators. More sectors were added to the revised PEAP, which included roads, education, health, the modernisation of agriculture, including the environment, private sector competitiveness, water and sanitation, and justice, law and order. This PEAP, therefore, provided a Comprehensive Development Framework (CDF)[7] for Uganda. And in 2000 it was accepted by the World Bank and the IMF as Uganda's Poverty Reduction Strategy Paper (PRSP).

In 2004, the second modification of PEAP was undertaken to include findings from the latest research studies, the second community PPAs, and fresh consultations with stakeholders. The widest consultations were held with numerous stakeholders about progress and implementation challenges. These stakeholders included government sector working groups, civil society, the private sector, parliament and development partners. The modified PEAP was organised under five pillars: economic management; production, competitiveness and incomes; security, conflict resolution and disaster management; good governance; and human development. In addition to the emphasis on functionality and implementation, two new issues were added in 2004: security and conflict resolution; and cross-cutting issues such as HIV and AIDS, environment and gender.

3.4.4 The Poverty Action Fund

In 1997, the Government of Uganda introduced the PAF to restore donor confidence in how pro-poor funds were going to be spent. This was particularly important since Uganda was to benefit from the debt relief funds under the Highly Indebted Poor Countries (HIPC) initiative. To ensure the smooth operation of PAF in improving pro-poor expenditure monitoring and management, external consultations were undertaken during its preparation. It is believed that PAF and the Multilateral Debt Fund instituted by Nordic donors are closely related in structure (Morrissey and Verschoor 2006).

The PAF framework incorporates sector planning and allocations, thereby increasing the effectiveness of pro-poor spending. PAF is regarded as a 'virtual fund' because it is part and parcel of the national budget (MFPED 2004). PAF forms a subset of the national budget that

[7] The CDF is a holistic, overarching framework which covers macro- and microeconomic, financial, structural, social, institutional, environmental, and human resource considerations that enable a country to transform society and the economy to reduce poverty effectively.

is considered to contribute directly to poverty reduction: primary education, primary health care, water and sanitation, agriculture and rural roads. This part of the budget is specially treated in that its share of the total budget has been rising, it is protected from within-year budget cuts, and it is subjected to much stricter reporting and monitoring requirements than other parts of the budget. Although the development of PAF has been beneficial to Uganda through the restoration of donor confidence in pro-poor spending, its special treatment has led to some implementation challenges, such as the distortion of budget allocations towards specific social sectors favoured by donors, reduced flexibility in the budgeting process, and the concentrated deployment of scarce monitoring resources at the expense of other components of the national budget.

3.4.5 Ownership of the PRS

Although external consultancy and advice were widely sought in the preparation of both PEAP and PAF, the Government of Uganda has been highly instrumental in the initiation and implementation of these programmes. Mackinnon and Reinikka (2000) hail Uganda as 'one of the first low-income countries to prepare a comprehensive national strategy for poverty reduction using a participatory approach'. It is thought that the development of pro-poor expenditure policies in Uganda occurred due to 'pure policy learning, supported (in policy design) by external agents' and that Uganda 'owns' both PEAP and PAF (Morrissey and Verschoor 2006). Uganda has been considered a leader in formulating a strategy to monitor and deliver pro-poor expenditures. It is believed that Uganda's experience contributed considerably to the design of the PRSPs[8] by the IMF and the World Bank.

The deep commitment to poverty reduction by the political leadership in Uganda has been attributed to its history and the donor reward system (Morrissey and Verschoor 2006). Since the late 1980s, Uganda has increased its social spending. This occurred because the government became 'reform-minded' and agreed to adopt structural adjustment programmes, which were introduced by the IMF and the World Bank as conditions for their loans. In the mid-1990s, when poverty reduction became a major concern of most donors, Uganda was again enthusiastic in following external advice regarding the identification of strategic sectors for pro-poor expenditure. Second, it is argued that the commitment of the political leadership in Uganda to poverty reduction came from 'donors rewarding previous reform intentions immediately and generously'. For instance, Uganda became the first country to receive a stock debt rescheduling from the Paris Club in 1995. Uganda also became the first country to qualify as eligible for debt relief under the HIPC initiative in 1997 and a year later became the first country to obtain debt relief under this initiative. In 2000, Uganda qualified for enhanced HIPC debt relief worth USD 1.3 billion and Paris Club debt relief worth USD 145 million.

3.4.6 Implementation of the PRS

PEAP is a national planning framework to guide detailed medium- and long-term sector plans, district plans and the budget process in eradicating poverty. Under PEAP, sectoral or sub-sectoral programmes have been developed for education, health, roads, water (including urban and rural water and water for production), justice, law and order (criminal and commercial

---

[8] PRSPs substituted structural adjustment programmes and were introduced in 1999 by the World Bank and IMF as new preconditions for loans and debt relief under the HIPC initiative. To qualify for HIPC debt relief, pro-poor development strategies were required to be designed through involvement of stakeholders.

justice reform), sub-sectors of environment (land and wetlands), and social development. A sectoral plan for agriculture is at an advanced stage of development. Government has also strengthened the intersectoral linkages between expenditures in the productive sectors by the introduction of cross-cutting strategies, the Plan for Modernisation of Agriculture (PMA) and the Medium-Term Competitive Strategy (MTCS). The PMA ensures that expenditures geared toward the enhancement of rural incomes are looked at as a whole. The MTCS plays the same role for the productive sectors outside agriculture.

For each of the PEAP pillars, the government has set up plans intended to eradicate poverty as well as identifying a set of actions or strategies that will be carried out as shown below.

Pillar 1: Economic management

- Boost economic growth to 7% over the medium term by removing bureaucratic barriers to investment, improving transport infrastructure and utility services, and modernising agriculture among others.
- Reduce the public sector deficit to 6.5% of GDP by 2009/10 and keep its share constant thereafter by emphasising the quality rather than the quantity of public expenditure, negotiating budget support grants, and increasing revenue collection by the Uganda Revenue Authority.
- Stimulate growth in private sector investment to 21% of GDP and in exports to 16.1% of GDP by 2013/4 by reducing commercial bank holdings of Government securities, mobilising deposits and savings, establishing a credit reference bureau, promoting microfinance institutions (MFIs), reforming the pensions sector, and maintaining macroeconomic stability and a liberal trade policy.
- Keep inflation at 5% by controlling monetary growth.

Pillar 2: Enhancing production, competitiveness and incomes

- Promote agricultural research, extension, and marketing through support of National Agricultural Research Services, National Agricultural Advisory Services, and the Strategic Export Programme (SEP), respectively.
- Develop transport infrastructure through the maintenance of roads, rehabilitation of railway lines and regional links, and expansion of Entebbe International Airport.
- Expand electricity generation by building two more dams, Bujagali (250 MW) and Karuma falls (200 MW), and expanding the rural electrification programme. Other sources of energy, such as solar and thermal energy, are being considered.
- Encourage petroleum exploration and investment in mining. Private companies have been licensed to explore for petroleum and a new Mineral Policy and Mining Law has been established to promote investment in mining.
- Promote tourism, including cultural and domestic tourism. Government will continue to support the promotion of Uganda as a tourist destination.
- Advance science, technology, and industrialisation through the creation of incentives such as Innovation Awards for technological innovation and development.
- Under the Microfinance Outreach Programme, the government plans to expand microfinance in remote areas and to finance agriculture by funding capacity-building and matching grants.
- Promote the development of medium-, small-scale and micro-enterprises through the

development of a cost-effective way of delivering services to them, review the method of taxation used for this sub-sector; and reduce bureaucratic obstacles to their operations.

- Promote the sustainable use of environmental resources by instituting land reform, protecting central forest reserves, supporting district and community forests, and protecting wetlands and wildlife.
- Enhance the productivity of workers through the reform of vocational education and monitoring of the working conditions of workers.

Pillar 3: Security, conflict-resolution and disaster management

- Restore peace and security in the North and North-East. This requires bringing to an end the rebel insurgency in the North and persistent cattle rustling in the North-East. The government is using multiple strategies: protecting the security of the population using national and militia forces; providing amnesty to rebels who surrender; peace negotiations with rebels; disarming and controlling small arms movement in Karamoja; and supporting peace-building initiatives in Karamoja.
- Strengthen disaster preparedness and recovery programmes. Since disaster programmes are not budgeted for, Government will allocate funds to such programmes in a more flexible manner. The Northern Uganda Social Action Fund (NUSAF) has also been put in place to finance projects identified by communities in an effort to assist them to recover from insecurity.

Pillar 4: Good Governance

- Strengthen democracy, justice, and the rule of law. The government adopted a multi-party dispensation in 2005. The Uganda Human Rights Commission has been set up to protect against violations of human rights. Access to justice will be improved by recruiting more police and judicial officers. The efficiency and effectiveness of justice will be improved by strengthening local council courts, reducing case backlogs, strengthening prison farms, and promoting dispute resolution in the case of commercial justice.
- Improve public accountability and transparency. To this effect, the government has introduced better monitoring and financial controls, including the Integrated Financial Management System, procurement reforms and the publication of transfers to local governments. The government also intends to investigate and act against corruption and other dubious practices, such as money laundering. Furthermore, enhancement of salaries of public servants through public sector reform is thought to improve the efficiency of service delivery.

Pillar 5: Human development

- Improve the quality of health care; the prevention and treatment of malaria, HIV and AIDS, diarrhoea and other diseases; and the raising of public awareness about proper nutrition, sanitation and hygiene, and family planning. Under the first Health Sector Strategic Plan (HSSP I), priority areas are hygiene and sanitation; immunisation; malaria control; information, education and communication; reproductive health; and HIV and AIDS. The government has also upgraded the infrastructure, abolished user fees in public facilities, provided subsidies to the not-for-profit sector, upgraded training and enhanced drug availability. Under HSSP II, the government will continue to emphasise the following areas: health education and promotion, environmental health, control of diarrhoeal diseases, school health and community health, internally displaced populations and extension work from other sectors.

- Improve access to primary, secondary, and tertiary education; improve the quality and efficiency of education; and expand vocational education. Access to education will be improved through the continued provision of schools and classroom facilities, training of teachers in special needs, and supporting private community secondary schools, introducing student bursaries. The quality and efficiency of education will be improved by training more teachers, implementing the use of the mother tongue in lower grades, increasing the relevance of the curriculum, multi-grade teaching, double-shift teaching, and providing incentives for teachers in hard-to-reach areas. A school feeding programme is also being developed to target children in selected areas to improve school retention and educational performance.
- Increase access to safe drinking water and enable every district to reach the same level of coverage by 2015. The government has developed sector investment plans for urban and rural water supply and has assumed responsibility for most of the costs of rural water supply.
- Promote social development by revitalising the community development function and by strengthening functional adult literacy, social protection for vulnerable groups and the analysis of gender in sectoral ministries.

3.4.7 Milestones of the PRS

In 1997, when the first PEAP was prepared, many targets were set through a process of intense consultations by means of the Poverty Monitoring Network, among others. These national targets guide resource allocation and activities in the PEAP sectors. Later, when PEAP was revised in 2004, it incorporated the MDGs to the extent that the two programmes are now closely related.[9] Compared to PEAP, the MDGs are broad global goals for poverty eradication, including Universal Primary Education (UPE), gender, child and maternal mortality, HIV and AIDS, environmental sustainability and partnership principles. These programmes have in common the general objective of holding the government and the donor communities responsible for poverty reduction progress.

Although the use of PEAP targets predominates over the MDGs, the latter play three important roles. First, MDG targets have been fully embraced by certain sectors, such as education. Second, the MDGs have been used to supplement the national poverty monitoring indicators, especially in relation to HIV and AIDS, malaria and tuberculosis. Finally, the MDGs have become a yardstick by which Uganda makes international comparisons and measures its own performance against that of similar countries around the globe.

When the goals of the two programmes are systematically compared, some of them are very similar, except that their quantitative targets differ. In general, the PEAP targets related to poverty, UPE, HIV and AIDS, and water are more ambitious than the MDG targets. By contrast, the MDG targets for gender equality in education, infant mortality, and maternal mortality are more ambitious than those set in PEAP. It is believed that the prospects for achieving the MDGs are good. However, it is doubtful whether the resources will be sufficient to achieve the targets for maternal mortality and education (MFPED 2004).

---

[9] The MDGs stem from the Millennium Declaration of the UN General Assembly in 2000 with the aim of achieving them by 2015.

The monitoring and evaluation system of PEAP was designed for two main purposes. First, it is essential to monitor progress in order to provide continuing information to key agents involved in the process. Encouraging a two-way flow of information between beneficiaries, service providers and policy makers is an essential component of PEAP. In this way, the design and implementation strategies can be continually modified to build on what works and to avoid repeating mistakes. Second, the monitoring strategy will help to build accountability. Where targets are set, the government will expect to account for its successes or failures in achieving them, though it is understood that these successes and failures sometimes depend on factors outside government control.

The government has established an elaborate system to monitor and evaluate the implementation and progress of PEAP. This system was developed in 2001 and is referred to as the Poverty Monitoring and Evaluation System (PMES) (MFPED 2004). Under the PMES, there are 33 priority indicators for the implementation of PEAP, and each of these indicators has baseline and target levels. While the baseline level has been set for 2002/03, two target levels, one in 2007/08 and the other in 20013/14, have so far been instituted. The structure of the PMES also requires analysing these indicators at the following levels: input, output, process, outcome, and impact. Although the degree of regularity and accuracy of information about these indicators varies, it is obtainable. Furthermore, institutions responsible for poverty monitoring have also been identified in the PMES. Three types of data are used for monitoring purposes: national survey data from the Uganda Bureau of Statistics (UBOS); available data from sector ministries; and qualitative data from community PAPs.

Nevertheless, the PMES faces challenges: an imperfect flow of appropriate information to top decision-makers; weak M&E coordination activities; an inadequate performance-based public management culture; and incomplete and underused information. The government has devised ways of dealing with the above challenges. First, it has instituted the National Integrated M&E Strategy (NIMES) in the Prime Minister's office. The NIMES system is a framework to synchronise the existing systems to minimise duplication of effort and improve timeliness, quality of data generated, and the actual use of M&E information by decision-makers. Second, a variety of methods are used to collect data, including censuses and surveys, administrative data, PAPs, beneficiary assessments, economic data and research studies. Third, outputs of the monitoring system will be produced periodically. Fourth, reports and papers will be widely disseminated to the various sectors. Lastly, NIMES has a National Coordination Committee (NCC) accountable to the Technical Implementation Coordination Committee. The NCC comprises three working groups: spatial/geographical information systems, district information systems, and research and evaluation.

Uganda has placed special emphasis on poverty analysis and monitoring. Some of the major efforts include the establishment of the UBOS as an autonomous institution with a network to the lowest levels; the institutionalisation of annual household surveys, service delivery surveys and poverty assessments; and the establishment of a Poverty Monitoring Strategy and Framework. Since 1992, Uganda has used international expertise to analyse household survey data to ensure the integrity of the findings while building capacity at the same time. This has led to the establishment of comprehensive poverty trend data and determinants in the country. However, it can be argued that the inclusion in the poverty analysis of external pressures such as globalisation, climate change, and other external shocks remains a major challenge (Muduuli 2001).

Although Uganda launched PEAP in 1997, numerous policy papers were subsequently produced to ease its modification. In 2001, the United Nations Development Programme (UNDP), the World Bank and other development partners assisted Uganda in completing the PRSP process by sponsoring the Uganda Participatory Poverty Assessment Project. Another major contribution by UNDP to the PRSP process was the Uganda Vision 2025 that was produced in 1999.[10] This was incorporated into the revised PEAP and into the PRSP processes afterwards to provide the vision necessary under the CDF. These efforts helped Uganda to become the first country to benefit from the debt relief facility under the enhanced HIPC initiative in 2000. In addition to its involvement in designing the PRSP, the UNDP participated in other related activities such as revising the PAF, formulating the Plan for the Modernisation of Agriculture and the National Poverty Forum.

The UNDP also assisted in setting up a District Resource Information System in 15 districts and in the UBOS. In the second phase of the participatory poverty assessment, which commenced in 1999, the UNDP supported and strengthened the capacity of district authorities and non-governmental organisations for poverty-focused participatory planning and monitoring. In 2001, using the Policy Analysis and Poverty Monitoring Project resources under the CCF and tapping its headquarters' regional programme funds, the UNDP was able to embark on analytical studies for the benefit of the national planning and policy-making process. In the same year, the first joint audit exercise took place and after that the World Bank extended the activities to other districts in the country.

The other development partner that has assisted Uganda in considerable measure in its efforts to eradicate poverty is the African Development Bank (AfDB). The AfDB has co-funded various projects under PEAP such as water and sanitation, education and health services, and economic empowerment of the poor (New Vision 2006). In 2000, the AfDB funded the establishment of the Microfinance Support Centre (MSC).[11] The MSC was incorporated in 2001 as an autonomous apex body in charge of implementing the Rural Microfinance Support Project. The MSC targets MFIs across the country delivering financial assistance to the economically active poor, comprising mostly women. In education, the AfDB has funded Education I & II projects. The Education I project started in 1991 and aimed to strengthen scientific and technical teacher education. The Education II project was started in 2001 to support the education strategic plan. In early 2006, having achieved high primary school enrolment rates due to UPE, the AfDB agreed to fund the Education III project, intended to boost post-primary education and training in business, technical and vocational skills. In the health sector, the AfDB has partially funded Health Sector Rehabilitation Projects I & II, both of which aimed at renovating and constructing health units throughout the country. In 2001, the AfDB also funded the government's support to the Health Sector Strategic Plan Project, aimed at strengthening the provision of mental health and primary health services countrywide. Lastly, since 1996, when the Road Sector Development Programme (RSDP) was initiated, the AfDB has co-funded numerous national and district road network projects.

[10] Uganda Vision 2025 reflects the country's history, core values and aspirations in objectives and goals which are achievable. The theme for Vision 2025 is 'Prosperous people, harmonious nation and beautiful country'.
[11] The MSC has a dual mandate of providing sustainable financial services based on sound business principles through viable institutions and capacity building to MFIs to enable them deliver financial services to the economically active poor (mostly women) on a sustainable basis.

Realising its inability to fight poverty alone, Uganda has embraced regional cooperation initiatives such as the New Partnership for Africa's Development,[12] the Common Market for Eastern and Southern Africa (COMESA), the East African Community (EAC), and the Inter-Governmental Authority on Development (IGAD). In fact, Uganda considers foreign trade and investment to be important stimuli to economic growth and that is why it is involved in economic integration with regional ventures. To harmonise the regional trade regime, tariff barriers between the EAC member states are gradually being dismantled. Uganda extends preferential tariff treatment to members of COMESA. As far as IGAD is concerned, crucial issues such as land degradation, desertification, and food security are high on the agenda since they are directly linked to poverty. In sum, foreign trade policies are expected to encourage trade and investment between Uganda and other EAC and COMESA countries. However, regional trade arrangements between the above countries tend to focus on manufactures and to a lesser extent on agricultural produce because the latter is more sensitive.

Uganda is also one of the beneficiaries of the US market access initiative, African Growth and Opportunity Act, which has permitted it to export duty-free textiles and apparel to the American market. Furthermore, Uganda has benefited from the EU's Everything But Arms initiative as well as from other Generalised System of Preferences schemes, such as those of Canada and Japan. Uganda is also a member of the World Trade Organization (WTO), which provides an important forum through which its voice can be heard on trade issues. However, Uganda still faces some challenges during WTO talks, including strengthening the capacity of negotiators, ensuring a common position and continuing efforts to reduce tariff and non-tariff barriers.

The development of PEAP and the subsequent qualification for debt relief by Uganda under the HIPC initiative could have partly resulted in the impressive achievements in poverty reduction as shown in Table 3.3. The HIPC savings were set aside for pro-poor expenditure in priority sectors such as primary education and health services, through PAF. In the late 1990s, expenditure on primary education rose by 307%, primary health care by 227%, agriculture by 186% and roads by 279% (Morrissey and Verschoor 2006). Moreover, the share of PAF in the total national budget more than doubled from 17% in 1997/98 to 35% in 2003/04 (MFPED 2005).

However, poverty eradication still remains a great challenge for the government of Uganda. Some problems have been identified as affecting the implementation of the PRS, including persistent insecurity, limited public accountability, human development problems, poverty insensitive public transfers, lack of safety nets for the elderly, and unsustainable external debt (MFPED 2004; Ssewanyana et al. 2004; Morrissey and Verschoor 2006; Mukasa and Masiga 2003; APEJ 2003).

First, improvement of regional income inequality can only be realised if security is first restored in the war-torn regions in the North and North-East. Persistent cattle raiding and rebel activity in these regions have resulted in a loss of resources and assets, food insecurity

---

[12] NEPAD's role is to promote the accelerated transformation of African economies through good political and economic governance.

and displacement of people to camps, where they depend almost entirely on humanitarian assistance. Peace in these regions will allow Internally Displaced Persons to return home, where they again can become active in the economy. The government has endeavoured to end the insecurity in these regions through the use of arms. However, it has been blamed for preferring 'powerful' ministries, such as defence, to 'weak' ministries, such as agriculture, in budget allocations (Morrissey and Verschoor 2006). At the moment, peace talks are being held between the rebels and the government in the hope that they will bring to an end more than 20 years of war and suffering. Cattle raiders are also being disarmed voluntarily, although this strategy has not borne much fruit.

Second, Uganda's decentralised system of service delivery is marred by limited transparency and public accountability at the local authority level. Corruption and mismanagement of pro-poor funds have hindered the proper distribution of these funds to the intended beneficiaries. The public expenditure tracking surveys of service facilities that were pioneered in 1996 revealed that a large proportion of funds meant for non-wage primary education expenditure were misappropriated by local bureaucrats. The government then stepped up its efforts to enhance transparency by disseminating information, both through the media and by posting public spending information at schools and at the district level. Subsequent surveys in 1999–2000 revealed that the proportion of non-wage primary education funds received by schools increased to 90% from a mere 20% in 1995. Thus, the dissemination of information and transparency has been found to be a cost-effective way of mitigating systemic problems in service delivery. Two other strategies that have been applauded for their role in increasing the transparency of local authorities include making public the salaries of public sector workers and setting output targets (for schools, roads, health clinics) for public service delivery.

Third, human development challenges persist: poor quality and high drop-out rates in the UPE, lack of a post-primary education strategy, high mortality and population growth rates. Uganda has achieved major increases in pupil enrolment in primary education, but quality and drop-out rates remain its major threats. Increased primary school enrolment under the UPE suggests the need for a similar strategy for post-primary education. HIV and AIDS prevalence has fallen dramatically, but has recently levelled out at about 6%. In addition, progress in reducing child and infant mortality and promoting family planning has been disappointing. Thus, the government needs to improve the quality of primary education and reduce drop-out rates, expand post-primary education, and reduce infant and child mortality. The government also needs to improve the accessibility of and demand for family planning services as well as raising public awareness of the dangers of HIV and AIDS and producing many children.

Fourth, government expenditure has also been criticised for not sufficiently addressing regional inequalities. According to Africa Policy E-Journal (2003), the government's current transfer formula of allocating 85% of transfers according to the size of the district population and 15% according to geographical location does not take poverty into consideration. It is further revealed that in the distribution of transfers to local governments by region, the Western region receives the largest share (27%), followed closely by the Eastern (26%), the Central (25%) and the Northern (22%), where poverty is highest. Had the transfer allocation formula reflected poverty across districts, in addition to population and size of district, more transfers would have gone to the northern districts. If such a poverty-sensitive distribution formula were adopted, it would probably allocate 29% to the Northern region, 26% to the Western, 23% to the Central, and 22% to the Eastern.

Fifth, the PRS in Uganda has been focused on infrastructural development, health and UPE, as well as the development of specific projects or programmes, including the PMA, immunisation programme, food and nutrition, water and sanitation among others. Although poverty reduction policy initiatives have targeted all categories of the poor, including women, youth and children, the disabled and the elderly, they have been criticised for being less beneficial to the elderly (Mukasa and Masiga 2003). The only poverty eradication initiatives targeting the elderly in Uganda so far include pension and National Social Security Fund schemes. However, these schemes target only retired civil servants, who constitute only a small percentage of the elderly in Uganda who need social protection and income security.

Lastly, Uganda's external debt remains unsustainable as measured by the ratio of Net Present Value (NPV) of debt to exports of goods and services, which stood at 280% at the beginning of 2004/05. The HIPC debt relief threshold for sustainability is 150%. The main reason for Uganda's external debt being unsustainable is the slower than expected growth in exports and an increase in the NPV of debt arising from increased disbursements, especially from multilateral creditors. Consequently, it remains government policy to limit annual borrowing as one means of achieving debt sustainability. The government is also promoting exports as a lasting solution to this problem. In this regard, efforts are being made to address supply bottlenecks, especially infrastructural and institutional reforms, which are expected to increase the country's international competitiveness and boost export earnings.

3.5 CONCLUSION

The development of PEAP in 1997 and its subsequent revisions in 2000 and 2004 show the deep commitment of Uganda's top leadership to fighting poverty. Although wide consultations were made with external technical advisors, the government undoubtedly owned the policy direction, hence justifying the characterisation of PEAP as home-grown. Moreover, the government immediately translated the plan into its budget and medium- and long-term expenditure frameworks.

Pro-poor expenditures rose sharply after the formation of PEAP in 1997. Consequently, there was a substantial reduction in poverty nationwide in the 1990s, although from 2000 onwards there were mixed results. The poverty head count fell from 56% in 1992/93 to 34% in 1999/00 but rose to 38% in 2002/03. However, the poverty head count declined again to 31% in 2005/06. On the other hand, the Gini coefficient, a measure of income inequality, rose from 0.36 in 1992/93 to 0.39 in 1999/00 and then further to 0.43 in 2002/03, reflecting an increase in income inequality at the national level over this period. By 2005/06, the Gini coefficient had dropped slightly to 0.41.

Economic growth, backed by policies aimed at income redistribution, will further reduce poverty in Uganda. Policies that address income inequality need to embrace the provision of high quality social services to rural areas, for example, UPE, health, and community services. However, in areas where there is persistent insecurity such as northern and eastern regions, the restoration of peace should be prioritised.

To achieve poverty reduction through economic growth, the growth of the agricultural sector is crucial given the fact that it employs the largest proportion (73%) of the population.

Therefore, to spur rural income growth, commercialisation of smallholder agriculture is a prerequisite. Given the direct link between cash crop production and rural incomes, prospects for better rural incomes will depend on increased cash crop production. However, prospects for increased cash crop production will, in turn, depend on better and more stable market prices. Other existing challenges include the declining budgetary allocations to agriculture both at national and local government levels, and the vulnerability of agricultural producers to the vagaries of nature, such as drought, pests, and diseases.

Growth in the service sector is also important in poverty reduction since it employs about 23% of the population, particularly in urban areas. Moreover, it is the largest and the fastest growing sector of the economy. Thus, those investments within the service sector which create more employment opportunities should be encouraged or supported.

3.6 FURTHER RESEARCH

Major determinants of income inequality in Uganda between 1992/93 and 2002/03 have been found to be geographical location, sector of employment, education of the head of the household, and lack of access to community services (Ssewanyana et al. 2004). However, an empirical study is yet to be done to investigate the factors explaining the persistence of income inequality.

Uganda has intervened with a number of projects/programmes in its effort to fight poverty. Some of them, for example, economic recovery programmes, decentralisation and the public expenditure tracking system, have been assessed regarding their efficacy in reducing poverty. However, other programmes, such as the SEP, the NUSAF and the school feeding programme, have not yet been assessed in this respect.

REFERENCES

APEJ (2003), 'Africa: Economic Lessons, 1'. *Africa Policy E-Journal*, 2 August, http://www.africaaction.org/docs03/eca0308a.htm

Appleton, S. (2001), *Poverty Reduction during Growth: The Case of Uganda, 1992–2000*, Nottingham, UK: University of Nottingham, http://www.uppap.or.ug/docs/simonpaper.pdf

Balihuta, M. and Sen, K. (2001), *Macroeconomic Policies and Rural Livelihood Diversification: A Uganda Case-Study* (LADDER Working Paper no. 3), Norwich: University of East Anglia, Livelihoods and Diversification Directions Explored by Research, http://www.odg.uea.ac.uk/ladder/doc/wp3.pdf

Deininger, K. and Okidi, J. (2002), *Growth and Poverty Reduction in Uganda, 1992–2000: Panel Data Evidence*, paper presented at the 2002 annual conference on Africa at the Centre for the Study of African Economies, Oxford, Kampala: Economic Policy Research Centre.

James, R., Francis, P., and Pereza, G. (2001), *Institutional Context of Rural Poverty Reduction in Uganda: Decentralisation's Dual Nature* (LADDER Working Paper no. 6), Norwich: University of East Anglia, Livelihoods and Diversification Directions Explored by Research, Overseas Development Group, http://www.odg.uea.ac.uk/ladder/doc/wp6.pdf

Mackinnon, J. and Reinikka, R. (2000), *Lessons from Uganda on Strategies to Fight Poverty*, WB Policy Research Working Paper no. 2440, Washington D.C.: World Bank, http://econ.worldbank.org/docs/1195.pdf

MFPED (2006), *Background to the Budget for Financial Year 2006/07*, Kampala: Ministry of Finance Planning and Economic Development, http://www.finance.go.ug

MFPED (2005), *Background to the Budget for Financial Year 2005/06*, Kampala: Ministry of Finance Planning and Economic Development, http://www.finance.go.ug

MFPED (2004), *Poverty Eradication Action Plan 2004/5–2007/8*, Kampala: Ministry of Finance Planning and Economic Development, www.finance.go.ug

Mijumbi, P. and Okidi, J. (2001), *Analysis of Poor and Vulnerable Groups in Uganda*, (EPRC Occasional Paper no. 16), Kampala: Economic Policy Research Centre, with support from DFID (London).

Morrissey, O. and Verschoor, A. (accessed 2006), *What does Ownership Mean in Practice? Policy Learning and the Evolution of Pro-Poor Policies in Uganda*, http://www.dsaconf03morrissey.pdf

Muduuli, M. C. (2001), *Uganda's Poverty Eradication Action Plan: National Sustainable Development Strategy Principles Tested*, paper presented at the International Forum on National Sustainable Development Strategies (NSDSs), Accra, 7–9 November, http://www.dip.go.ug/english/peap/muduuli_joburg.doc

Mukasa, E. and S. Masiga (2003), *Poverty and Ageing*, Regional Workshop, http://www.un.org/esa/socdev/ageing/workshops/tz/uganda.pdf

Okurut, F. N., J. J. A. O. Odwee, and A. Adebua (2002), *Determinants of Regional Poverty in Uganda*, (AERC Research Paper 122), Nairobi: African Economic Research Consortium, November, http://www.aercafrica.org/documents/rp122.pdf

Okwi, P. (1999), *Poverty in Uganda: A Multivariate Analysis*, (EPRC Research Series no. 22), Kampala: Economic Policy Research Centre.

Ssewanyana N. S., A. J. Okidi, D. Angemi, and V. Barungi (2004), *Understanding the Determinants of Income Inequality in Uganda*, CSAE WPS/2004-29, http://www.bepress.com/cgi/viewcontent.cgi?article=1229&context=csae

The New Vision (2006). *ADB – Uganda's Development Partner*, Kampala: The New Vision, Special Pullout, April 28, http://www.newvision.co.ug

UBOS (2006), *Uganda National Household Survey: 2005/06*, Kampala: Uganda Bureau of Statistics, A Report on the Socio-economic Module.

UBOS (2003), *Uganda National Household Survey: 2002/03*, Kampala: Uganda Bureau of Statistics, A Report on the Socio-economic Survey.

CHAPTER 4

POVERTY PROFILE AND THE EVOLUTION OF POVERTY REDUCTION STRATEGIES IN ZAMBIA

Thomson Kalinda

4.1 INTRODUCTION

Zambia is a large country covering about 752,620 km². It is a landlocked country sharing borders with eight countries, namely Tanzania and the Democratic Republic of Congo to the North, Malawi and Mozambique to the East, Angola and Namibia to the West and Botswana and Zimbabwe to the South. Zambia has nine provinces and is a unitary multi-party democracy headed by a republican president. The provinces are headed by deputy ministers responsible for the coordination of all government business in the province. Zambia has a population of approximately 11.7 million with an annual growth rate of about 2.9%. A large proportion of the population (67%) resides in the rural areas and their livelihoods are largely based on agriculture (Government of the Republic of Zambia 2006a).

In Zambia, poverty is widespread in both urban and rural areas. Between 1996 and 1998, poverty increased from 69.2% to 72.9% of the population. Poverty in the rural areas was higher (83.1%) than in the urban areas (56%). In the rural areas, poverty levels among small-scale farmers remained almost constant, that is, from 84.4% in 1996 to 84% in 1998. However, poverty levels among medium-scale farmers increased from 65.1% in 1996 to 71.9% in 1998. This could be partially attributed to the loss of the government services they used to enjoy. The only positive development is that poverty among large-scale farmers decreased from 34.9% in 1996 to 15.6% in 1998 (Central Statistical Office 1999).

In view of the high levels of poverty, the government formulated a Poverty Reduction Strategy Paper (PRSP) (2002–2004) and identified 'poverty reduction and economic growth' as the overall objective for the economy in 2001. This meant that all sectors of the economy were expected to design and implement programmes that would make a significant contribution to poverty reduction and economic growth. The goal of the government was to reduce poverty to 50% of the population by the year 2004 (Government of the Republic of Zambia 2002a).

Despite the PRSP and positive growth trends during the last few years, Zambia is yet to record major declines in income poverty levels. According to the Living Conditions Monitoring Survey (LCMS) IV of 2004, as much as 68% of the population fell below the national poverty line, earning less than ZMK111,747. Poverty levels fell slightly in 2004 compared to 1998, when poverty stood at 73%. The depth and severity of poverty also remain high despite the slight decline since 1998. At the national level, the depth of poverty dropped to 36% from 40% in 1998, while the severity of poverty declined to 23% from 26% in 1998. Extreme poverty (covering people earning less than ZMK 78,223 per month) fell from 58% in 1998 to 53% in 2004. The declining depth and severity of poverty was driven primarily by rising per capita consumption amongst the poorest non-farm households. This represents a deviation from the experiences of 1991–1998, during which time non-farm poverty rose rapidly (Central Statistical Office 2005a).

This chapter attempts to describe the genesis, development, implementation, and achievements of the poverty reduction strategy in Zambia. The chapter is organised as follows. After this introduction, Section 4.2 presents an overview of the recent performance of the Zambian economy as well as the status of poverty in the country. Section 4.3, which is divided into several subsections, presents poverty trends in Zambia and various aspects of its poverty reduction strategy process, highlighting the policy-making process and implementation with regard to national poverty reduction and concomitant programmes. The last section presents a conclusion.

4.2 OVERVIEW OF RECENT PERFORMANCE OF THE ZAMBIAN ECONOMY

Over the last few years, Zambia has achieved an impressive record in macroeconomic growth and stability. Growth has accelerated in recent years, averaging 3.9% per year between 1998 and 2004, and represents a reversal of the economic stagnation experienced during the 1990s. Exchange rate stability has improved with the local currency appreciating against convertible currencies in the last 6 months, and both the country's fiscal balance and balance of payments position have recorded improvements. The inflation rate has also gone down from over 30% in 2000 to single digit levels of about 8.5% by June 2006 (Government of the Republic of Zambia 2006b). Growth over the last few years has been especially strong, with the overall economy growing in excess of 6% in 2003 and 2004 (Table 4.1). Although most sectors have contributed positively to growth, the recent period has been dominated by the rapid expansion of mining and construction. The renewed growth of the mining sector is a result of recapitalisation and new investments following the privatisation of state-owned mines in 2000 and of favourable conditions in world commodity markets. The construction sector has also recorded rapid growth as a result of private construction activities, especially in residential housing around the main urban centres and in facilitating mining sector investments (Government of the Republic of Zambia 2005).

Table 4.1: Annual Gross Domestic Product (GDP) Growth Rates by Sector, 1998–2004

Type of sector	Share[1] (1998)	Annual growth rate (constant 1994 prices)							Average (1998–2004)
		1998	1999	2000	2001	2002	2003	2004	
GDP (factor cost)	100.0	-1.4	3.1	3.4	4.6	4.6	6.0	6.8	3.9
Agriculture	18.4	1.2	10.1	1.5	-2.5	-1.7	5.0	4.3	2.6
Mining	10.2	-25.1	-24.8	0.1	14.0	16.4	3.4	12.7	-0.5
Manufacturing	11.8	1.9	2.8	3.5	4.2	5.7	7.6	3.6	4.2
Energy	3.4	0.6	2.5	1.2	12.6	-5.2	0.6	-1.8	1.5
Construction	5.4	-9.1	3.2	6.5	11.5	17.4	21.6	32.0	11.9
Trade and transport	27.4	4.7	4.8	2.3	4.7	4.2	5.8	5.2	4.5
Tourism	2.2	3.8	-6.2	12.3	24.4	4.8	6.9	5.9	7.4
Other services	21.2	3.8	9.4	6.0	3.2	3.4	3.2	2.8	4.6

[1] Contribution to GDP in 1998 measured in 1994 prices.
Source: Central Statistical Office (2005b).

Manufacturing and tourism have grown strongly in recent years, averaging 4.2% and 7.4% respectively. Manufacturing has benefited from new and sustained investment that began in the late 1990s. However, much of this growth has been concentrated in food processing and textiles, such that there is still little high-value manufacturing taking place in the country. Tourism growth has been driven by a small number of sizable private investments and through concerted marketing efforts by private enterprises. However, the tourism sector remains small and has faced a number of constraints, including inadequate infrastructure, a strict regulatory framework, and high production costs. Such constraints are also felt elsewhere in the economy (Government of the Republic of Zambia 2005).

Unlike the industrial sectors, agriculture has not performed well in recent years, with wide fluctuations in production and a low average growth rate of only 2.6%. This reflects considerable variation in weather patterns as well as inadequate infrastructure and generally poor market access. Much of the growth that has taken place has been driven by cash crops such as cotton and tobacco, and has been concentrated in specific areas of the country.

Given the strong performance of mining and construction, it is not surprising that recent growth has been investment-driven (Table 4.2). Investment growth has averaged over 10% since 1998 and has been accelerating alongside construction and mining. Other components of demand-side GDP have not grown as strongly. Government expenditure has been erratic, with rapid declines during the late 1990s offsetting a subsequent period of faster growth. Similarly, export growth has fluctuated in response to sharp movements in world copper prices. By contrast, import growth has been slow and has declined on average since 1998. Most importantly, growth in private consumption expenditure has been well below the average population growth rate of 2% (Government of the Republic of Zambia 2005).

Table 4.2: Annual GDP Growth Rates by Expenditure Type, 1998–2004

Expenditure type	Share[1] (1998)	Annual growth rate (constant 1994 prices)							Average (1998–2004)
		1998	1999	2000	2001	2002	2003	2004	
GDP (market prices)	100.0	-1.9	2.2	3.6	4.9	3.3	4.2	6.4	3.2
Government	13.5	-14.8	-19.4	-21.6	44.7	2.3	19.3	6.4	2.4
Private consumption	72.9	-1.3	3.0	2.3	-14.2	14.8	4.4	-2.9	0.8
Investment	17.1	9.6	8.4	8.4	15.1	17.2	18.9	2.2	11.4
Exports	38.1	4.9	4.9	-14.4	28.3	-22.3	-16.3	21.2	0.9
Imports	-41.6	4.6	1.6	-20.1	1.2	1.8	1.7	-6.4	-2.2

[1] Contribution to GDP in 1998 measured in 1994 prices.

Source: Central Statistical Office (2005b).

Despite the strong overall performance of the economy, higher levels of GDP growth have not translated into significant declines in poverty. Poverty remains high at about 70% and has changed little since 1998 (Figure 4.1). These recent trends raise concern over whether stagnant poverty outcomes are possible in the context of such high economic growth. However, as seen above, recent growth has been investment-driven with significant declines in per capita private consumption. Since private consumption or household expenditure is the measure on which poverty estimates are based, it is not surprising then that poverty has remained largely unchanged in spite of high per capita GDP growth rates. The country's recent performance therefore suggests that, in terms of poverty reduction, the structure of growth may be as important as the level of growth.

4.3 POVERTY TRENDS IN ZAMBIA

Like in most other developing countries, poverty in Zambia is characterised by low income and expenditure, high mortality and morbidity, poor nutritional status, low-educational attainment, vulnerability to external shocks, and exclusion from economic, social and political processes. Though poverty is particularly widespread in the rural areas, there are significant regional differences in levels of poverty and in the relative importance of different aspects of poverty. Those particularly at risk to the many dimensions of poverty are young children and youth, the very old, women, those in large households and those involved in subsistence agriculture, livestock production, and small-scale fishing. While some progress has been made in the fight against poverty since independence, poverty in Zambia remains a persistent problem, as shown in the preceding subsections.

4.3.1 Income poverty

Poverty is acknowledged to be a multidimensional phenomenon and for this reason, effective measures to address it require conceptualising it not only as a lack of income or shortfall in expenditure required to achieve a certain minimally acceptable level of living standard, but also as a lack of capabilities that individuals require in order to live meaningful and valued lives in their societies. This is predicated on access to food and other basic amenities, on access to essential services, such as basic health and education, and on access to care and protection from abuse, especially for children, young women and men as well as other particularly vulnerable people. The status of poverty indicators is provided and summarised in Figures 4.1–4.3 to provide trends on income poverty in Zambia.

Figure 4.1: Proportion of People below the Poverty Line

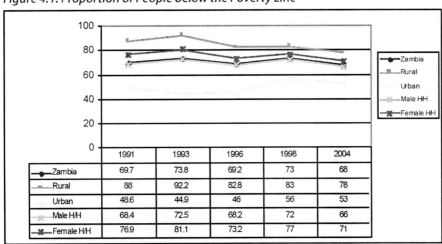

	1991	1993	1996	1998	2004
Zambia	69.7	73.8	69.2	73	68
Rural	88	92.2	82.8	83	78
Urban	48.6	44.9	46	56	53
Male H/H	68.4	72.5	68.2	72	66
Female H/H	76.9	81.1	73.2	77	71

Source: Central Statistical Office (1991; 1993; 1996; 1999; 2005a).

Figure 4.2: Proportion of People Living in Extreme Poverty, 1991–2004

	1991	1993	1996	1998	2004
Zambia	58.2	60.6	53.2	58	53
Rural	80.6	83.5	68.4	71	65
Urban	32.3	24.4	27.3	36	34
Male H/H	56.5	58.7	51.5	56	51
Female H/H	67.6	70.5	60.4	65	71

Source: Central Statistical Office (1991; 1993; 1996; 1999; 2005a).

Figure 4.3: Extreme Poverty Trends by Province, 1991–2004

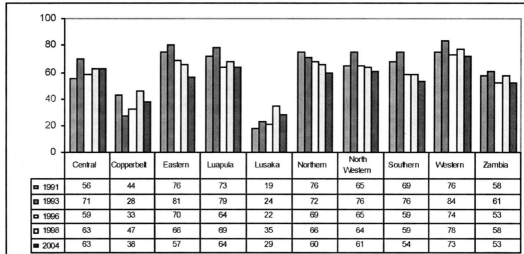

	Central	Copperbelt	Eastern	Luapula	Lusaka	Northern	North Western	Southern	Western	Zambia
1991	56	44	76	73	19	76	65	69	76	58
1993	71	28	81	79	24	72	76	76	84	61
1996	59	33	70	64	22	69	65	59	74	53
1998	63	47	66	69	35	66	64	59	78	58
2004	63	38	57	64	29	60	61	54	73	53

Source: Central Statistical Office (1991; 1993; 1996; 1999; 2005a).

From these figures, it can be seen that there was a reduction in poverty between 1993 and 1996. However, this reduction was reversed in 1998 to nearly the same levels obtained in 1991 in the case of extreme poverty and slightly higher in the case of overall poverty. Between 1998 and 2004, poverty in rural and urban areas declined by 5% and 3%, respectively. The incidence of poverty in the rural areas fell from 83% in 1998 to 78% in 2004, while poverty in the urban areas declined to 53% from 56% in 1998. The rural incidence of extreme poverty fell from 71% in 1998 to 65% in 2004. In urban areas, the incidence of extreme poverty declined by 2% from 36% to 34%. Extreme poverty also fell from 58% in 1998 to 53% in 2004 (Figures 4.1 and 4.2).

In terms of the current status of poverty, high levels of poverty continue to be associated with more remote provinces such as Western Province (83%), Luapula (79%) and North-Western Province (76%). The incidence of poverty was lowest in more urbanised regions such as Lusaka (48%) and the Copperbelt Provinces (56%). While the proportion of the population living in poverty did not vary much among the provinces, there were quite significant variations in terms of the proportion of the population living in extreme poverty across the provinces. The rate of extreme poverty varied from 29% in Lusaka Province to 64% in Luapula Province (Figure 4.3). The incidence of extreme poverty was also high in rural areas where two-thirds of the population was extremely poor compared to only one-third in the urban areas. From Figures 4.1 and 4.2, it can be observed that the incidences of both poverty and extreme poverty were much higher in rural areas as compared to urban areas during the period 1991–2004. This has led to the observation that although poverty is widespread and all places in Zambia are affected by high-poverty levels, it remains predominantly rural. The rural areas are at a particular disadvantage, not only because more of the poor and deprived in the population live there, but also because the rural areas continue to lack social services and other economic infrastructure, such as roads of a reasonable quality, that would help them take advantage of various opportunities to develop themselves emanating in the new liberalised environment. Nevertheless, poverty was rising much faster in the urban than in the rural areas, which is attributable to the job losses and rising food prices that characterised the 1990s. It is also observed that female-headed households are more likely to be poor than male-headed households, although the incidence is high even in the case of the latter.

Given this trend, one can see that the challenge of reducing income poverty for Zambia is still a major one. The Millennium Development Goal (MDG) target of halving poverty by 2015, when looked at in the context of recent economic trends, also seems very ambitious. While government programmes such as the PRSP and the Transitional National Development Plan (TNDP) emphasised high economic growth as a precondition for the reduction of extreme poverty and vulnerability, the strong overall performance of the economy in terms of high GDP growth has not translated into significant declines in poverty. The contribution of GDP growth to poverty reduction has been very small due to institutional and structural constraints that have limited its trickle-down effects.

This is not to say that there is no potential. On the contrary, some potential is there but the achievability of the targets depends on the extent to which current efforts can help make growth pro-poor. In the last 15 years, the agricultural sector, which stands to be the most pro-poor sector for poverty reduction in the country (supporting the livelihoods of more than 75% of the country's population), has been left behind in terms of development. And although some efforts have been underway since 2001, their impact on the economy has not been discerned yet. Major breakthroughs are therefore still needed to facilitate the growth of economic activities to boost employment and income-raising opportunities as well as to increase agricultural productivity so as to make food products accessible to the poor. Zambia's agricultural sector offers the best option for achieving the development objective of increasing food production and rural incomes. With a land area of 752,620 km^2, Zambia's abundant agricultural resources are underutilised with only 16% of the estimated 9 million hectares of arable land being cultivated. The demand for reasonably fertile land, relative to population pressure, is much more favourable than most of Zambia's neighbours. Zambia has an estimated 25% of the Southern African region's surface water resources. However, only 9% of the irrigation potential of 423,000 ha is being utilised. These underutilised land and water resources need to be fully exploited in order to achieve growth in the agricultural sector (Government of the Republic of Zambia 2002a).

4.3.2 Non-income poverty

The preceding subsection presented the trends in Zambia's income-based poverty indicators. However, there are a number of non-income or social dimensions of poverty that are also important for household welfare. This section presents recent trends in the non-income poverty indicators in Zambia. Table 4.3 summarises selected non-income poverty indicators.

Table 4.3: Selected Non-Income Poverty Indicators, 1990–2004

	1991	1993	1996	1998	2001	2002	2004
Health and nutrition indicators							
Infant mortality rate (per 1000 live births)	107.3	-	-	109	-	95	-	-
Under-five mortality rate (per 1000 live births)	191	-	-	197	-	186	-	-
Births attended by health staff (% of total)	51	38	-	47	-	-	45	-
Stunting, 5 years and under (%)	40	-	-	42	-	47	-	50
Underweight, 5 years and under (%)	25	-	-	24	-	28	-	20
Wasting, 5 years and under (%)	5	-	-	4	-	5	-	6
Education indicators							
Gross primary enrollment (%)	98.7	99	92.8	98	95	83.3	86.6	-
Net primary enrollment (%)	70	-	-	81	80	70.5	72	-
Adult literacy rate of people ages 15+ (%)	68.1	69.1	71.1	74.2	75.2	79	70	
Access to basic public goods and services							
Access to safe water (%)	34.9	-	-	-	-	49.1	-	56.6
Access to electricity (%)	8.9	-	-	-	-	13.8	-	16.2

Sources: Central Statistical Office (various reports); Government of the Republic of Zambia (2002a); Ministry of Education (2004).

Trends in the nutritional status of children

Food insecurity and poverty are some of the main factors that cause malnutrition among children in Zambia. The Demographic and Health Surveys (DHS) in 1992, 1996 and 2001/02 and the LCMS IV of 2004 collected data on the nutritional status of children. An analysis of trends in these data shows a decline in the nutritional status of children. The proportion of children under five who are stunted increased from 40% in 1992 to 42% in 1996 and to 47% in 2001/02. By 2004, the proportion of children under five who are stunted further increased to 50%. The proportion underweight also rose, but less significantly, from 25% in 1992 to 24% in 1996 and 28% in 2001/02. By 2004, the proportion of underweight children had slightly declined to 20%. However, the proportion of children who are wasted remained more or less steady, declining from 5% in 1992 to 4% in 1996 and rising again to 5 and 6% in 2001/02 and 2004 respectively. These trends in nutritional status imply that the problem of malnutrition in Zambia is one of chronic food shortages. This situation also reflects the economic deterioration and increased poverty that has been experienced in the country in recent years.

Infant and child mortality

The 2001/02 Zambia Demographic and Health Survey indicates a decline in mortality rates for both infants and under-five children compared to the deterioration in the same indicators experienced during the 1990s. During the 1990s the mortality rate for children under 5 years old increased from 191 deaths per 1000 live births in 1991/92 to 197 deaths in 1996. However, by 2001/2 the mortality rate for under-five children recorded a decline to 186 deaths per 1000 live births. The infant mortality rate also increased in the first half of 1990s from an average of 107 per 1000 live births recorded in 1992 to 109 deaths per 1000 live births in 1996. However, between 1996 and 2001/2 there was an improvement with infant mortality declining to 95 deaths per 1000 live births (Gaisie et al. 1993; Central Statistical Office et al. 1997; 2003).

Maternal health status

Complications related to pregnancy and birth are a serious health problem for women and newborn children in Zambia. The DHS estimated the maternal mortality ratio as standing at 649 per 100,000 live births in 1996. This ratio, however, went up to 729 per 100,000 live births in 2001/02, implying that more Zambian women have died of pregnancy-related complications in recent years compared to past decades (Gaisie et al. 1993; Central Statistical Office et al. 2003). The top six contributors to the high maternal mortality ratio in Zambia are post-partum haemorrhage, malaria, HIV and AIDS, hypertensive disorders, abortions, and the lack of access to quality health services.

Maternal mortality is directly related to the availability of quality health services in a given population. The DHS has shown that up to 60% of Zambians live within 5 km of a health facility. This percentage has remained much the same over the past decade while the maternal mortality ratio has continued to rise over the same period. Antenatal and postnatal attendance also has a direct bearing on maternal mortality. The Zambia Demographic and Health Survey estimated that over 80% of pregnant women visit an antenatal clinic at least three times during their pregnancy. However, less than 60% subsequently return to deliver at the clinic. Post-natal problems such as sepsis, anaemia, and haemorrhage contribute significantly to maternal mortality. These trends suggest that access to quality reproductive health services in Zambia is a major problem. The proportion of births attended by skilled health workers in the country has been declining in the 1990s and recent years. The DHS reveals that the proportion of births attended by skilled health workers in Zambia declined continuously during the 1990s from 51% in 1992 to 47% in 1996 and down further still to 45% in 2002 (Gaisie et al. 1993; Central Statistical Office et al. 1997; 2003).

HIV and AIDS and other infectious diseases

The HIV prevalence rate as measured through the sentinel surveillance of pregnant women in Zambia has demonstrated a gradual drop over the past decade. Available statistics reveal that HIV prevalence among pregnant women dropped gradually from about 19.7% in the mid-1990s to 18% in 2001 (National HIV and AIDS Council 2002). Overall, the HIV prevalence remains high. The Demographic and Health Survey indicates that adult HIV prevalence was about 16% in 2001/02. In urban areas, the prevalence rate among 15–49 year-olds was more than 23% while in rural areas it was about 11%. The Demographic and Health Survey also found that women are 1.4 times more likely to be HIV-infected compared to men. Prevalence among women is higher in the younger age groups than it is among men and it peaks earlier. HIV infection rates among young women aged 15–19 and 20–24 years are 3.5–4 times higher than those for young men in the same age categories. Prevalence among women is highest between the ages of 25 and 34. By contrast, male prevalence is highest among those aged 35–39 years. Only in the older age groups is the proportion of HIV-infected men higher than the proportion of HIV-infected women (Central Statistical Office et al. 2003).

According to the Demographic and Health Survey, HIV infection rates are very low among the 5–14 age group. Since prevalence is so low among these young people, programmes targeted at this group provide a special opportunity to prevent infection and affect the future course of the epidemic. The National HIV and AIDS Intervention Strategic Plan recognises the importance of this 'window of hope' and calls for prevention programmes for both in-school and out-of-school youth (National HIV and AIDS Council 2004).

Education and literacy achievements

Progress in education and literacy attainments during the 1990s presents a mixed picture (Table 4.3). In 2002 it was estimated that net enrolment was about 72%, a slight improvement from 70% in 1990. Some progress has also been made in achieving gender parity in primary education in the country. There has been an increase in the net enrolment and progression rate of girls in primary education. During that time the gross enrolment rate showed a deterioration, having declined to about 87% in 2002 from 99% in 1990. Geographical disparities in enrolment indicators, however, continued to be high with some rural provinces such as Eastern recording net enrolment rates below 60%. Completion rates in primary schools during this period have nevertheless shown an improvement. For instance, the primary school completion rate increased from 53% in 1990 to 63% in 2003 (Ministry of Education 2004).

Access to safe water and sanitation

With respect to access to clean and safe water sources, there has been some improvement in recent years. In 1990, about 35% of households had access to safe drinking water and by the year 2000, the percentage had increased to 49%, and further to about 57% by 2004 (Central Statistical Office 2000; 2005a). However, access to this service in rural areas is lower than in urban areas as only 38% of the rural people have access to safe drinking water whereas it is 86% in the latter (Central Statistical Office 2005a;b).

On the other hand, access to proper sanitation in Zambia is poor. In 1990, only 16% of the households had access to improved sanitation and by 2004, the proportion of these households had dwindled to about 14%. The proportion of rural households with access to proper sanitation has remained unchanged at about 1.7% between 1990 and 2004. For the urban population, the proportion of households with access to proper sanitation has decreased from about 42% in 1990 to 33% in 2004 (Central Statistical Office 2005a).

4.4 POVERTY REDUCTION STRATEGY PROCESS IN ZAMBIA

As part of the World Bank and International Monetary Fund (IMF) requirements, Zambia adopted, in May 2002, a PRSP. Accordingly, Zambia's PRSP focused on measures to achieve strong sustained economic growth. A growing economy that creates jobs and tax revenues for the state was considered to be a sustainable and powerful tool for reducing poverty. The open and participatory nature of the PRSP approach was regarded by many as its defining characteristic and its most significant achievement. PRSPs have often led to an improved dialogue within the various parts of government and between governments and domestic stakeholders. There is some evidence that the active involvement of civil society influenced PRSP content, particularly in drawing attention to social exclusion, the impoverishing effects of poor governance, and specific policy issues (Government of the Republic of Zambia 2002a).

4.4.1 Ownership and Participation

The PRSP in Zambia was prepared after extensive consultations involving the Cabinet, the legislature, government bodies, the private sector, academia, non-governmental organisations (NGOs), donors and the provinces. The Ministry of Finance and National Planning (MoFNP) was tasked with the responsibility of being overall coordinator of the process of producing the PRSP. Within the Ministry, a PRSP secretariat drawing members from the Ministry itself, the Ministry of Community Development and Social Services (MCDSS), and the Bank of Zambia provided day-to-day coordination. Members of this secretariat were later absorbed into the newly established Planning and Economic Management Department (PEMD) which, towards the end, also assumed the overall responsibility of coordinating the completion of the PRSP. The PRSP secretariat worked closely with other government ministries and the latter provided the chairpersons of the Sector Advisory Groups (SAGs). This ensured that while overall participation in the PRSP preparation embraced the whole society, the process also became deeply grounded within government. This was critical for smooth implementation (Government of the Republic of Zambia 2002a).

The government team that coordinated the preparation of this PRSP worked closely with civil society. Civil society organisations' representatives were members of the PRSP sector working groups described above. On top of this, they formed an umbrella organisation called Civil Society for Poverty Reduction (CSPR), which drew members from civil society groups. They established their own PRSP working groups on poverty themes that largely coincided with those of the government, although not entirely. Civil society working groups generated ideas, which they passed on to their members sitting in the government working groups, which used them as discussion inputs. Although specialised technical assistance was required in certain areas, it was the government's intention to ensure that the PRSP preparation and implementation was done by Zambians themselves through an extensive consultative process. This was to enhance local ownership of the plan and thus increase the chances of its successful implementation (Government of the Republic of Zambia 2002a).

Involving many stakeholders in the preparation of this document enriched it and deeply grounded its ownership in the country. Stakeholders were involved at every stage of its preparation, including at the level of conceptualising its roadmap through a national sensitisation workshop. This collaboration was extended into the formation of SAGs, drawing participants from different interest groups into designing sector-specific programmes for poverty reduction, which became the main ingredients of this PRSP. The document also benefited from wide consultations with rural areas and political leaders and from previous consultative processes (World Bank 2005).

The zero draft of the PRSP comprised the outputs of eight working groups, each addressing a specific sector. The membership of each working group comprised representatives from the government, NGOs, the private sector, churches, donors, academia, and professional associations. These initial outputs were discussed amongst a broader group of stakeholders at the national level, and the revised documents were discussed at provincial level consultation workshops.

It is worth noting that the provincial consultation was with the poor. The participants were the provincial leadership; the District Administrators; a few experts from sectors such as agriculture, health and education; a representative of traditional leaders; representatives of NGOs; churches; and the poor themselves. In each provincial PRSP consultative conference, the CSPR, NGOs, churches and other civil society organisations were actively involved in consultations regarding poor peoples' views on the causes of poverty and how they should be addressed. The CSPR participated alongside the government teams that went around in the provinces to solicit views from participants on issues of poverty reduction at different levels, including the meaning of poverty, its causes, what outsiders could do to help reduce it and what the local people could do to reduce it. As a wrap-up of these provincial discussions, the delegates produced a list of priority interventions for poverty reduction. These priorities were reflected in the PRSP (Government of the Republic of Zambia 2002a).

The draft PRSP document was then produced for consultation with the donor community. Substantial changes were made between the first and second drafts, and again in the final draft. The changes were made in order to reduce the initially over-ambitious budget and to ensure that the final document would be well received by the international community (World Bank 2005).

Following the preparation of the PRSP (2002–2004), the government accepted it as Zambia's development planning and resource programming tool and, as such, it was the overall framework for national (both government and non-government) planning and interventions for development and poverty reduction. It was to roll over every 3 years and would continue to solicit broad stakeholder input into its planning, implementation, monitoring and evaluation (M&E). It was the nation's medium-term development framework. The PRSP was not independent of other public planning instruments and processes such as national development visioning, public investment programming, sector investment programmes and strategic frameworks, as well as the national budgeting process.

4.4.2 Institutionalisation and implementation

The PRSP was published in May 2002 and officially launched 2 months later. As mentioned earlier, the preparation of the PRSP was coordinated by the MoFNP through a specially established unit headed by a Consultant Coordinator. The unit was subsequently absorbed into the PEMD of MoFNP. The PEMD coordinated and monitored the implementation of the PRSP and managed the preparation of the Fifth National Development Plan (FNDP).

The PEMD is the Department in charge of national planning, PRSP implementation, and economic management. The Department had the responsibility for PRSP M&E. M&E guidance was provided by the Interministerial Technical Committee, headed by the Director of PEMD (Government of the Republic of Zambia 2002a).

In order to ensure that the implementation of the PRSP was on course and that the desired results were achieved, M&E was undertaken. Monitoring involved tracking key indicators over time and space with a view to seeing what changes had taken place in the indicators following the implementation of the PRSP. Since the central objective of the PRSP was to reduce poverty, evaluations would enable an assessment of the impact on poverty of interventions under the PRSP. Thus, the monitoring system was expected to provide the basic input data into either PRSP evaluation as a whole or specific programme components or policies.

The primary aim of Zambia's poverty monitoring system was to track progress being made in the achievement of the goals and objectives set out in the sectoral chapters, using an appropriate mix of intermediate and final indicators. The intermediate indicators were mostly composed of factors that were under the control of implementing agencies such as line ministries. On the other hand, final indicators were mostly composed of aspects of welfare not directly under the implementing agency's control. Quarterly reports and an annual PRSP report were produced to monitor progress towards PRSP implementation (Government of Republic of Zambia 2002a; 2004a).

4.4.3 Time perspective and sequencing of PRSP implementation

The quality of implementation of the PRSP (2002–2004) was hampered by a lack of timely information and dialogue between MoFNP and the implementing agencies, both in government and outside. This deficit was attributable to the initially low profile that was given to PRSP implementation in the start-up period (2002 to mid-2003), and to the subsequent problems of always being behind schedule and trying to catch up. Timeliness on the part of MoFNP was essential for effective implementation. The lack of timeliness also reduced the time available for effective dialogue. The management and subsequent performance of the PRSP's SAGs were a good example of this, as constant lateness damaged the opportunity to develop a shared vision and team spirit among them.

The timing of the development of the PRSP may have undermined political commitment to its implementation in 2002–2003. The presidential elections in the last days of December 2001 heralded a change in political leadership. From the beginning, the new administration under President Levy Mwanawasa had plans to revive some key planning functions that had been abolished in the early 1990s under President Frederick Chiluba's administration. In January 2002, President Mwanawasa instructed the Ministry of Finance to develop a TNDP (2002–2005) as a temporary measure while a new 5-year plan was created. The TNDP was signed by the President in October 2002, and explicitly absorbed the PRSP into a broader framework, with some modifications (World Bank 2005).

The TNDP was linked to the PRSP in four significant ways. First, it shared the same theme with the PRSP. Second, it drew heavily on the invaluable work of the PRSP working groups by converting the PRSP chapters into the TNDP format. Third, it encompassed areas not adequately covered by the PRSP. That is, the consolidated TNDP took the PRSP as the core aspect of the plan and included other sectors that had not been included in the former. These included the Judiciary; Law and Order; Foreign Relations; Defence and Security; Policy Making; Science and Technology; Information Services; Population and Development; and Local Government, Housing and Urban Development. Finally, it extended the horizon of the PRSP by a year (Government of the Republic of Zambia 2002b).

The TNDP included the thematic chapters from the PRSP. However, as noted above the format had changed, and to some extent the contents had changed as well. The structure of the TNDP was, in comparison to the PRSP, difficult to follow. The changes in substance, even where they were not very great, had the unfortunate effect of reducing the levels of ownership amongst stakeholders who had been involved in the PRSP Working Groups. These events may help to explain the low priority given to the PRSP in 2002 and 2003. In itself this would not have mattered had the TNDP simply taken over the PRSP inside a broader framework. However, the problem was that the TNDP had been hastily prepared, had changed the PRSP chapters too far to preserve ownership amongst sectoral stakeholders and was not given much credence by the international community (World Bank 2005). In reality, both the PRSP and TNDP programmes were implemented concurrently since they were fundamentally similar. The TNDP guided the implementation of the poverty reduction programme in the last year (2005) of the plan period.

4.4.4 Poverty analysis and the PRSP

Through the Central Statistical Office, several surveys and studies were undertaken in the 1990s which provided information on trends in the various dimensions of poverty in Zambia. A number of other studies were undertaken in Zambia that included participatory poverty assessments, whereby the poor were able to express their own conception of poverty and how it could be addressed. The first comprehensive analysis was the 1994 World Bank report, *Zambia Poverty Assessment*. Moreover, under the periodic sector performance analysis by the Institute of Economic and Social Research that monitored the operations of the Agricultural Sector Investment Programme, participatory assessments also revealed the 'voices of the poor' regarding poverty as it relates to agriculture. Similarly, under the MoFNP and in the context of the Study Fund, several phases of *Beneficiary Assessments* were financed and undertaken to bring out the views of the poor. In addition to this, the PRSP preparatory process also involved countrywide consultations regarding poor peoples' views on the causes of poverty and how they should be addressed (Government of the Republic of Zambia 2000; 2002a).

The data from these studies and consultations with the poor and vulnerable groups showed that in general, poverty levels had increased during the decade. This, to some extent, provided the impetus to address the problem of poverty in the country through interventions like the PRSP. The PRSP therefore identified economic growth as the primary engine for national development, without which poverty reduction would be impossible. The plan notes that 'little can be achieved to reduce poverty unless measures are taken to revive Zambia's economy' (Government of the Republic of Zambia 2002a). While evidence from around the world shows that economic growth is essential for poverty reduction, there remains debate about the mix of policies most likely to lead to inclusive pro-poor growth, and the relevant levels and composition of public spending. In the case of Zambia, it was assumed that growth would reach the poor through increased opportunity to earn or to farm, better infrastructure, and increased access to schools and health services.

Given that economic growth was identified as a prerequisite for poverty reduction, it became the central focus of the PRSP. The plan was based on a growth promotion analysis, with little focus on how the different policies and investment priorities would influence the composition of growth and hence the extent of poverty reduction or the key impediments to pro-poor growth. There was also a lack of attention to and analysis of the various risk factors that affect the Zambian economy in the PRSP. The country was hit by serious shocks in the 1990s (e.g. climate shocks, macro-price shocks) and the economy suffered as a result. Despite these experiences, and despite the fact that security was highlighted as one of the three pillars of poverty reduction in the 2000/01 World Development Report, the PRSP made no attempt to identify key production risks and assess potential impacts on growth, nor to assess consumption risks and links with the well-being of children, the elderly, and other poor and vulnerable groups. More generally, the vulnerabilities and risk aversions of the poor were not considered, a factor which in itself may threaten the potential success of the strategies identified. The barriers to participation and the poverty spirals that entrap the poor were not assessed. The absence of well-conceived livelihood strategies for the poor was noted in the PRSP but not addressed. Although the PRSP strategy and spending priorities did include health and education, little emphasis was given to the needs of the vulnerable groups (e.g. the elderly, female-headed households) and the most destitute (World Bank 2005).

The lack of specifically pro-poor analysis and planning in the PRSP was overlooked by the government. For instance, the PRSP largely ignored the informal sector and its important role in the provision of jobs and incomes for the poor. The informal settlements in most Zambian towns and cities are diverse and dynamic, with enormous economic potential that can be used as a basis to create new jobs and reduce urban poverty. However, the administrative and economic environment in Zambia's urban areas neither recognises nor supports this potential. Neither the government nor most urban dwellers recognise the informal sector as a longer-term source of livelihoods and even of wealth. Instead, many are still waiting for formal sector employment. The same is true for local authorities that continue to enforce outdated regulations that hinder rather than enable the growth of informal economic activities. As a result, many of the urban poor consider their current (informal) economic activities to be temporary coping mechanisms, and they have little incentive to invest or build on them for the longer term. The lack of a pro-poor focus during the PRSP period provides food for thought as the country is just starting to implement programmes in the FNDP (2006–2010). Zambia's economy is still characterised by extreme dualism between the rich and poor. Even though inequality has fallen over the past few decades, it still remains well above that of many other low-income countries and there is therefore a need to address these disparities (World Bank 2005).

4.4.5 Linking the PRSP with the budget

In order to reorient spending towards PRSP objectives and priorities, the MoFNP used to issue and still issues the Call Circular to all government controlling officers describing the budget procedures for the following year. This provides guidelines on how the provincial administration system, line ministries and other government institutions should prepare their work plans. With the PRSP, all activities outlined in operational and capital budgets from ministries were oriented towards realising the objectives and targets of the PRSP. The implication was that all controlling officers and technical staff in line ministries and provinces were expected to be well versed in the goals and targets of the PRSP. The goals in the PRSP were now clearly linked to resources and performance. In preparing provincial and sectoral budgets, planning officers were expected to refer to the PRSP for broad policy goals, programmes and targets. For capital expenditure, reference would be made to the Public Investment Programme. Expenditure ceilings were established that broadly reflected priorities and available resources in the medium term (Government of the Republic of Zambia 2002a).

The MoFNP, through the PEMD, would analyse and scrutinise all budget submissions from line ministries to ensure that they were consistent with the objectives of the PRSP, as budget preparation was one of the core functions of the PEMD. It was important that funding by MoFNP through the Budget Office was made based on activities to achieve PRSP goals. In addition to this and as a way of improving expenditure planning, management and tracking systems, a Medium Term Expenditure Framework (MTEF) was developed in collaboration with line ministries, the donor community and civil society. The MTEF was based on the medium-term framework established under the PRSP and the medium-term resource envelope (both government and external). During the consultations for the PRSP, stakeholders emphasised the need for a longer-term development framework as the seeming lack of a coordinated approach to development planning and coordination had been of concern (Government of the Republic of Zambia 2002a).

4.4.6 International partnership

There was debate over the extent to which the PRSP process was 'donor driven'. Certainly the inception of the PRSP process was – at the outset – largely in response to the World Bank. In line with other countries, the need had been identified for a comprehensive poverty reduction package, as part of the justification for agreeing to debt relief. The PRSP planning process in Zambia gained active participation across parts of government, civil society, NGOs and the international community. By the time the document was published, in May 2002, the contents had been discussed and debated quite extensively.

The absence of growth and the huge debt burden on the Zambian economy made external funding a necessity. External funding constituted, for instance, 89% and 84% respectively of total spending in the water and sanitation sector in 1995 and 1996, compared to 31% in 1990. In 2001, 53% of the national budget was funded from outside or external sources (Government of the Republic of Zambia 2004a). External funding, however, had tended to create a paradoxical situation in Zambia. Funds from international cooperating partners would be forthcoming only if the country was current on debt servicing. As a result, nearly half the inflow of external assistance had tended to flow out again in the form of debt service payments. External funding also depended on the donors and the Zambian government being congruent in their views on economic and political governance. The lack of such congruence had led to a drastic reduction in donor assistance since the latter half of the 1990s. In any case, Zambia is today dangerously dependent on aid, and still cannot finance all her needs. If donor support is reduced further, then poverty levels are likely rise sharply (Saasa and Carlsson 2002).

In the initial years of implementing the PRSP, there was a widespread belief in the government that the USD 1.2 billion PRSP budget could not be funded domestically, and that it would largely be funded by donors. The PRSP document was quite explicit about this – it observed that 'most of the existing domestic revenue will remain committed to running government, with hardly any room left for spending on PRSP programmes beyond those that are already running'. It was argued that international donors were already expected to release around USD 1 billion over the 3-year period of the plan, and that therefore 'it is donor financial assistance that should finance the PRSP' (Government of the Republic of Zambia 2002a). It was observed that donor activities were not yet aligned with the PRSP, a matter that was identified as a topic for future discussion. Deeper analysis might have shown that significant levels of donor funding were already fully committed over the 3-year period, tied to non-PRSP programmes, public sector reform, technical assistance contracts and balance of payments support. The belief that donors should pay for the implementation of PRSP may have been responsible for the low levels of disbursement in 2002 and 2003. Some high-level public statements were made to the effect that if the donors did not fund these activities, they could not expect the PRSP to be implemented. This in a way caused confusion in the international community, as some interpreted the statements as suggesting that poverty reduction was seen as their responsibility and a low priority for the Zambian government (World Bank 2005).

However, by 2004 many of the active international donor agencies in Zambia had begun the process of harmonising their financial assistance with the PRSP. For instance, the World Bank used the same strategic priorities as the PRSP in developing its most recent Zambia Country Assistance Programme. In the same vein, representatives from the donor community participated in the reactivated PRSP SAGs involved in the formulation of the FNDP (World Bank 2005).

By late 2003 and throughout 2004, however, disbursements for the PRSP budget were regular. The Zambian government attributed this significant improvement in performance to the introduction of the MTEF and Activity Based Budget systems. In addition, the improvements coincided with Zambia's loss of the Poverty Reduction Growth Facility programme, and the subsequent provisions of the Staff Monitored Programme (SMP) agreed with the IMF. The full monthly disbursement to PRSP programmes was a key component of the SMP, essential to regaining the PRFG and subsequently qualifying for debt relief under the Heavily Indebted Poor Countries (HIPC) (World Bank 2005).

With regard to external aid, inflows during the period 2002–2004 amounted to USD 2,332 million. This was above the PRSP target of USD 804 million or 67% of the planned budget of USD 1,200 million. On an annual basis, external aid declined from USD 754 million in 2002 to USD 406 million in 2003 and rose to USD 519 million in 2004. In 2005, inflows increased to USD 652 million. Despite external aid inflows being in excess of the PRSP targets, aid management was still weak, thereby adversely affecting its effectiveness. Key weaknesses are the unclear procedures regarding how best to mobilise, receive, plan/budget and manage external resources; inappropriate systems of monitoring programme/project implementation; and, consequently, inability to determine the level of impact and weak coordination within the government system in the area of aid management. This has resulted in many line ministries becoming marginalised in the process. It is noteworthy that serious efforts were initiated to make aid more effective. Under the Harmonisation in Practice Initiative, the government and its main cooperating partners initiated a process that attempts to reduce transaction costs in aid receipt and management. The operationalisation of a Joint Assistance Strategy for Zambia is currently under discussion. An Aid Policy and Strategy was also developed and is awaiting Cabinet approval. With respect to debt, the government started a process of strengthening its capacity for debt management (Government of the Republic of Zambia 2006a).

A major development during 2005 was Zambia's reaching the Completion Point under the HIPC initiative, resulting in debt forgiveness/cancellation. In addition to this, in 2005 Zambia also became eligible for debt relief under the G8 initiative, which proposed to cancel 100% of all debts owed to the IMF, the African Development Bank and the World Bank. Following the debt relief provided as a result of the Enhanced HIPC initiative, Zambia's foreign debt came down to USD 4 billion in 2005 from USD 7.1 billion at end 2004. When the G8 commitments are effected through the Multilateral Debt Relief Initiative, it is expected that Zambia's debt will reduce to around USD 700 million (Government of the Republic of Zambia 2006a).

4.4.7 Role of regional groupings

The planning and implementation of poverty reduction strategies and programmes is an issue or prerogative for individual countries. Be that as it may, participation in international trade arrangements is essential in facilitating income growth and therefore poverty reduction. Worldwide experience indicates that success in economic expansion in small countries hinges on export growth. Exports not only create a vent for domestic surpluses but also expand domestic incomes and, therefore, enhance purchasing power, leading to expanded markets for domestic produce. This is true for Zambia, which has a small population with insufficient purchasing power to absorb expanded domestic output. The implication is that production and services in the agricultural, tourism, mining, and manufacturing sectors need to expand into export markets and trade if they are to sustain growth. The ability of countries like Zambia to benefit fully from regional and global trade is, however, limited by various barriers and inequalities in the terms of trade among the various trading partners.

Zambia considers international trade to be an important stimulus to economic growth and hence its trade policies have aimed at contributing to poverty reduction. The trade policy objectives have been pursued through involvement in economic integration with regional economic communities. The country is a member and signatory to some regional economic or trade communities such as the Southern African Development Community (SADC) and the Common Market for Eastern and Southern Africa (COMESA), as well as global trade organisations such as the World Trade Organization. Regional economic communities like COMESA play an important role as alliances in negotiating for better terms of trade with the rest of the world.

The importance of trade to Zambia's growth is clearly illustrated in the agricultural sector. Since the mid-1990s, the agricultural sector has shown some vibrancy in terms of diversification with significant increases in the production of crops like cotton, tobacco, horticultural and floricultural products. Increased production of these commodities has mainly been due to the support currently provided to farmers by private outgrower companies. Due to the increased production and diversification, the agricultural sector has increased its share of exports. Primary agricultural products make the largest contribution to agricultural exports. On average, exports of products such as sugar, tobacco, cotton lint, coffee, maize and others contribute significantly to non-traditional exports. Other major contributors to agricultural exports are processed foods and textiles. Processed foods are largely maize meal, which is exported to the neighbouring Democratic Republic of Congo. The textile industry has also experienced strong demand from the regional market due to the American Growth and Opportunity Act programme. This has been a remarkable achievement for the agricultural sector and it underlines the pivotal role agriculture and trade can play in the growth of the

Zambian economy.

Against such a background, Zambia has been supportive of trade harmonisation through the gradual removal of tariff barriers in the region by organisations such as SADC and COMESA. Zambia also extends preferential tariff treatment to other COMESA member countries. Under the PRSP and other programmes, the government has been examining its economic and trade positions with a view to arriving at what is best for the country in the light of the country's membership of regional trade-enhancing protocols under COMESA and SADC. The relevant sector ministries and trade promotion institutions have given appropriate support in order to address issues that are critical for ensuring that the benefits of trade accrue to local producers and thus contribute to income growth and poverty reduction.

4.4.3 Economic growth versus 'welfarist' orientation

As pointed out earlier, Zambia has been experiencing a number of chronic and acute socio-economic problems or shocks that have included the economic structural adjustment programme, the impact of the HIV and AIDS pandemic, and droughts. Almost all measures of the quality of life in Zambia indicate that most households are highly vulnerable due to these shocks. For instance, the overall poverty levels are very high with about 70% of the population living below the poverty datum line. Due to the economic restructuring programmes, there have been high levels of retrenchment in the formal sector, particularly in the mining industry. Today, formal employment accounts for less than a fifth of the workforce. The impact of HIV and AIDS has also been tragic with approximately 16% of the population aged 15–49 years infected by HIV. It is also estimated that almost 10% of the population has so far died from AIDS, already leaving over 600,000 orphans. Child malnutrition levels and stunting are amongst some of the highest in the world (Government of the Republic of Zambia 2002a).

Against such a background, welfare and social protection measures can play a critical role in managing both chronic and acute shocks, which are threatening to increase or deepen existing poverty in Zambia. There are no comprehensive government social assistance programmes. However, the PRSP and Highly Indebted Poor Country debt relief process have provided opportunities for the government to develop more effective and coherent welfare and social protection strategies. Several priority pro-poor programmes were proposed and implemented under the PRSP to offer relief to the poor and vulnerable. These included agricultural development and rural infrastructure development to improve food security, agricultural input subsidies, free basic education, funding of home-based care and the establishment of a revolving fund to introduce the treatment of HIV and AIDS patients with Anti-Retroviral drugs (ARVs). Several related project activities, such as the Public Welfare Assistance Schemes (PWAS), the Micro Financing and Food for Work Programmes, were designed and carried out by both government and non-government organisation countrywide. All these programmes were aimed at alleviating and reducing the level of poverty among the poor and vulnerable segments of society as well as at achieving maximum impact in the delivery of social services to the poor.

In terms of social security, the Ministry of Labour and Social Security provides some social assistance (retrenchment benefits and pensions), but these are reserved for those in formal employment and are not particularly effective given the small proportion of the population who are in formal employment. Other existing social assistance interventions are chiefly located within the MCDSS. Unfortunately the MCDSS is weak and suffers from severe funding constraints (poor disbursement from the central budget, in part due to delayed HIPC disbursements) and low capacity. The MCDSS has been implementing the PWAS, with funding from GRZ and the EU, which is aimed at enabling the most vulnerable individuals to fulfil their basic needs (health, education, food, shelter) through a voucher system and local community support. The PWAS has been successful in designing an effective and equitable community-based targeting system. The targeting systems are currently being redesigned for urban areas where it still remains difficult to identify beneficiaries. Currently, the PWAS only reaches about 200,000 beneficiaries due to funding constraints. Its targeting structure has been used by NGOs such as Programme against Malnutrition and by other ministries for food supply programmes.

4.4.9 Sector emphasis

Zambia's PRSP covered both the productive and the social sectors. The poverty reduction strategy presented in the PRSP (2002–2004) had five pillars: improved economic performance (in agriculture, industry, mining, and tourism); improved provision of social services (education and training, health and nutrition); improved infrastructure (transport, communication, roads, energy, water, and sanitation); action on cross-cutting issues (environment, gender, HIV and AIDS); and improved enabling environment (macroeconomic management and governance).

The major focus was on measures to achieve strong and sustained economic growth, that is, 'a growing economy that creates jobs and tax revenues for the state is a powerful tool for reducing poverty'. The PRSP highlighted the importance of increasing the level and quality of investment, expanding infrastructure throughout the country, and promoting the commercialisation and expansion of Zambia's export sectors. The PRSP also looked at the enabling conditions for economic growth, including, for example, sound economic management, good governance, and investing in a range of infrastructural services.

The Zambian government recognises that agriculture is important in reducing poverty because the majority of the rural people derive their livelihood from agriculture-related activities. The PRSP and the TNDP and policy statements emphasised the need to tackle poverty and unemployment as a way of enhancing household food security. In line with this commitment, the government started to implement some programmes that are likely to have a positive impact on reducing poverty and hunger or food insecurity. One such programme is the Fertiliser Support Programme, which was started in the 2002/03 farming season. The programme aims at improving access for smallholder farmers to agricultural inputs by rebuilding the asset base of farmers through direct income transfers (subsidy) of inputs for smallholder farmers. The government supports selected beneficiary farmers with the cost of inputs. That is, the government pays the suppliers a 50% down payment on the inputs supplied and the remaining 50% is paid by farmers. The programme impact has been immediate with the country recording bumper maize harvests in some agricultural seasons when the rainfall has been normal. Increased production has enabled the country to attain some level of food self-sufficiency and this will greatly assist in reducing poverty and hunger.

The government has also shown commitment to investing in and promoting technologies such as conservation farming and irrigation as a way of reducing the risk of crop failure and increasing production among both large-scale and smallholder farmers. Other poverty reduction programmes that were and are still being implemented are the Livestock Restocking and Animal Draught Power programme aimed at restocking livestock in order to reduce poverty by restoring breeding stock and increasing animal draught power. Animal Draught Power assists in eliminating labour constraints, improves on timely tillage operations and increases the area cultivated per household (Government of the Republic of Zambia 2004b). The other major areas of intervention through poverty reduction programmes have been the promotion of commercial agriculture through outgrower schemes. The rationale behind the promotion of outgrower schemes is to enable small-scale farmers benefit from commercial farmers' expertise in the production and marketing of high value agricultural products.

Under the PRSP and HIPC initiative, the government has also continuously reinvested the savings from debt write-offs in social sectors such as education and health to support programmes aimed at poverty reduction. In the education sector, the implementation of various reforms and development programmes for improving the quality of education in the country has led to considerable improvement in enrolment rates, school completion rates and in gender parity in education. In the health sector, several interventions aimed at reducing the morbidity and mortality rates due to preventable diseases have been implemented as part of the poverty reduction programmes and it is expected that these will impact positively on the ultimate attainment of goal 5 of the MDGs. For instance, there have been major programmes to combat malaria since the mid-1990s, which have included measures such as implementation of the Roll Back Malaria programme in both rural and urban areas. This has involved the free distribution of insecticide-treated bed nets, malaria prophylaxis for young and pregnant women, comprehensive residual household spraying against mosquitoes, etc. (Ministry of Health 2004).

In the water and sanitation sector, some poverty reduction policies and programmes were and are still being implemented with the aim of attaining the MDG target of improved access to safe water and sanitation. The government recognises the importance of sustainable management of the country's water resources and has formulated various policy reforms and programmes in order to improve the water sector. For instance, all urban water supply and sanitation schemes have since been transferred to local authorities. Commercially viable utilities have been established to manage the urban water systems. Cooperating partners have also pledged financial resources for the improvement of water and sanitation in peri-urban and urban areas. Capacity building activities to develop skills in water supply and management through community empowerment have also been funded and implemented by the government and donors. At the regulatory level, the National Water Supply and Sanitation Council has been established to regulate the service providers in order to for them to provide good services to consumers and to guard against consumer exploitation (Government of the Republic of Zambia 2004a). To improve access to safe water and sanitation in rural areas, the government has embarked on the Rural Water Supply and Sanitation programme. Activities undertaken in this programme include the improvement of water supply and sanitation in drought-prone areas, where 271 boreholes were drilled at the cost of ZMK18.7 billion. The government also embarked on water resource infrastructure development programmes, especially in drought-prone areas. This programme involved dam construction and rehabilitation in rural areas in all the nine provinces. To this effect, 62 earth dams were completely rehabilitated in 2003 at a cost of about ZMK1.8 billion (Government of the Republic of Zambia 2004a).

4.4.10 Themes and cross-cutting concerns

Several issues relevant to growth and poverty reduction cut across economic and social boundaries, such as the HIV and AIDS pandemic, environmental degradation, and governance. Zambia's PRSP considered the key priorities of the HIV and AIDS pandemic, environmental degradation and gender to be cross-cutting issues. Several strategies and actions to address the cross-cutting issues of HIV and AIDS, gender and the environment were implemented under Zambia's PRSP. The challenges of HIV and AIDS on Zambia are obvious. Principally, AIDS threatens the country's capacity-building efforts because it strikes the educated and skilled as well as the uneducated. Consequently, it reverses and impedes the country's capacity by shortening human productivity and life expectancy. From the time that the first AIDS case was diagnosed in Zambia, four national plans have been developed in response to the epidemic by the government. The first and second plans were implemented by the Ministry of Health, while the third involved all ministries since a multi-sectoral response is perceived as being more effective. After an extensive consultative process, a national strategic framework has been developed, validated and costed. The current framework is being coordinated by the National HIV and AIDS Council, which follows a multi-sectoral approach in the fight against the epidemic (National HIV and AIDS Council 2002).

In addressing the HIV and AIDS pandemic, the PRSP set several objectives and prioritised interventions. The first-level priority programmes included the following:

- *Reduction of new HIV and AIDS infections*: In order to reduce the number of new HIV cases, the programme promoted safe sex practices among the high-risk groups such as youth, men, sex workers and prisoners. This was to be achieved through several means, such as multi-sectoral behaviour change communication campaigns and improved free condom distribution by the government.
- *Reduction of the socio-economic impact of HIV and AIDS*: The main focus here was on individuals and families at the workplace and in homes and on the whole of Zambian society. The government promoted positive and healthy living among the asymptomatic HIV-positive people. This was achieved through the expansion of access to quality voluntary counselling and testing services; support of community home-based care to improve the quality of life of people living with AIDS; support to ARV treatment, mainly by providing funds to introduce a pilot guided scheme on the use of ARVs in public health centres (Government of the Republic of Zambia 2002a).

The second-level priority HIV and AIDS programmes under the PRSP included the following interventions:

- Improvement of the quality of life of orphans and vulnerable children through the expansion of existing programmes, and of targeting high-risk groups with peer education, drama, condom promotion/distribution, and other interpersonal outreach activities.
- Improvement of the management and treatment of sexually transmitted infections in order to reduce the risk of HIV transmission.
- Expansion of access to quality prevention of mother to child transmission programmes.
- Improved access to prophylaxis against TB and drugs for other opportunistic infections – the programmes promoted positive and healthy living among asymptomatic HIV-positive people (Government of the Republic of Zambia 2002a).

In terms of gender issues, the PRSP was implemented within the context of an already existing integrated institutional framework for policy formulation, coordination, resource mobilisation and utilisation, implementation, and M&E. At the national level, various actors are involved in gender mainstreaming activities. These include the national gender machinery, namely, the Gender in Development Division (GIDD), the Gender Consultative Forum, sector ministries, Parliament and civil society organisations. GIDD is responsible for coordinating the implementation of the National Gender Policy, and for facilitating research and resource mobilisation for implementing gender and poverty programmes. The division also liaises and networks with national, regional and international organisations. It monitors and evaluates the implementation of poverty policies, programmes and projects to ensure that they are gender responsive. The Gender Consultative Forum advises GIDD on gender issues while sector ministries mainstream gender into their respective programmes and budgets. The Gender Focal Points facilitate this process. At provincial level, the Provincial Development Coordinating Committees facilitate the implementation of gender-responsive poverty reduction programmes and projects. At district level, the District Development Coordinating Committees facilitate the implementation of gender-responsive poverty reduction programmes, projects and activities (Government of the Republic of Zambia 2002a).

The PRSP recognised the very important role that issues of gender play in poverty reduction and sustainable development. In order to enhance equitable access to productive resources for both women and men, the PRSP proposed, by way of strategy, to remove barriers to their economic participation, design special economic schemes, and reduce women's workloads through the provision of appropriate technologies. Emphasis was placed on the combination of access to assets and increased returns from the various activities. In order to ensure access to productive resources, the following strategies are proposed and implemented:

- Enactment and enforcement of laws that remove barriers to the economic participation of women, particularly relating to property rights, asset holdings, inheritance laws and credit policies.
- The design of special economic schemes for poor women and men, taking into account the multiple responsibilities of women.
- Analysis from a gender perspective of policies, programmes and plans with respect to their impact on poverty and equality between women and men and adjusting them as appropriate.
- The formulation and implementation of policies and programmes that enhance women's access to financial, technical, extension and marketing services.
- The provision of access to land, appropriate infrastructure and technologies that enhance women's income and promote household food security (Government of the Republic of Zambia 2002a).

With regard to the environment, the PRSP articulated and implemented the following actions as a means of integrating environmental concerns within the activities and programmes:

- Review the policy framework for integrating environmental management and poverty reduction within the ongoing process of preparing a national environmental policy. This would provide an update of the National Environmental Action Plan (NEAP), with special emphasis on poverty reduction.
- Review ongoing programmes in environmental management with a view to strengthening the addressing of the environment/poverty nexus.
- Expand, possibly to national level, pilot programmes that proved successful in improving the environment while at the same time enhancing the sustainable livelihood of the poor.

- Develop complementary pro-poor/pro-environment programmes within the existing and future policy framework.
- Develop a framework for assessing the environmental impacts of sector-specific poverty reduction strategic policies, programmes and action plans (Government of the Republic of Zambia 2002a).

Some environmental programmes and policies were already in place and were being implemented before the PRSP. For instance, to help monitor and enforce environmental legislation and regulations, the Environmental Protection and Pollution Control Act was enacted in 1990, and led to the subsequent establishment of the Environmental Council of Zambia in 1992. In the same vein, in 1994 the NEAP was approved which provided updated information and environmental policy actions in an attempt to redress the imbalance between development and the environment. Under the PRSP, various development programmes were strengthened in order to mainstream environmental issues in enhancing growth and poverty reduction. For instance, in 2003 the government revamped the environmental policy development process in order to harmonise all the regulations and sectoral policies in the tourism, environment and natural resources sector. Furthermore, the Zambian government is still working towards the domestication of some of the international conventions it has ratified.

4.5 CONCLUSION

Poverty and income inequality persist in Zambia despite efforts to eliminate them through the national poverty reduction strategy and concomitant programmes. The poverty problem in Zambia is in both the urban and rural areas but it is predominant in the latter. While efforts to fight poverty and deprivation continue, poor linkages between macroeconomic achievements and poverty reduction remain major challenges which limit faster progress. Despite the overall strong performance of the economy, higher levels of GDP growth have not translated into significant declines in poverty. Poverty remains high at about 70% and has changed little since the 1990s. Poor macro-micro linkages and unevenness in the distribution of the benefits of growth in the rural and urban areas also remain suggestive of a need to identify the missing links for more broad-based and equitable growth to be achieved.

With respect to non-income poverty indicators, progress has been mixed. With regard to health indicators, progress has been mixed and the challenges emanating from the impact of the HIV and AIDS pandemic on health achievements and the economy continue to be great. An analysis of trends in the nutritional and health status of children shows a decline in the nutritional status of children. These trends in nutritional status imply that the problem of malnutrition in Zambia is one of chronic food shortages. This situation also reflects the increased poverty that has been experienced in the country in recent years. The maternal mortality rate has continued to grow, implying that more Zambian women have been dying of pregnancy-related complications in recent years compared to past decades. Other health indicators, such as new tuberculosis and malaria infections, reveal that these have been increasing in Zambia in recent years.

With regard to education indicators, net enrolment, gender parity, and completion rates in primary schools have shown an improvement in the past decade. However, in terms of literacy the country has experienced retrogression with the literacy rate declining. The implementation of various educational reforms and development projects for improving the education sector in the country is responsible for the considerable improvement in enrolment and school completion rates and in gender parity in primary education. However, issues surrounding staff shortages in primary schools, particularly in rural areas, the quality of the education offered, and the adequacy of learning facilities to meet education needs commensurate with the contemporary labour market still remain major challenges.

With regard to water and sanitation indicators, access to safe drinking water in Zambia increased slightly between 1990 and 2004, mainly due to various initiatives that have been ongoing with government and donor-supported programmes. However, access to proper sanitation in Zambia still remains poor. The proportion of households with access to proper sanitation has been on a declining trend in the last decade. This implies that more intensive efforts are still needed to improve the quality of education, health care and nutrition as well as water and sanitation services offered to the Zambian population in order to make progress in poverty reduction and attain sustainable development.

The PRSP (2002–2004) was designed with the objective of poverty reduction and economic growth with a target of reducing poverty. The PRSP is a conditionality under the HIPC initiative. The PRSP was prepared through a very consultative process to enhance ownership and sustainability. This entailed broad-based consultations across the country, involving diverse stakeholders – civil society, academia, NGOs, donors, and traditional leaders. The thrust of the PRSP was to achieve sustained annual economic growth of 5–8% in the medium term, which would allow for increased real spending on poverty reduction programmes. Agriculture, tourism, manufacturing, and mining were identified as key potential growth sectors for raising income for poverty reduction on a sustainable and equitable basis. The PRSP and HIPC debt relief process has provided opportunities for the government to develop more effective and coherent pro-poor programmes, which were proposed and implemented under the PRSP to offer relief to the poor. These have included, among several others, agricultural and rural infrastructure development to improve food security, free basic education, the funding of home-based care and the establishment of a revolving fund to introduce anti-retroviral drug treatment to people living with HIV and AIDS.

A major development during 2005 was Zambia's reaching the Completion Point under the HIPC initiative, resulting in debt forgiveness/cancellation. In addition to this, in 2005 Zambia also became eligible for debt relief under the G8 initiative, which proposed to cancel 100% of all debts owed to the IMF, the African Development Bank and the World Bank. The Zambian government recognises the need to mainstream poverty reduction into its economic policies and has accordingly reinvested the savings from debt write-offs in social sectors such as education and health to support programmes aimed at poverty reduction. It is broadly recognised that the development and implementation of poverty reduction programmes is a serious challenge for low-income countries like Zambia, in terms of both analysis and organisation. Continuing efforts are therefore needed to learn and share good practices among countries. There is also a need for patience, perseverance and realism about what can be achieved in the short run, while helping countries to build their capacities to implement sound poverty reduction policies and monitor progress over the medium and long run.

The experience in the preparation of Zambia's PRSP and other poverty reduction programmes set a good precedent in stakeholder participation and the collaboration with stakeholders continued to shape other national development programmes, such as the FNDP (2006–2010), which was prepared and drafted over a period of about 2 years and was officially launched in January 2007. Stakeholder participation in programme planning and implementation is critical to the success of the programmes. The SAGs played a critical role in the preparation and planning of the FNDP. It is important for line ministries and other representatives from government to participate fully in SAG planning activities as well as in M&E responsibilities. Through such consultations, much greater effort must be made to identify and act on core development priorities that are essential to improving the livelihoods of the poor and vulnerable groups. It is not sufficient just to set priorities; these priorities must be reflected across the programmes and actual budget allocations and expenditures in order to ensure the effective implementation of poverty reduction programmes. The new plan must also be realistic in terms of what it can achieve over the 5-year planning horizon, and programmes included in the FNDP should have a realistic budget and realistic expectations of human resource capacity in implementing agencies and ministries.

REFERENCES

Central Statistical Office (1991), *The Social Dimensions of Adjustment: Priority Survey I*, Lusaka: Central Statistical Office.

Central Statistical Office (1993), *Social Dimensions of Adjustment: Priority Survey II Tabulation Repor*, Lusaka: Central Statistical Office.

Central Statistical Office (1996), *Living Conditions Monitoring Survey*, Lusaka: Central Statistical Office.

Central Statistical Office [Zambia] and Ministry of Health and Macro International Inc. (1997), *Zambia Demographic and Health Survey, 1996*. Calverton, MD: Central Statistical Office and Macro International Inc.

Central Statistical Office (1999), *Living Conditions in Zambia 1998*, Lusaka: Central Statistical Office.

Central Statistical Office (2002), *2000 Census of Population and Housing: Presentation of Selected Indicators*, Lusaka: Central Statistical Office.

Central Statistical Office [Zambia], Central Board of Health [Zambia], and ORC Macro (2003), *Zambia Demographic and Health Survey 2001–2002*, Calverton, MD: Central Statistical Office, Central Board of Health and ORC Macro.

Central Statistical Office (2005a), *Living Conditions Monitoring Survey Report 2004*, Lusaka: Central Statistical Office.

Central Statistical Office (2005b), *National Accounts*, Lusaka: Central Statistical Office.

Gaisie, K., A. Cross, and G. Nsemukila (1993), *Zambia Demographic and Health Survey, 1992*, Columbia, MD: University of Zambia, Central Statistical Office, and Macro International Inc.

Government of the Republic of Zambia (2000), *2000 Mid-Year Economic Review*, Lusaka: Ministry of Finance and Economic Development.

Government of the Republic of Zambia (2002a), *Poverty Reduction Strategy Paper*, Lusaka: Ministry of Finance and National Planning.

Government of the Republic of Zambia, (2002b), *Transitional National Development Plan: 2002–2005*, Lusaka: Ministry of Finance and National Planning.

Government of the Republic of Zambia (2004a), *Monitoring and Reporting Progress in the PRSP by Means of the Refined Indicator System*, Lusaka: Planning and Economic Management Department, Ministry of Finance and National Planning.

Government of the Republic of Zambia (2004b), *National Agricultural Polic*, Lusaka: Ministry of Agriculture and Cooperatives.

Government of the Republic of Zambia (2005), *Pro-Poor Growth through Rural Development, Job Creation and Technological Advancement*, Research Brief prepared by the Macro Sector Advisory Group. Lusaka: Ministry of Finance and National Planning.

Government of the Republic of Zambia (2006a), *Fifth National Development Plan: 2006–201'*, Lusaka: Ministry of Finance and National Planning.

Government of the Republic of Zambia (2006b), *Macroeconomic Indicators*, Lusaka: Ministry of Finance and National Planning.

Ministry of Education (2004), *Education Management Information System*, Lusaka: Planning Unit, Ministry of Education (Hosted @ ZamSED).

National HIV and AIDS Council (2002), *National HIV and AIDS Intervention Strategic Plan 2002–200'*, Lusaka: National HIV and AIDS/STI/TB Council.

National HIV and AIDS Council (2004), *The HIV and AIDS Epidemic in Zambia*, Lusaka: National HIV and AIDS/STI/TB Council.

Saasa, O. and J. Carlsson (2002), *Aid and Poverty Reduction in Zambia: Mission Unaccomplished*, Uppsala: Nordic Africa Institute.

World Bank (2002), *World Development Report*, Oxford: Oxford University Press <Query>

World Bank (2005), *Zambia: Poverty and Vulnerability Assessment*, Discussion Draft, Africa Region, World Bank, Report No. 32573-ZM.

CHAPTER 5

POVERTY STATUS AND EVOLUTION OF POVERTY REDUCTION POLICIES AND STRATEGIES IN BOTSWANA

Charity K. Kerapeletswe

5.1. Introduction

Botswana is a landlocked country in Southern Africa. It shares borders with South Africa to the south and southeast, Namibia to the northwest, and with Zambia and Zimbabwe to the northeast. The surface area of Botswana is 582,000 km^2 with the Kalahari Desert constituting 77% of the total area. The climate is sub-tropical, with summer temperatures ranging from 19° to 33°C and in the winter from 0° to 23°C. Average annual rainfall in the northeast is about 650 mm, decreasing to less than 250 mm in the extreme southwest. The population of Botswana is 1.7 million with a growth rate of 2.4% in 2006 (Central Statistics Office (CSO) 2001; 2006).

Botswana is often hailed as one of Africa's success stories of sustained economic growth, which is grounded in good governance, political stability and prudent macroeconomic management. From humble beginnings as one of the poorest countries in the world at the time of attaining independence in 1966, Botswana harnessed diamond rents in the 1970s as an engine of growth and the economy dramatically progressed to its classification in the late 1990s as a 'middle-income country' by the World Bank. GDP growth has averaged 6% per annum in real terms over the post-independence period and per capita GDP has grown sixfold. This impressive performance record continues to earn the country high international ratings. The country has since 1998 been ranked the least corrupt country in Africa by Transparency International's corruption perception index.

By contrast, strong economic growth is associated with high unemployment level and income poverty, which is particularly serious in rural areas. Consequently, migration to urban areas has been a key individual strategy for escaping poverty in rural areas. A study by the Botswana Institute for Development Policy Analysis (BIDPA) in 1997 reported that the national poverty rate had declined from 59% in 1984/85 to only 47% in 1994/95. The incidence of poverty subsequently declined to 30.2% in 2005/06 (CSO 2006). Another feature is the highly skewed income distribution with a Gini coefficient of almost 0.6, implying that the benefits of growth are not equitably distributed (CSO 2005). The HIV and AIDS epidemic presents another challenge for poverty reduction by eroding achievements in socio-economic development. The most recent sentinel survey shows that HIV prevalence is 32.4%. In spite of tremendous challenges, Botswana aims to halt and reverse the spread of HIV and AIDS by 2016.

Poverty reduction has been the focus of government policies for many years, with modest success. In the past the government has sought to reduce poverty through a variety of policies and programmes, including social safety nets, income transfer programmes for the poor and the disadvantaged and expanded access to basic services for a significant proportion of the population. Notwithstanding these efforts, there is still a high level of poverty in Botswana. The National Poverty Reduction Strategy (NPRS) of 2002 is geared to addressing poverty in line with the national long-term development strategy called the National Vision 2016, which seeks to eliminate extreme poverty by the year 2016.

This chapter presents a socio-economic profile of Botswana and its poverty status and explains the evolution of poverty reduction policies and strategies. It elaborates the poverty reduction strategies that have been and are currently being pursued. The section following the introduction presents a macroeconomic overview; thereafter a demographic profile is given. Subsequent sections cover social development; poverty status and profile; national poverty reduction strategies; stakeholder views of national poverty reduction strategies; details of the nationwide strategies; the voluntary sector; and a conclusion.

5.2 Macroeconomic performance and analysis

The macroeconomic situation bears decisively on the prevalence of poverty and the prospects for poverty reduction. This section presents a broad overview with regard to key parameters.

Botswana has experienced four decades of high real per capita income growth, in the last decade of more than 7% per annum on average (see Figure 5.1). Sound macroeconomic policies and prudent use of diamond revenues have made Botswana one of the fastest-growing countries in the world over the three last decades and it has now achieved middle-income status, making it globally the best economic performer over that period.

Figure 5.1: GDP Growth Rate (percent)

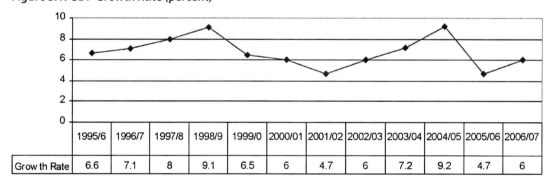

	1995/6	1996/7	1997/8	1998/9	1999/0	2000/01	2001/02	2002/03	2003/04	2004/05	2005/06	2006/07
Growth Rate	6.6	7.1	8	9.1	6.5	6	4.7	6	7.2	9.2	4.7	6

The economy of Botswana has undergone structural change from primarily an agricultural subsistence one in 1966 when agriculture accounted for 40% of the country's Gross Domestic Product (GDP) to one that is predominantly dependent on mineral revenue, specifically diamonds. Over the years the contribution of the minerals industry to GDP has burgeoned from virtually zero in 1966 to almost 45% in 2004/05 (see Figure 5.2). Apart from being the world's leading diamond producer, the country produces copper, nickel, cobalt, coal, gold and soda ash, albeit not on the scale of its diamond industry. Other sectors such as tourism grew by 4%, which is a potential source of growth and employment, especially in rural areas.

Figure 5.2: Sectoral share of GDP 2004/05

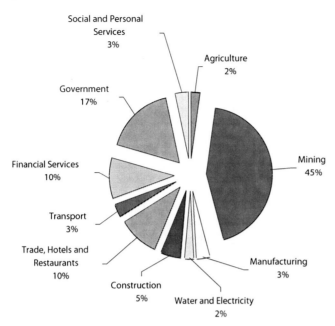

Growth in GDP per capita shows an upward trend. In 1966, Botswana had a per capita GDP of USD 660. Over the years it has increased almost tenfold to USD 6,203 (see Figure 5.3).

Figure 5.3: Trends in GDP Per Capita

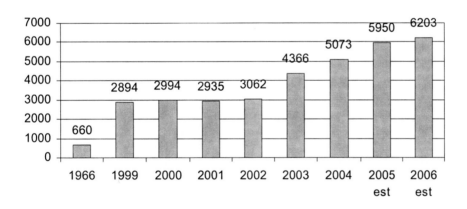

Previously, the government of Botswana used the exchange rate to support the competitiveness of domestic producers. In May 2005, there was a 12% devaluation of the Pula to boost exports. This entailed a temporary surge in inflation (Figure 5.4), which slowed down to 7.2% in March 2007 (CSO 2006).

Figure 5.4: Trends in Annual Inflation (Percent)

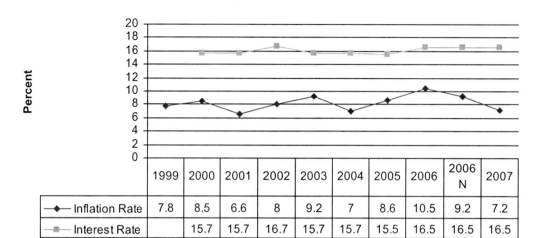

	1999	2000	2001	2002	2003	2004	2005	2006	2006 N	2007
—◆— Inflation Rate	7.8	8.5	6.6	8	9.2	7	8.6	10.5	9.2	7.2
—■— Interest Rate		15.7	15.7	16.7	15.7	15.7	15.5	16.5	16.5	16.5

The rise in inflation was attributable to the increase in administered prices, including the reintroduction of fees in government secondary schools and fuel prices, which were increased three times in the first half of the year in response to high international oil prices. The Bank of Botswana used interest rates to inhibit borrowing in an attempt to curb inflation. However, in response to the devaluation in 2005, the prime lending rate shot up to 16.5%. Botswana is an import-dependent economy and hence changes in exchange rates have cost effects. The interactive effects of increases in domestic prices due to inflation and devaluation increase inflation and the cost of living for the poor.

The economy faces the serious challenge of a high unemployment rate. Unemployment has been increasing since 2002 and currently stands at 23.8%, while at the same time there are shortages of skills. The problem is above all prevalent among youth in the 15–19 and 20–24 age groups. Unemployment is also gradually increasing among university graduates. This may suggest a mismatch between the skills on offer and the demands of the labour market. With a high unemployment rate it will be difficult, if not impossible, to alleviate poverty and inequality in Botswana over the longer term.

5.3 DEMOGRAPHIC PROFILE

The Botswana population is 1,680,863, which is perceived as small (CSO 2001). A small population provides a small market base, which makes it difficult to foster a diversified and stable economy. Its advantage is in spreading resources over a small number of people, which may result in adequately meeting the needs of everyone. Botswana's population growth rate was at 3.5% in the 1980s and 2.5% in 2001 and ultimately -0.04% by 2006 (UNDP 2006). Life expectancy at birth declined from 65.2 years in 1993 to 56 years in 2007 with male life expectancy being 53 and 59 years for females (Population Census 2001)

In 1966, the Botswana population was largely rural (94%) and also mobile, commuting between villages, land areas and cattle posts. With the rapid expansion of economic activities in the mid-1970s and the 1980s, the settlement pattern changed from predominantly rural to largely urban.[13] By 1991, the spatial distribution had changed to 54.3% urban and 45.7% rural, respectively (Government of Botswana 2000).

Figure 5.5: Geographical Distribution by Rural–Urban Population Mobility

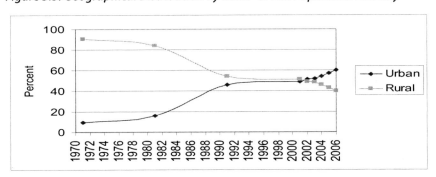

By 2002 the population distribution between urban and rural was even but by 2006 it had changed to 60% urban and 40% rural (Figure 5.5). This complete shift in population settlement pattern primarily reflected the influx of migrants from the rural areas rather than a natural increase in the existing urban population. Rural–urban migrants are attracted by job opportunities in urban centres or pushed out by the hardships in the rural areas, or both. The urbanisation process in Botswana presents a variety of urban challenges, such as housing, health care, transportation, utilities, employment and an increase in urban poverty.

In conclusion, Botswana presents a paradoxical performance in socio-economic indicators. A steady growth of GDP has been in parallel with an increase in unemployment and declining life expectancy. In addition, there has been a transformation of settlement patterns, from largely rural to mainly urban. What are the implications of these contrasting features for poverty reduction?

5.4 POVERTY STATUS AND PROFILE

Notwithstanding its impressive economic performance, Botswana is still riddled with a high level of poverty and unemployment, indicating that growth alone is hardly sufficient to achieve poverty reduction on any significant scale. While growth is the key to poverty reduction, poverty may also hamper sustained growth. According to Perry et al. (2006), a 10% drop in poverty levels, other things being equal, can increase economic growth by 1%. In turn, a 10% increase in poverty levels will lower the growth rate by 1% and reduce investment by up to 8% of GDP. This is so because the poor are in no position to engage in many of the profitable activities that stimulate investment and growth, thus creating a vicious circle in which low growth results in high poverty and high poverty, in turn, results in low growth.

---

[13]   A settlement is defined as urban for statistical purposes if 75% or more of its workforce are in non-agricultural activities and its population is at least 5,000. According to this definition, all the major villages in the country were classified as urban villages.

5.4.1 Income poverty

A 1997 study on Poverty and Poverty Alleviation, undertaken by the BIDPA, reported that the national poverty rate had declined sharply from 59% in 1985 to 47% in 1994. In 2002/03 national income poverty was estimated at 32.89%, and subsequently in 2005/06 at 30.2%. While poverty reduction was rapid between 1985/86 and 1993/94, it significantly slowed down between 1993/94 and 2005/06 (see Figure 5.6).

Figure 5.6: Head Count Ratio (1985 - 2006)

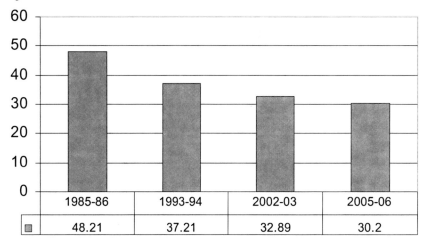

	1985-86	1993-94	2002-03	2005-06
	48.21	37.21	32.89	30.2

5.4.2 Poverty and rural/urban disparities

There are disparities in poverty incidence by geography, gender and ethnicity. In some parts of the country poverty is endemic and many depend on destitution payments by the state for their livelihoods. This situation persists mostly in the smallest settlements inhabited mainly by people referred to as remote area dwellers (RADs), who reside in settlements and cattle posts, as well as villages. The RAD households are still highly dependent for their survival on rapidly depleting natural resources. The BIDPA study estimated that at least 62% of the poor or the very poor lived in rural areas. Overall, 48% of rural households were estimated to be poor or very poor.

Botswana is divided into administrative districts (see Figure 5.7). The most severe poverty is recorded in the rural southwest (Ghanzi and Kgalagadi Districts), and in western parts of Kweneng and Southern Districts, where most of the Basarwa and other ethnic minorities live.[14] There some 71% of the population were found to be poor in 1997, and 59% were classified as very poor. By 2002/03, the poverty headcount had declined to 51.5% in Kgalagadi and 44.23% in Southern and 33.97% in Kweneng Districts.

---

[14] The San people of Botswana, who constitutes an ethnic minority.

Figure 5.7: Administrative District Distribution of Poverty

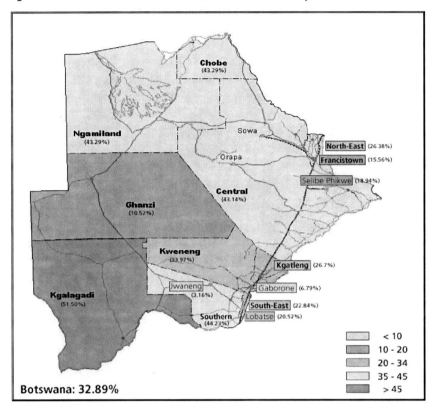

Source: UNDP (2004).

The incidence of poverty is also high in other districts, such as Ngamiland (43.29%), Chobe (43.29%) and Central (43.14%). Poverty is highly concentrated in the districts in the northwest of Botswana and less in urban districts, especially in Jwaneng, which has the lowest poverty incidence of 3.16% only. This may be attributed to the fact that Jwaneng has one of the largest diamond mines in the country.

5.4.3 Poverty and gender

In Botswana poverty is complexly gendered, as men and women are often poor for different reasons, experience poverty differently and have differing capacities to withstand and/ or escape poverty. Gender inequalities and gender power relations interact with other inequalities and power relations to produce these differences. Studies have shown that female-headed households (FHHs) are poorer than male-headed ones. Almost 50% of FHHs are poor, compared with 44% of male-headed households (BIDPA 2000). In rural areas, both male and FHHs experience the same poverty rate. This can be explained partly by the fact that many of the FHHs are seasonal. Males from such households may have migrated to urban areas in search of jobs. The designation FHH may thus cover several different types of household.

Measured against other countries with a comparable per capita income, Botswana has been more successful in addressing capability poverty than income poverty. Sustained public investment has greatly improved the quality of and public access to services such as education, health care and safe drinking water. However, the national rate of income poverty is relatively high for a country with Botswana's per capita income, partly due to skewed income distribution. According to the CSO (1996), the poorest 40% of the population received 12% of total income, the middle 40% had 29% and the richest 20% had 59% of the national income. The distribution of income is more uneven in rural areas and least uneven in urban areas (CSO 1996). The outstanding economic growth has failed to influence the income disparities, as evidenced by the country's Gini coefficient of almost 0.6 in 2005 (Figure 5.8).

Figure 5.8: Trends in Income Distribution (Gini Coefficient)

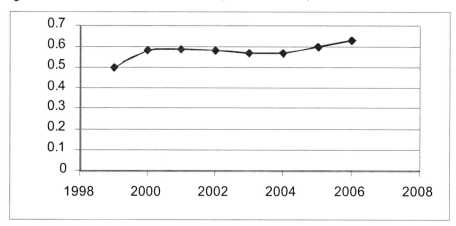

The poverty situation reflects the words of the late President Sir Seretse Khama in a message marking the fifth anniversary of independence in 1971 when he stated:

> Unless we introduce clear and consistent policies which provide for social justice, development will enrich a minority of our citizens and leave the lives of the majority practically untouched….We must make every effort to ensure that our strategy is based on social justice and this means that rural development must have a high priority (*Daily News*, 1 October 1971).

It is critical, therefore, that the government focuses on the skewed distribution as part of a strategy for poverty reduction.

5.5 NON-INCOME POVERTY

Botswana has achieved significant improvement in social development. The years following independence saw an extraordinary social transformation. The average citizen of Botswana benefited from the phenomenal economic growth through the provision of social services in the form of health facilities, free education, clean water and other welfare services.

5.5.1 Human development

The country's success in terms of human development is reflected in its Human Development Index (HDI), compiled by the United Nations Development Programme (UNDP) on the basis of life expectancy, per capita income and education. The HDI for Botswana rose from 0.5 in 1975 to almost 0.7 in 1990, placing it among the few top countries in the developing world. However, this score has been declining over time due to the impact of HIV and AIDS. Figure 5.9 shows that the decline in Botswana's HDI has been dramatic, from 0.674 in 1990 to 0.614 in 2001, placing it among only four countries (the others being the Russian Federation, Moldova and Lesotho) to witness such a marked fall (Institute for Security Studies 2005).

Figure 5.9: *Trends in Human Development Index*

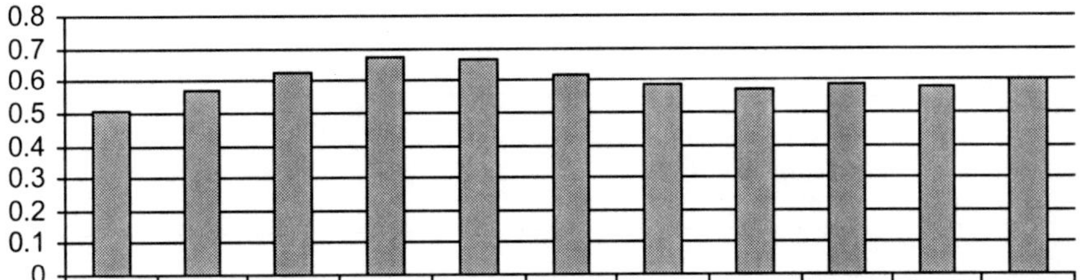

	1975	1980	1985	1990	1995	2001	2002	2003	2004	2005	2006
	0.509	0.573	0.626	0.674	0.666	0.614	0.59	0.57	0.59	0.58	0.6

Life expectancy at birth (Figure 5.10), which was slightly above 40 years in 1966, was estimated to have risen to 67 years in 1996 (Botswana Government 2006). However, it plummeted to 56.3 years during the 1995–2000 period and is currently 40 years, which is 32 years lower than the life expectancy projected in the absence of AIDS.

Figure 5.10: *Life Expectancy at Birth*

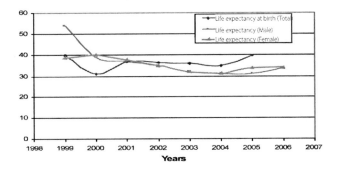

5.5.2 Education and literacy

Education has been a priority for Botswana since independence. Remarkable achievements have been made in primary and junior secondary schools alike. At both levels enrolment rates are close to 100%, with girl pupils outnumbering boys. Adult illiteracy has fallen below 20% for both males and females (Figure 5.11). It is estimated that in 2003, 81.2% of the population were literate, with a larger percentage of females (81.5%) than males (76.1%) being literate (see Figure 5.11). Literacy levels in urban areas, where most of the newspapers and other information channels are based, tend to be higher than in rural areas: in 2000, 83.3% of those in urban areas were literate compared with 64.1% in rural areas (UNDP 2005).

Figure 5.11: Literacy Rate (Percent)

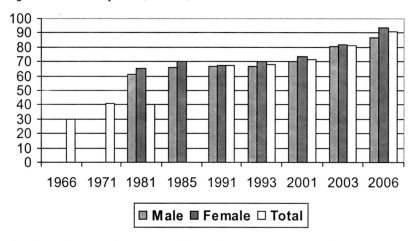

The data show a clear upward trend. The literacy rates for adults (15 to 65+) increased from 68.9% in 1993 to 81% in 2003 and reached almost 90% in 2006. The 2004 Status Report of the Millennium Goals concludes that Botswana has achieved universal access to primary education, which currently consists of a 10-year basic education system (Republic of Botswana/United Nations 2004). Women's literacy is of crucial importance in addressing wider issues of gender inequality.

5.5.3 Health care

Botswana has achieved remarkable advances in the health status of its population since 1966. There has been expansion of health services through government investment in health infrastructure and in the training of health personnel (Figure 5.12). Health expenditure in the past two decades has averaged 5–8% of the national budget. Given the need to serve a sparsely distributed population, most of the investment in physical health infrastructure has gone into developing an extensive primary health care (PHC) outreach system.

Figure 5.12: Public Spending on Health

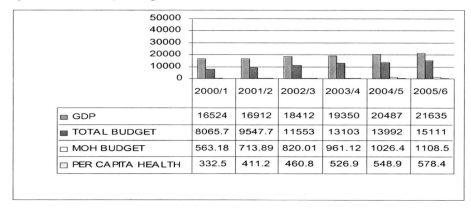

	2000/1	2001/2	2002/3	2003/4	2004/5	2005/6
GDP	16524	16912	18412	19350	20487	21635
TOTAL BUDGET	8065.7	9547.7	11553	13103	13992	15111
MOH BUDGET	563.18	713.89	820.01	961.12	1026.4	1108.5
PER CAPITA HEALTH	332.5	411.2	460.8	526.9	548.9	578.4

The steady increase in health spending reflects the commitment of the government to providing improved health services and fighting HIV and AIDS. Botswana's health care services were hospital-based until 1973, when the government accepted PHC as the most appropriate strategy for the attainment of health for all. The concept PHC is based on promotive, preventive, curative and rehabilitative health care services. This strategy has been followed in the past in national development plans as well as in the current NDP 9 (2003/04–2008/09). Access to health care is generally good, with almost 90% of the rural population now living within 15 km of a primary health clinic (EU 2006). There is a standard BWP2 (USD 0.40) charge for outpatient treatment and first-line hospital care, but many sections of the population are exempted from payment: pregnant women, TB patients, HIV and AIDS patients and children under 12 are entitled to free treatment.

There has been a significant improvement in health and survival indicators. Infant mortality fell from 95 to 56 deaths per thousand between 1970 and 1995. However, this figure has subsequently risen to 80 deaths per thousand, as a direct consequence of HIV and AIDS. The infant mortality rate has been reduced from 80 per 1000 births in 2000 to 54 per 1000 births in 2006 and under-five mortality increased from 58 per 1000 births to 101 per 1000 births (Figure 5.13)

Figure 5.13: Infant and Under-Five Mortality Rate (Per 1000 births)

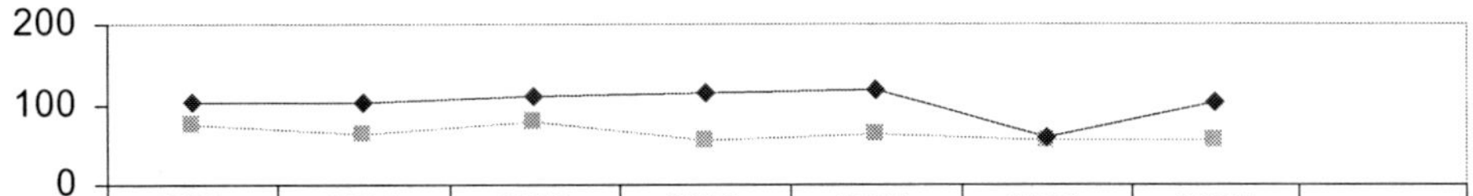

	2000	2001	2002	2003	2004	2005	2006	
Infant Mortality	74	63	80	53.7	64.7	54.5	54	
Under 5 Mortality	101	101	110	112	116	58	101	

One of the factors influencing the indicators is the fact that some 99% of births are attended by a trained health worker. Maternal mortality, however, which stands at 330 per 100,000 live births, is still relatively high for a middle income country (Figure 5.14).

Figure 5.14: Maternal Mortality Rate (Per 100,000)

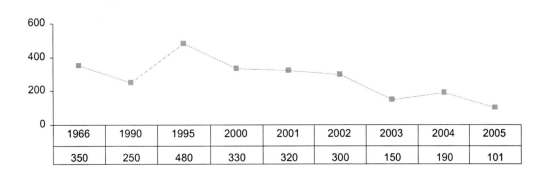

1966	1990	1995	2000	2001	2002	2003	2004	2005
350	250	480	330	320	300	150	190	101

Health care services tend to be more easily accessible in urban areas than in rural areas. These disparities reflect, in part, the long distances which people have to travel in remote areas to reach health facilities, which reinforces household poverty.

5.5.4 Water and sanitation

Access to safe drinking water has been expanded to virtually the entire country, with almost 100% of the population currently enjoying access to safe drinking water (Figure 5.15).

Figure 5.15: Access to Safe Drinking Water

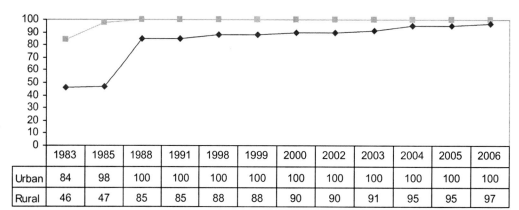

	1983	1985	1988	1991	1998	1999	2000	2002	2003	2004	2005	2006
Urban	84	98	100	100	100	100	100	100	100	100	100	100
Rural	46	47	85	85	88	88	90	90	91	95	95	97

In 1983, almost 84% of urban dwellers had access to safe drinking water, rising to 100% by 1988. Similar progress has been made in rural areas. In 1983, only 46% of the rural population had access to safe drinking water. By 2000, however, the coverage had reached 90% and 97% by 2006.

Equally impressive achievements have also been registered in the expansion of sanitation and other social and economic infrastructures (Figure 5.16). The government of Botswana provides sanitation services with the aim of improving the general public health conditions of the Batswana. A major step in that direction has been the passage of the Waste Management Bill of 1998, in terms of which a sanitation and waste management department was established.

Figure 5.16: Access to Sanitation

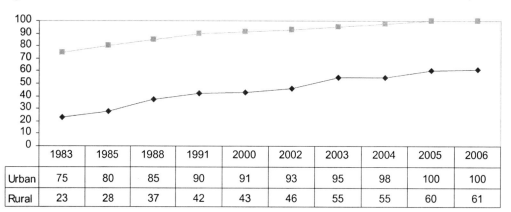

	1983	1985	1988	1991	2000	2002	2003	2004	2005	2006
Urban	75	80	85	90	91	93	95	98	100	100
Rural	23	28	37	42	43	46	55	55	60	61

The provision of adequate sanitation facilities countrywide remains a challenge owing to rapid urbanisation of the population. In 1983 only 51% of the population were using adequate sanitation facilities. By 2006, almost 80% of households were using adequate sanitation facilities. There are disparities between rural and urban areas (see Figure 5.16). Nonetheless, access to sanitation in rural areas has been improving over time through the government's intervention programmes under which rural households were subsidised to build latrines.

5.5.5 HIV and AIDS

Botswana faces high rates of HIV and AIDS, which increases the incidence of poverty due to the inability of the sick to work or to the demanding care for the sick, as well as to the loss of breadwinners for many households. The most recent sentinel survey shows that HIV prevalence had decreased from 37.4% in 2003 to 32.4% in 2006. HIV prevalence is high among the group aged 15–19 years, but decreased from 22.8% in 2003 to 17.8% in 2005. The Prevention of Mother to Child Transmission Programme provides drugs to 73% of pregnant HIV-positive women. Patients enrolled for anti-retroviral drug treatment in 2005 increased to 54,378 compared to 32,835 in 2004. In 2004, there were an estimated 260,000 people living with HIV. The 2004 Botswana AIDS Impact Survey showed the overall HIV prevalence rate to be 17.3% (population-based rate). There are some 60,000 registered orphans and about 200,000 orphans are projected for 2010 (CSO 2005; UNAIDS 2006).

The economic and social impacts of HIV and AIDS are potentially devastating. If not tackled through appropriate measures requiring significant budgetary allocations, the HIV and AIDS pandemic will act as an obstacle and constraint to the development of Botswana. The national policy on HIV and AIDS came into being in 1993. Activities related to HIV and AIDS were budgeted for under different ministries. Since the formation of NACA in 2000, it has handled all HIV and AIDS budgetary allocations. Table 5.1 shows HIV and AIDS budget allocations for 2001/02 through 2005/06.

Table 5.1: Budget Allocations to HIV and AIDS

	2002/3	2003/4	2004/5	2005/6
HIV and AIDS budget, percent of health budget	41.9	24.1	19.5	12.6
HIV and AIDS budget, percent of total budget	1.87	1.20	0.98	0.65

The share of HIV and AIDS budget allocations as a percentage of the total budget was almost 2% in 2002/03 and has since hovered around 1% of the total budget. Over the coming years, HIV and AIDS is likely to exacerbate the existing shortages of skilled labour, putting pressure on all sectors of activity (e.g. health services, secondary and tertiary level education, business services) which already rely on the costly import of expatriate skills. Overall, HIV and AIDS may affect the Botswana economy in terms of a declining labour force; a decline in labour force productivity; a decline in overall GDP growth; and a decline in the growth of demand for labour power.

5.5.6 Gender

Gender equality is an important part of human progress. Gender inequalities are measured by the Gender-related Development Index and the Gender Empowerment Measure. In Botswana, the Gender Equality Index was 0.80 in 2005, up from 0.72 in 1993 (UNDP 2006), indicating some progress in reducing gender inequalities in education enrolment, employment and decision-making. Nevertheless, a very high proportion of very poor households are headed by women and a high proportion of non-poor households are headed by men in Botswana (BIDPA 1997). The adoption of the Policy on Women in Development in 1995 was meant to address these discrepancies. Poverty reduction strategies should embrace a better understanding of the potential impact of interventions on the welfare of men and women, gender equity and gender distribution in Botswana. Generally, the gender distribution of the Botswana population shows that there were more women than men in all economically active age groups.

5.6 DETERMINANTS OF POVERTY IN BOTSWANA

Poverty is rooted primarily in Botswana's adverse physical conditions and narrow economic base. This situation is exacerbated by a range of social disadvantages and problems that adversely affect the poor. In order to formulate and target successful poverty alleviation strategies it is important to look at these causes in more detail.

At the root of the problem of rural poverty lies a structural limitation of agriculture. There is a lack of agricultural diversity. A combination of poor soils, drought, extreme variations of temperature and unreliable rains is not conducive to arable agriculture. Despite a wide range of agricultural support and extension programmes in the past, there has been no sustained improvement in crop yields. The contribution of agriculture to GDP sharply dropped from 40% in 1966 to only 2% 2006. Although this is partly due to an increase in the share of mining, agriculture has also declined in real terms. Consequently, the majority in rural areas live below the poverty line and survive primarily on a mixture of low-return subsistence agriculture, remittances and subsidies.

Lack of cash income is the single most important cause of poverty in Botswana. This is exacerbated by the narrow economic base of mineral exploitation, which is not labour intensive and provides only 3.5% of formal employment. In addition, it has not created significant spin-offs in other areas of the economy, apart from in the public sector. With such a narrow economic base and limited opportunities for productive work, the country has a high unemployment rate.

The outstanding achievement in expanding access to education did not translate into skills development. Hence, Botswana faces a challenge of unemployment and skills shortage. This situation is predicted to get worse as the HIV and AIDS epidemic takes its toll on the existing workforce. The education system has not been able to equip school leavers adequately with the diverse and high level of skills required by the job market as a whole.

Traditionally, inequality in Botswana was managed through a practice whereby those who had more wealth often helped those less well off by means of various well established traditional institutions, such as the mafisa: pooling of resources, sharecropping and extended family systems.[15] There have been major changes in these traditional social safety nets. The

---

[15] Mafisa is a traditional system of loan of animals, especially cattle.

traditional extended family system has been weakened due to rapid rural-urban migration, especially of young adults. While many urban dwellers remit money back to their kin in the rural areas, they are not physically present any more to assist less able-bodied family members and neighbours. As a result, poor people in rural areas have lost much of their social safety nets. In urban areas some rural migrants have not found the employment and wealth they had hoped for and without their extended family they have ended in destitution.

Women tend to have less power in gender relationships than men. Previously, the provisions of the law allowed the husband to manage and control the family estate without the knowledge and consent of his wife, thus reducing her to the status of a minor. Married women must have their husband's consent before loan applications can be approved. Recent changes in legislation have attempted to address this issue. The 1999 Affiliations Proceedings Act provides for a minimum BWP100 a month to be given by the father for the maintenance and education of the child. This amount can be adjusted up or down according to the court's view of the father's circumstances. The Marital Bill of 2005 repealed the marital power of the husband, giving women equal say in the disposal of the couple's assets.

Poverty and HIV and AIDS mutually reinforce each other; reduced incomes owing to the loss of able-bodied persons to AIDS cause a deepening of poverty. Poverty affects FHHs more than those headed by men and aggravates the vulnerability of women to HIV infection.

5.7 Evolution of Poverty Reduction Strategies and Policies in Botswana

Poverty reduction has long been pursued in Botswana. The government's commitment to poverty alleviation is demonstrated by its endorsement of a series of United Nations global declarations for the improvement of human conditions. Most notably, Botswana is a signatory to the Millennium Declaration of 2000, and to the Copenhagen Declaration and Programme of Action for Social Development (1995), whose central goal has been the elimination of poverty through the enhancement of productive employment and fostering of social integration. Botswana is also signatory to the International Convention on the Rights of the Child (1990); the International Convention on the Elimination of all Forms of Discrimination Against Women (1979); the SADC Gender and Development Declaration; the International Conference on Population and Development (1994); and the World Food Summit (Rome 1996).

In terms of domestic policy, a national desire to reduce and ultimately eliminate poverty has been articulated, directly or indirectly, in a number of policy documents, including, but not limited to, National Development Plans, Vision 2016, the National Policy on Rural Development, and recently the NPRS. The government of Botswana has adopted a three-pronged strategy towards poverty reduction:

1. stimulation of economic growth through economic diversification, employment creation, income generation, citizen economic empowerment, and citizen entrepreneurship development;
2. investment in infrastructural development and social services to enhance health and education outcomes as well as to stimulate economic growth;
3. the adoption of a system of social safety nets as direct measures to assist the ultra poor and vulnerable groups.

The Long-Term Vision for Botswana 2016: Towards Prosperity for All, otherwise known as Vision 2016, outlines the aspirations of Botswana for the year 2016, which are more ambitious than the MDGs. Vision 2016 is based on seven pillars which are complementary to the MDGs (Table 5.2). All pillars affect well-being, either directly or indirectly, and thus have a bearing on poverty reduction.

Table 5.2: Vision 2016 and the MDGs

Vision 2016 Pillars	Millennium Development Goals
1. An educated and informed nation	*MDG 2: Achieve Universal Primary Education* *With a primary school enrolment rate of 106%, Botswana has achieved this goal. Vision 2016 thus sets higher priorities in the dimension of quality, relevance and access (10 years of basic education)*
2. A prosperous, productive and innovative nation	*MDG 1: Eradicate Extreme Poverty and Hunger* *MDG 7: Ensure Environmental Sustainability* *The key elements of this vision pillar are sustainable growth and diversification*
3. A compassionate, just and caring nation	*MDG 1: Eradicate Extreme Poverty and Hunger* *MDG 6: Combat HIV and AIDS, Malaria and other Diseases. This vision pillar's main priorities are poverty, inequality and social safety nets; and health and HIV and AIDS*
4. A safe and secure nation	*MDG 1: Eradicate Extreme Poverty and Hunger* *MDG 3: Promote Gender Equality & Empower Women. This pillar addresses some broader issues of human security, e.g. disaster preparedness, to deal with, amongst others, drought, animal diseases and floods, national defence, and crime, (including violence against women and children)*
5. An open, democratic and accountable nation	*MDG 8: Develop a Global Partnership for Development. The fifth pillar focuses on leadership, which is the main prerequisite for international development cooperation, especially FDI, and to a lesser extent aid and trade*
6. A moral and tolerant nation	*MDG 3: Promote Gender Equality & Empower Women. The key elements of this pillar are values – morality and tolerance. Under tolerance, the vision gives priority to the elimination of discrimination against women, children, the aged and the disabled and speaks against sexual harassment*
7. A proud and united nation	*MDG 8: Develop a Global Partnership for Development. Promotes nationhood based on shared values and shared aspirations. An important element of this vision pillar, which is also essential to MDG 8, is good governance and participation*

From independence in 1966, successive National Development Plans (NDPs) have prioritised the eradication of poverty through sustained economic diversification and employment creation. All NDPs published after 1997 are themselves guided by Botswana's 'Long Term Vision for Botswana: Towards Prosperity for All'. The National Development Plan (NDP 9), whose theme is 'Towards Realisation of Vision 2016: Sustainable and Diversified Development through Competitiveness in Global Markets', covers the period 2003–2009. The policy thrust of NDP 9 includes:

- economic diversification, employment creation and poverty alleviation;
- macroeconomic stability, financial discipline and public sector reform;
- environmental protection, rural development, human resource development, the fight against HIV and AIDS, science and technology development, and disaster management.
- Both Vision 2016 and NDP 9 recognise the importance of the agricultural sector for the growth of the national economy, the creation of employment opportunities, the improvement of food security and the alleviation of poverty, particularly rural poverty.

5.7.3 National Poverty Reduction Strategy

The government prepared a national strategy for poverty reduction (NPRS) in April 2003, which takes a broad developmental view with several interrelated thrusts and rapid economic growth as central to eradicating poverty. It flags the priority areas of NDP 9 and aims to ensure a poverty focus within NDP 9 and sector implementation. The strategy itself is not time-bound. The Botswana NPRS is not a 'Poverty Reduction Strategy Paper' in its usual meaning and bearing. Rather, NDP 9 and its expenditure framework remain the reference point of the NPRS. Half-yearly reports to Cabinet on the implementation of the strategy are planned.

A major feature of the NPRS is that Botswana is one of the few African countries that has not been subjected to a Structural Adjustment Programme under World Bank auspices. Botswana is actually one of the only two African countries that are net creditors of the Bretton Woods institutions and hence external assistance is playing a very limited role in the development efforts of Botswana. The strategy is home-grown without reference to IMF and World Bank conditionalities.

The strategy rests on:

- macroeconomic policies fostering stability, economic growth, and foreign and domestic investment;
- pro-poor spending;
- protection of essential items (food, clothing, shelter) from inflationary pressures;
- promotion of tourism with a view to increasing employment opportunities for the poor based on existing resources;
- more sustainable, efficient and targeted safety net packages;
- the effective participation of the poor in the planning of anti-poverty schemes;
- the fight against HIV and AIDS;
- monitoring mechanisms including poverty surveys and capacity building of the CSO.

Through the NSPR, the government underscores the importance of broad-based economic growth as a means to promote sustained poverty reduction. The key areas of development under the NSPR (during NDP 9) include:

- enhancement of sustainable livelihoods;
- human capabilities and participation in programmes by beneficiaries;
- strengthening of local government institutions;
- creation of an environment conducive for investment.

The NSPR accentuates the need for the government to continue to use social safety nets to target the most needy and vulnerable segments of society. The government's approach to poverty reduction has always encompassed four complementary elements:

- Aggressive investment in human capital formation;
- Infrastructure development;
- Employment creation;
- Social safety nets.

Implementation efforts so far include strengthening the institutional framework for overseeing, coordinating and monitoring poverty-related initiatives. A Multi-Sectoral Committee on Poverty Reduction, comprising representation from both within and outside government, has been established. In addition, early in 2005 a Poverty Reduction Programme Advisor was attached to the Ministry of Finance and Development Planning to work with other ministries and stakeholders to help them sharpen the anti-poverty components of their programmes. As part of the implementation process, some are being implemented under NDP 9 that directly contribute to poverty reduction and welfare improvement for the Batswana by providing employment opportunities.

5.8 STAKEHOLDER VIEWS OF THE NPRS

Stakeholder views on NPRS formulation, comprehensiveness, political underpinnings, legitimacy and popular support, cross-cutting issues and other indicators were obtained through structured interviews with 40 stakeholders. The respondents included officers from research institutions, the donor community, civil society organisations, government officials, and parliamentarians. An interview guide was a major tool used for this research exercise.

Opinions about the degree of participation and national ownership differed widely and the most vocal emerged from civil society. Almost 75% of the respondents indicated that the NPRS was really participatory when it was formulated. House to house surveys were conducted through the use of social workers to profile the poor. However, it seems that most non-state agencies, especially civil society organisations, were not involved in undertaking the analysis of the poverty situation in the country. The involvement by civil society organisations was not perceived to have been genuinely participatory but rather reactively consultative.

As for issues relating to monitoring and evaluation systems, most respondents were aware that Ministry of Finance and Development Planning has a Poverty Reduction Unit with a Programme Advisor which is in charge of monitoring and evaluating the implementation of the NPRS.

Stakeholders were asked how comprehensive they perceived the PRS to be. Almost all respondents (97%), except some civil society organisations, considered the NPRS to be quite comprehensive. Those knowledgeable about it indicated that the document covers quite a lot of issues, different classes of people and factors of poverty. The strategy was said to be very wide-ranging, despite a reservation that being comprehensive does not necessarily translate into effectiveness. It was argued that the formulation may be good but implementation may prove to be daunting. Some argued that the NPRS lacks strategic direction and focus, which makes it ineffective.

As to whether the strategy occupies a central place in the government's anti-poverty activities, the preponderant response (65%) was that the NPRS dominates the government's poverty reduction efforts, while 35% indicated that the NPRS is one among several parallel programmes instituted by the government. Those who argued in favour of a pro-poor growth approach asserted that the NPRS is bound to fail to reach its intended objectives because it offers incentives to being dependant on government assistance rather than aiming at pulling people out of poverty towards self-reliance.

Almost all international agencies interviewed indicated that they were consulted throughout the processes of formulating and implementing the NPRS. However, 30% indicated that they did not know about the origin of resources for the NPRS while 10% indicated that it will be dependant on external sources and almost 70% believed that the PRS would not depend on external resources.

This implies that the NPRS is largely dependant on the government's own resources. However, donor agencies emphasised that external funding is mainly for HIV and AIDS programmes and the government does not depend on these donations to fund the NPRS. Currently, only the EU and the Food and Agriculture Organization have ongoing programmes related to agriculture and rural development, and thus to the NPRS.

The time period covered by the NPRS is largely unknown to most respondents (including some members of parliament). However, most of them presume that it must be based on Vision 2016, the NDP and the MDGs. According to a majority of respondents, most programmes within the NPRS have targets so that their implementation goals have been clearly set. Indeed, the NPRS is not time-bound but provides a framework within which poverty reduction programmes are implemented.

Many countries of the world have formed, expanded or strengthened a variety of regional integration arrangements in the last decade. Likewise, Botswana is a member of several regional economic groupings, including the Southern African Development Community (SADC) and the Southern African Customs Union (SACU).

More than 50% of the respondents disagree that regional groupings play a significant role in national anti-poverty efforts. They reckon that regional groupings concentrate on variables such as economic growth and trade liberalisation, ignoring poverty issues. On the other hand, about 70% of the respondents indicated that organisations like SADC and SACU are useful to join because they have certain collective objectives, which enhances the efforts of individual member countries to achieve their national targets. Those who believed regional grouping make a difference argued that membership had assisted Botswana to set targets for its poverty reduction efforts. They emphasised that achieving poverty reduction in Botswana has become easier partly due to regional strategies and membership of international organisations.

While some respondents did not really know much about the poverty reduction strategy document and its initiation, almost 46% of them answered that the impetus to formulate the PRS came from the government, in realisation that a strategy is needed to fight the extent of poverty in the country in a concerted and coherent manner. About 24% of respondents associated the urge to formulate the strategy with the Millennium Declaration, while about 30% believed that the formulation of the NPRS was influenced by regional agreements.

Half of the respondents were sceptical about the political commitment to the implementation of the NPRS. If political commitment had been genuine, poverty would have been drastically reduced in the past. However, half of the respondents indicated that there is political will to implement the NPRS, as reflected in national budget allocations. Almost every government ministry has a poverty reduction unit. Civil society argued that although the government's commitment is reflected clearly in the budget allocations there are also implementation limitations because it is common among government departments to fail to utilise allocated funds fully and to return them at the end of budgetary year.

Findings show that the NPRS seems to be widely supported. However, respondents pointed out that popular programmes are often used to gain political mileage. People tend to support the programmes from which they benefit most, without building capacity to fend for themselves. The fear is that the NPRS, given its popularity, may fail to be analysed critically when its shortcomings appear.

Lack of a clear implementation strategy is perceived to render the NPRS ineffective. Especially the targeting leaves out some groups, such as small-scale farmers' associations, youth and people with disabilities. However, members of parliament interviewed indicated that the NPRS document does address targeting issues. Some respondents from civil society argued that since civil society organisations were not involved in the drafting of the NPRS, the document does not reflect their interests.

When asked 'How well integrated into the institutional set-up of your country is the implementation of the PRS?', about half of the respondents claimed that the strategy is not well integrated while the other half said they have no idea one way or the other. Those who thought that it is well integrated into the institutional set-up of the country said that the MFDP has a Rural Development Department which administers the NPRS. It is also the responsibility of every ministry to include the NPRS into its annual work plans and activities.

Some 88% of the respondents believed that the macroeconomic framework of the NPRS is a home-grown product. A follow-up question on the origins of the framework revealed that 52% of the respondents had no idea where the framework came from. Others argued that the macroeconomic framework of the NPRS is only home-grown on paper while, in practice, it is influenced by Bretton Woods ideas and that the strategy is not much different from the World Bank's.

Generally, the NPRS is perceived to pursue both economic growth and welfarist objectives at the same time. The poor are perceived not to be using their most abundant resource – labour – and hence respondents suggested that labour-intensive projects need to be implemented under the NPRS to encourage beneficiaries to work hard and not expect government handouts on a permanent basis.

The NPRS's economic growth orientation is epitomised in Vision 2016, which emphasises self-reliance. In addition, there are citizen empowerment programmes designed to assist people to exit from social safety nets and to become more self-reliant. About half of respondents from the civil society organisations involved in the formulation of the NPRS favoured a welfarist orientation while one-half favoured both, arguing that the two complement each other.

The distributional effects of economic growth in the NPRS are perceived to favour the poor only on paper. In practice, the benefits of growth tend to be open to all. Some parliamentarians expressed the view that the benefits from economic growth flow directly into social welfare programmes, which are distributed equitably through social services.

The findings show that the agricultural sector was given higher priority than others in the NPRS mainly because the majority of Batswana still derive a livelihood from agriculture. HIV and AIDS is also perceived as one of the prioritised concerns in the NPRS as it is one of the determinants of poverty. Infrastructural provision, specifically electricity, is also given priority to speed up rural development.

Earlier strategies of poverty reduction were biased towards women, especially in the agricultural sector through the Arable Lands Development Programme (ALDEP) and the Financial Assistance Policy programmes. The NPRS includes improved targeting of women through empowerment projects and programmes.

Table 5.3: Cross-Cutting Issues

Cross-cutting concern	Mitigation	Mechanism
HIV and AIDS Botswana suffers from one of the highest rates of HIV infection and AIDS in the world The HIV and AIDS pandemic has far-reaching impacts on Botswana's economic and social development	Curb the spread of HIV/AID and mitigate its economic and social impacts Policy analysis of HIV and AIDS and institutional strengthening HIV and AIDS preventive and curative health service Implement an awareness campaign	Establishment of the National AIDS Coordinating Agency and a National AIDS Council chaired by the President Establishment of a National Sexually Transmitted Diseases Referral, Research and Training Centre with a mandate to advise government on appropriate strategies
Gender Feminisation of poverty Inequitable division of labour, discrimination against women in the labour market Women's inadequate access to education and training Women continue to be disproportionately affected by unemployment Women's lack of economic resources and decision-making power in both public and private sectors A number of traditional laws enforced by tribal structures and customary courts restrict women's property rights and economic opportunities	Enhance women's rights in the labour market Implement targeted programmes to improve women's access to education and training Enhance women's participation in the public and private sector	Implement the National Policy on Women adopted in 1996 and the National Gender Programme Framework adopted in 1998 Implement the Plan of Action for the National Gender Programme Strengthen the relationship between government and women's NGOs Establish a National Council on Women (comprised of representatives from a wide range of organisations) as the country's highest coordinating and advisory body and think-tank on gender issues

Most of the respondents indicated that the NPRS considered several cross-cutting issues, such as the environment (Table 5.3). Furthermore, most government institutions prioritised HIV and AIDS in their planning. Technology was pertinent and, as a result, most government departments have now been computerised to speed up productivity. It is generally believed that if the mainstreaming of cross-cutting issues was implemented correctly and closely monitored, it would be effective.

5.9 ECONOMY-WIDE STRATEGIES FOR POVERTY REDUCTION

The government of Botswana has been aiming at reducing poverty and improving the welfare of the marginalised in Botswana through several policies and programmes. Some of these have already been discussed in the previous sections. Table 5.4 shows poverty and hunger reduction policies, strategies and programmes.

Table 5.4: Poverty and Hunger Reduction Policies, Strategies and Programmes

Instruments	Objectives
2003 National Strategy for Poverty Reduction (NSPR)	To link and harmonise anti-poverty initiatives, provide opportunities for people to have sustainable livelihoods through expansion of employment opportunities and improved access to social investment, and to monitor progress in poverty reduction
2002 Revised National Policy for Rural Development	To reduce rural poverty, promote sustainable livelihoods, stimulate rural employment and income generation, diversify the rural economy, reduce dependency on government, maintain and improve rural capital, increase agricultural productivity and promote participation in development
1984 Industrial Development Policy IDP (revised 1998)	To diversify the economy, foster the growth of the private sector, assist small-scale rural entrepreneurs, support growth and employment creation in towns and villages, and achieve higher levels of productivity
1982–2002 Financial Assistance Policy	To create employment opportunities and encourage investment in a range of economic activities
2002 Citizen Entrepreneurial Development Agency (CEDA)	To promote citizen entrepreneurship, support economic diversification and create employment opportunities
1980 Destitute Policy (Revised 2000)	To provide income support to people defined as destitute according to criteria used by the government
Policies, strategies and programmes to reduce hunger	
Labour-Based Drought Relief Programme	To provide work and income in rural areas for people whose livelihoods are temporarily disrupted by drought
1996 National Policy on Disaster Management	To provide a comprehensive framework for disaster management; reduce the potential loss due to disasters; ensure timely assistance to victims; and achieve rapid and durable recovery
The Revised National Food Strategy	To provide a framework for attaining national and household food and nutrition security through (a) the attainment of household income security; (b) physical and economic access of households to adequate supplies of safe and nutritionally adequate food; and (c) availability of food through import and production
The Strategic Grain Reserve	To store enough grain to meet the national requirement of cereals for at least 3 months
The Botswana Agricultural Board	To offer a favourable price regime and extended marketing services to isolated parts of the country through depots and cooperatives

5.9.1 National policy on rural development

In 1973 a Rural Development Policy was adopted to channel revenue from the exploitation of minerals into rural development and livelihoods. It was revised in 2002 to take account of other long-term government policy initiatives, development goals and aspirations, including Vision 2016. The policy now centres on livelihoods, land and natural resources, social protection, the institutional framework and development, capacity building, gender, HIV and AIDS, poverty and the environment. In essence, the policy occupies a central role in the reduction and eventual eradication of poverty in Botswana.

5.9.2 Community-based strategy for rural development

The community-based strategy for rural development was developed in 1997 with the aim to assist people living in rural communities to improve their livelihoods and reduce poverty. The implementation of the strategy is the responsibility of district-level institutions. The strategy aims at reorienting existing institutional arrangements in order to foster community self-mobilisation and ownership. The Ministry of Health promotes the strategy through the use of participatory methods for promoting health care. The Participatory Hygiene and Sanitation Transformation approach was piloted in seven community sites, three urban and four rural. This strategy requires effective collaboration among all stakeholders. It is yet to be seen what impact it will have on poverty levels.

5.9.3 Privatisation policy

Botswana's Privatisation Policy was approved by parliament in 2000. It is a home-grown policy intended to improve the productivity and enhance the efficiency of the economy, through the promotion of citizen empowerment and ownership of assets. Although it is not easy to ascertain its bearing on poverty reduction, it is envisaged as having positive spill-over effects on poverty reduction through employment creation and asset ownership.

5.9.4 Industrial development policy

The Industrial Development Policy of Botswana was adopted in 1984 and revised in 1998 to pursue key objectives such as economic diversification, greater local control of industry, and the spreading of economic activity throughout the country with diversification of the economy. The development of industries, especially if dispersed all over the country, would play a significant role in addressing Botswana's poverty problem.

5.9.5 National Food Strategy

The National Food Strategy was adopted in 1985 and revised in 1997. The main goal of the policy was to reduce the dependence on food supplies from external sources resulting from failure of domestic production to meet the basic food needs of the population and the persistently inadequate nutritional status of certain population groups. Several programmes were introduced, including research on improved traditional agriculture, credit and other assistance packages, and physical infrastructure and marketing assistance. Guaranteed food supplies in rural areas, drought relief and recovery measures, and a grain reserve were part of the strategy.

The agricultural policy on self-sufficiency was revised in 1991 to become a national food security policy which aims at ensuring food availability in the country. The policy plays a critical role in the alleviation of poverty in the sense that food shortages have direct implications for poverty and related health and nutrition issues.

5.9.6 Social service policies

The government has also embarked on programmes to provide social services as a means of reducing poverty by improving the capacities of the poor to increase their income-earning capacity and to protect their own health. The provision of education directly alleviates human capacity poverty and indirectly alleviates income poverty and broadens individuals' range of choices, as stipulated in the National Education Policy of 1991. In line with this, in 1987 school fees both at primary and secondary levels were abolished as an intervention aimed at encouraging and promoting education among all Batswana. A school feeding programme was also introduced to provide poor children who would otherwise have been at risk of malnutrition and starvation with a daily meal. Towards the end of 2005, the government introduced a cost recovery/cost sharing component of the education policy. An assessment of students was carried out countrywide to ensure that no student is denied access to education due to implementation of the cost recovery/cost sharing system.

The 1995 National Health Policy seeks to enhance the capacities of the poor to protect their own health. This policy is implemented through various additional policies and programmes. The provision of access to essential health care is catered for through the public health system, which comprises PHC facilities as well as referral hospitals. The PHC component is managed by the district and town councils and health teams, while the referral hospitals are owned by the government, mining companies and religious missions. In line with the poverty reduction strategy, Botswana's health care system is financed by taxes via public budgets. In 2002, the government introduced cost recovery of medical costs, with all foreigners being charged the full cost.

5.9.7 National policy on HIV and AIDS

The national policy on HIV and AIDS came into being in 1993 and outlines the national response to the pandemic. The strategic components are prevention of HIV/STD transmission; reduction of the personal and psycho-social impact of HIV and AIDS and STD; mobilisation of all sectors and all communities for HIV and AIDS prevention and care; and provision of care and reduction of the socio-economic consequences of HIV and AIDS (MoH 1993). Some of the measures intended to achieve these objectives include increasing access to voluntary counselling and testing, facilitating the participation of women and families in the PMTCT programme, and developing culturally appropriate behavioural change interventions. Others include expanding health care, addressing the needs of orphans and affected families and ensuring that all HIV and AIDS programmes and policies are in line with ethical, legal and human rights principles. The policy efforts have resulted in the formation of strategic partnerships between government and non-government stakeholders in order to address the pandemic and its effects through District Multi-Sectoral AIDS Committees, which are tasked to co-ordinate district- and village-level responses to HIV and AIDS.

5.9.8 National Policy on Women

The National Policy on Women in Development was adopted in November 1995. Its main goal is to achieve the effective integration and empowerment of women in order to improve their status and enhance their participation in decision-making and their role in the development process. The policy is consistent with the Vision 2016 pillar on enhancing a moral and tolerant nation, which envisages the elimination of all discriminatory practices on the basis of gender by the year 2016 (Presidential Task Group 1997).

Studies (BIDPA 1997; GOB and UNDP 2002) identify FHHs as particularly vulnerable to poverty in Botswana. The key causes of poverty within this vulnerable group are high income-dependency ratios and patriarchal legal and cultural practices (male-based inheritance rights), which limit women's access to resources. The National Gender Policy (NGP) framework and the National Plan were developed in 1998 to provide a blueprint for the implementation of strategies in the area of gender and development for NDPs 8 and 9. To reduce disadvantages that limit women's income and economic opportunities, the NGP and the National Plan recommended a review of all laws that discriminated against women. While this review was conducted in 1998, recommendations regarding the elimination of gender discrimination in job recruitment, the full payment of maternity leave and the development of legislation to address sexual harassment remain to be addressed.

Other policies in need of mentioning include the National Youth Policy of 1996, whose objective is to promote youth development based on three key goals/criteria. The first is to recognise and promote the participation and contribution of the youth in Botswana's socio-economic development. The second is to develop a coordinated contribution and participation by all stakeholders involved in youth development programmes and activities at grassroots and national levels, including non-governmental organisations. The third goal is to develop structures and strategies that are supportive of young people's initiatives and capable of promoting social responsibilities and national pride amongst the youth, as well as enabling families and communities to present positive role models.

5.9.9 Citizen Entrepreneurial Development Agency

The CEDA was introduced in 2002. It is expected to contribute to poverty reduction through employment generation and economic diversification. The general view is that CEDA does not cater for the poor. The application forms, according to critics, are very complicated and require technical expertise that most poor people do not possess. It is thus argued that CEDA's success in poverty reduction will be very limited. No major review of CEDA has been undertaken to determine its impact in creating sustainable employment and empowering citizens and ultimately reducing poverty.

5.9.10 Remote Area Development Programme

The Remote Area Development Programme (RADP) started in 1978 and initially targeted the Basarwa (San people). Its aim was to assist citizens of Botswana who live in settlements located far from centres of basic services and facilities. The basic premise of this programme was that the primary constraint to remote area development and poverty reduction was geographic remoteness, with inadequate access to basic social services. The revised programme of 2003 changed from the ethnic identification of beneficiaries to the geographical targeting of all people living in remote areas. The main aims of the programme are to establish permanent settlements, to promote productive economic activities, and to provide public services. According to BIDPA (2003), the RADP currently provides services to 64 settlements with a population of about 38,000 people. In terms of poverty reduction, RADP has made some impact through the provision of infrastructure and economic activities.

5.9.11 Specific agricultural programmes

The Botswana Agricultural Marketing Board was established in 1974 and mandated to purchase grain crops from farmers for sale to millers and other traders in the country. From its inception until 1991, the BAMB supported producer prices above border prices. The BAMB was also awarded a monopoly on sorghum imports, the major staple, to prevent private traders from importing at lower world market prices and out-competing the BAMB at miller level. Price support on producer prices was removed in 1991, and the BAMB would from then onwards price its major staples of maize and sorghum on the basis of import parity pricing. To further liberalise the grain industry, the BAMB's monopoly on sorghum imports was removed in 1992, to allow private sector participation in the importation of food grains.

The ALDEP was introduced in 1982 as one of the programmes targeting resource-poor households involved in rain-fed arable agriculture. Public assistance took the form of draught power (oxen, mules or donkeys), animal-drawn implements (ploughs, planters, cultivators and harrows), fencing materials, scotch carts, water catchment tanks and fertilisers. The link between ALDEP and poverty alleviation is clear. It was aimed at increasing the grain production and productivity of resource-poor households by providing access to productive assets. While ALDEP did lead to improved access to productive assets, particularly draught power, some of its intended outputs were not realised. A major failure of the programme was that the majority of producers did not utilise some of the implements they acquired from the programme, including planters, harrows and cultivators. The programme was reintroduced in late 2006.

The National Master Plan for Arable Agriculture and Dairy Development (NAMPAADD) was introduced in 2002 with the aim of improving the performance of the sector, while encouraging the sustainable use of the country's natural resources. The NAMPAADD, which is still at the early stages of operation, targets both traditional and commercial farmers in rain-fed arable agriculture (grain/cereal production), dairy and irrigated arable agriculture (horticulture). Production training farms, which have already been established, are intended to demonstrate to farmers the potential benefits of adopting modern technology and improved management practices, including mechanised farming. The NAMPAADD does not provide financial grants and subsidies. It only provides technical assistance and develops infrastructure to support agricultural development, for example, roads and electricity.

The 1980 Destitutes Policy stated that the government must confront the larger issue of providing programmes and opportunities which will enable persons to help themselves and not call upon government subsidies. A destitute was defined as (a) an individual without assets (defined as cattle, other livestock, land, cash), with disability or ill-health preventing him/her from ploughing, and lacking assistance from close family members; (b) an individual who is physically or mentally incapable of working due to old age, or physical or mental handicap; (c) a minor child or children whose parent(s) has (have) died or deserted the family, or is (are) not supporting his/her (their) family; or (d) an individual who is rendered helpless due to a natural disaster or temporary hardship.

The Destitutes Policy was revised in 2002 to take into account social and economic development in the intervening two decades, and the perceived changes in the circumstances of poor people. A destitute is now defined as an individual who, owing to disabilities or a chronic health condition, is unable to engage in sustainable economic activities and has insufficient assets and income sources. Insufficient assets and income sources are defined to mean (1) possessing not more than four livestock units (e.g. 4 cows), or (2) earning or receiving an income of less than BWP120 per month without dependents or less than BWP150 per month with dependents (MLG 2002). Other criteria pertain to mental or physical disability, terminal illness, and children under 18 years of age living under difficult circumstances (Revised Destitutes Policy 2002). The Policy was reviewed again in 2006 and to date there are 37,000 beneficiaries.

The social safety nets programmes are divided into three categories:

- social allowance programmes,
- social assistance programmes,
- social insurance programmes.

Social allowance programmes

The Orphan Care Programme was established in 1999 and reviewed in 2006. Its main goal is to respond to the immediate basic needs of orphans through the provision of food, clothing, education, shelter, protection and care. To be eligible, one has to be under 18 years of age and to have lost one or both parents, whether biological or adoptive. Assistance packages come in the form of food baskets amounting to BWP 216.60 per month, which are provided through local retailers. Each basket is based on the nutritional requirement by the age of the child. However, food baskets can cost up to BWP 300, depending on the prevailing local prices. Orphans are also provided with clothing, toiletry, transport fees, school fees, etc.

The Vulnerable Groups Feeding Programme was established in 1996 and reviewed in 2006. It provides fortified flour, *Tsabana*, for feeding children between the ages of 6–36 months. This flour is derived from sorghum and soya and fortified with essential vitamins and minerals. The programme is applicable in times of drought as determined by the district drought committees and the interministerial drought committee and the early warning technical committee. During non-drought years, the programme covers medically selected under-five children and pregnant and lactating women (including the anaemic, those not gaining enough weight, teenagers between 13 and 18 years and TB and leprosy patients). Universal coverage is implemented during drought years. Food ration packages comprise *Tsabana* for children between 6 and 36 months, dry skimmed milk for children aged 7–36 months and medically selected pregnant and lactating women, sunflower oil for children aged 6–60 months and fortified precooked maize for children aged between 37 and 60 months and TB outpatients.

The long-standing School Feeding Programme was established before independence with the aim of covering a third of the daily calorific requirement for children, by providing a single meal a day composed of sorghum meal, pulses, milk and vegetable oil. As from 2001 the government has added nine more food items to the old menu, provided during a mid-morning snack and at lunchtime. All children attending primary school are eligible.

The Old Age Pension programme was introduced in 1996 and subsequently reviewed in 2006. It provides a monthly pension to all citizens above 65 years of age. The payments of cash are made through several avenues in villages or settlements, which include over the counter collection of allowances at post offices and bank deposits if the beneficiary has a bank account. There were 89,000 beneficiaries of this scheme in 2005.

The World War II Veteran Grants programme was established in 1998 and reviewed in 2006. It was set up as a token of appreciation to those Batswana who fought in the Second World War. All veterans are eligible for benefits. In the event that a veteran dies, his widow receives the benefits. If both the veteran and his spouse are deceased, their children under the age of 21 receive the payment, which amounts to BWP 272 per month. There were 4,602 beneficiaries of this programme in 2006.

The Community Home-Based Care Programme was established in 1995 and reviewed in 2006. It was set up in response to the HIV and AIDS pandemic but covers patients with other conditions as well. Assessment guidelines used for the destitute programme are applied and baskets are provided to needy patients only. This programme provides optimal care for the terminally ill in their home environment. The majority of the caregivers are women, many of whom are the breadwinners of their households. Baskets are provided based on the recommendation of a doctor or dietician, thus no price is attached to the food basket. The monthly cost of the food basket ranges from BWP 200 to BWP 1,500 per patient.

Social assistance programmes

Through the Destitutes Programme, permanent rural destitutes receive food packages worth BWP 211.90 per month in rural and BWP 211.40 per month in urban areas (up to BWP 300 depending on the value of the approved ration). Temporary destitutes receive food rations worth BWP 181.90 in rural areas and BWP 181.40 in urban centres (up to BWP 300 depending on the value of the approved ration). Both classes of destitute receive BWP 61 in cash per month for personal non-food items. Provision is made for shelter if needed, medical care, occasional fares, funeral expenses, and exemptions are made from paying service levies, water charges, street licenses, school fees and tools required for rehabilitation.

The Labour-Based Drought Relief Programme was established before independence as part of the self-reliance (ipelegeng) programme. It was initially a food-for-work programme but it changed to wage payment in 1982. This programme provides temporary income support during periods of drought. Workers are engaged in labour-intensive programmes and receive a wage payment of BWP 10 per 6-hour day and supervisors receive BWP 16. In 2004 it employed 117,087, comprising 95,808 females and 21,279 males on a total of 1,345 projects. Unfortunately, this programme created a dependency syndrome. Instead of working hard as in the case of food for work, people perform minimal work at least to be able to earn a little money payable under the programme. The programme also has an adverse effect on agriculture as it takes away labour from the sector.

5.10 THE ROLE OF THE VOLUNTARY SECTOR

The Botswana Council of Non-Governmental Organisations has produced a position paper on poverty and poverty alleviation, which focuses on the advocacy and implementation role of its members. These organisations are well placed to target the poor while also providing an important mechanism for communities to voice their concerns. Income generation is a key focus for many voluntary agencies working in the field of poverty reduction. Groups such as Batswana Against Poverty and the Botswana Christian Council are involved in basket-making and weaving cooperatives. On a broader level, Emang Basadi NGO campaigns for greater equality for women and the removal of all cultural and legal barriers that hinder the advancement of women in Botswana.

5.11 CONCLUSIONS

The previous sections spell out the strategies that the government of Botswana is pursuing in poverty reduction. Some of them are welfarist in nature while others are geared towards economic empowerment linked to economic growth. Many programmes involve the provision of social services as a means of reducing poverty. There is also a growing recognition of the importance of private investment, particularly foreign direct investment, in the creation of sustainable employment, economic diversification and poverty reduction, which has led to the adoption of a privatisation policy. The majority of projects and programmes in NDP 9 directly contribute to poverty reduction and improved welfare for the Batswana. The effective implementation of NDP 9 projects and programmes is, therefore, central to the goal of eradicating poverty.

A major challenge is to improve income-earning opportunities for the poor. Efforts to tackle this issue include sustaining stable economic growth, together with a strong emphasis on diversification to create more jobs and reduce unemployment. At the same time the government is prioritising skills development and training to create a workforce that is willing and able to take up new employment opportunities. The challenge with respect to social safety nets is to ensure their effectiveness. If the programmes are welfarist in approach, this may create a perpetual dependence on the government. The government, therefore, needs to foster pro-poor growth strategies that stimulate increased employment and income-generating opportunities, specifically for the poor.

At the programme level there is fairly broad consensus that improvement is needed through ensuring wider participation by communities in the design and implementation stages. Current initiatives tend to be characterised by a top-down approach that works through structures which often exclude those most in need, particularly women and vulnerable groups. As a result, programmes are 'government-owned' and communities are not motivated to get involved. This ultimately militates against their success. Involving the poor in determining their own future is a challenge, but it also offers a great opportunity to help eradicate poverty and make one of Vision 2016's most important goals a reality. Unfortunately, the challenge of poverty eradication has been made even more daunting by the HIV pandemic.

The opportunities for Botswana in poverty reduction are set out clearly in policies and strategies. It is through Vision 2016 and the Botswana NPRS that the government aims at promoting the development of agriculture, rural development and poverty reduction. The fact that the government has clearly and unambiguously defined its objective is a big step forward towards addressing poverty.

Another opportunity for tacking poverty in Botswana derives from the efficiency of the civil service. The rapid economic development that Botswana has enjoyed over the last four decades is often associated with the dedication, motivation and efficiency of the civil service. With the objective of furthering its efficiency, the government has recently introduced a performance management system. The system requires periodical assessment of the achievements of civil servants to ensure that they are less marred by corruption and other administrative malpractices that lead to inefficiencies and a waste of resources.

Botswana is one of the few countries with a proven track record in managing its economy with prudence and efficiency. Botswana does not face a shortage of capital. It has demonstrated its ability to meet the capital requirements of its development plans. Its democratic tradition, the efficiency of its civil service, the participation of the people in the development processes, etc. indicate favourable conditions for reducing poverty as per Vision 2016 and the NPRS. There is no doubt that Botswana has the means to eradicate absolute poverty in the foreseeable future, other things being equal.

Generally, the macroeconomic framework contained in the NPRS is perceived to be a home-grown product. The formulation of the strategy was participatory except that the involvement of civil society organisations was not perceived to have been genuinely participatory but rather reactively consultative. The strategy is quite comprehensive and covers many of issues, as well as different classes of people and determinants of poverty. Although its formulation may have been good its implementation may prove to be daunting. The NPRS is perceived to lack a clear implementation strategy and a technical platform for its success, which may render it ineffective.

Political commitment to the strategy is unquestionable given the national budget allocations towards the implementation of poverty reduction programmes. Almost every government ministry has a poverty reduction unit. However, implementation constraints persist in government departments, which often fail to utilise allocated funds fully and thus return them at the end of the budgetary year.

The past efforts of Botswana in poverty alleviation demonstrate that a too welfarist approach to poverty reduction creates a perpetual dependence on government and limited success in poverty reduction. There is evidently a change under way from a welfarist approach to increased emphasis on economic growth as a means of poverty reduction, as epitomised in Vision 2016, which underscores self-reliance. In addition, the citizen empowerment programmes have been designed to assist people to exit from social safety nets and to be more self-reliant. The agricultural sector has been given higher priority than other sectors in the NPRS, mainly because the majority of Batswana still derive their livelihood from agriculture. HIV and AIDS is also perceived as one of the prioritised concerns in the NPRS as it is one of the determinants of poverty. Infrastructural provision, especially electricity, is also being given priority to speed up rural development. The NPRS considers several cross-cutting issues, such as the environment and gender.

However, an economic growth orientation for a poverty reduction strategy is not sufficient. There is need to expedite the implementation of the strategy and strengthen the institutional framework for overseeing, coordinating and monitoring poverty-related initiatives. The Multi-Sectoral Committee on Poverty Reduction, with representation from both within and outside government, is intended to provide periodic updates on the implementation of the poverty strategy. Although the government remains committed to the economic empowerment of the Batswana, the effectiveness of its policies and strategies depend on the beneficiaries of the NPRS initiatives committing themselves to capitalising appropriately on the government's promotion of their economic participation.

ERR

Charity K. Kerapeletswe

REFERENCES

BIDPA (1997), *A Study on Poverty and Poverty Alleviation in Botswana*, Gaborone: MFDP.

BIDPA (2000), *Financial Assistance Policy (FAP) Fourth Evaluation Report, Final Report for MFDP*, Gaborone: Government Printer.

BIDPA (2001), *Review of the Rural Development Policy*, Gaborone: Ministry of Local Government.

BIDPA (2002), *Economic Mapping for Botswana*, Gaborone: Ministry of Trade, Industry, Wildlife and Tourism.

BIDPA (2003), Review of Remote Area Development Program, Gaborone: Ministry of Local Government.

BIDPA (2004), *Diversification in Botswana's Agricultural Sector: Issues, Prospects and Challenges*. Unpublished Manuscript. Gaborone: Botswana Institute for Development Policy Analysis (BIDPA).

Central Statistics Office (CSO) (2002), *Statistical Bulletin Quarter* 1–4, 2002, Vol. 26, No. 4.

CSO (2004), *Household Income and Expenditure Survey 2002/03, Stats Brief*, Gaborone.

CSO (2006), *Statistical Brief*, Gaborone.

Department of Sanitation and Waste Management (2003), *National Master Plan for Waste Water and Sanitation*, Gaborone: Ministry of Environment Wildlife and Tourism.

Ministry of Health, *Draft National Plan of Action for Nutrition* (2004), Gaborone: Government Printer.

European Community (2002), *Republic of Botswana: Country Strategy Paper and Indicative Programme for the Period 2002–2007*, Brussels.

Family Health Division (2004), *Food and Nutrition Unit. Guidelines on the Vulnerable Group Feeding Program*, Gaborone: Ministry of Health.

Family Health Division (2004), *The Botswana PMTCT Newsletter*, Vol. 1 No.4, March, 2004, Gaborone: Ministry of Health, UNICEF and BOTUSA.

Gaolathe, B. (2007), *Botswana Budget Speech 2007*, Gaborone: Republic of Botswana.

Government of Botswana and UNDP (1997), *Botswana Human Development Report 1997. Challenges for Sustainable Human Development*, Gaborone: UNDP.

Government of Botswana and UNDP (2000), *Botswana Human Development Report 2000. Towards an AIDS-Free Generation*, Gaborone: UNDP.

Government of Botswana and UNDP (2002), *A Review of Anti-Poverty Initiatives in Botswana: Lessons For a National Poverty Reduction Strategy*, Gaborone: UNDP.

Government of Botswana (2003), *Botswana Second Generation HIV and AIDS Surveillance Report 2003*, Gaborone: National AIDS Coordinating Agency.

Government of Botswana (2003), *Botswana National Strategic Framework for HIV and AIDS 2003–2009*, Gaborone: National AIDS Coordinating Agency.

Government of Botswana (2004), *Botswana Millennium Development Goals Status Report 2004*, Gaborone: UNDP

Government Paper No. 1 of 2000, *Privatization Policy for Botswana*, Gaborone: Government Printer.

Government Paper No. 2 of 1973, *National Policy for Rural Development*, Gaborone: Government Printer.

Government Paper No. 2 of 1984, *Industrial Development Policy*, Gaborone: Government Printer.

Government Paper No. 2 of 1985, *National Food Strategy*, Gaborone: Government Printer.

MFDP (1997), *National Development Plan 8, 1997 – 2003*, Gaborone: Government Printer.

MFDP (2002), *Revised National Policy for Rural Development*, Gaborone: Government Printer.

MFDP (2003), *National Development Plan 9 2003–2009*, Gaborone: Government Printer.

Ministry of Local Government and Lands (1980), *National Policy on Destitutes*, Gaborone: Government Printer.

Ministry of Local Government (2002), *Revised National Policy on Destitute Persons*, Gaborone: Government Printer.

Ministry of Labour and Home Affairs (1996), *National Youth Policy*, Gaborone: Government Printer.

Ministry of Labour and Home Affairs (2000), *National Youth Plan of Action 2001–2010*, Gaborone: Government Printer.

MLGL (1999), *Short Term Plan of Action on Care of Orphans in Botswana 1999–2001*, Gaborone: Oakwood.

MLGL (2001), *Report on the Review Of Primary School Menu*, Gaborone: Government Printer.

MLGL (2004), *Destitute Report for September 2004*, unpublished report.

MoH (1993), *Botswana National Policy on HIV and AIDS*, Gaborone: Government Printer.

MoH (1998), *The Rapid Assessment of the Situation of Orphans in Botswana*, Gaborone: Oakwood.

MoH-FHD (2002), *National Sexual and Reproductive Health Program Framework*, Gaborone: Family Health Division.

Ministry of Agriculture (2002), *National Master Plan for Arable Agriculture and Dairy Development*, Gaborone: Government Printer.

Ministry of State President, Office of the President (1996), *National Policy on Disaster Management*, Gaborone: Government Printer.

Perry, G. et al. (2006), *Poverty Reduction and Growth: Virtuous and Vicious Circles*, Washington, D.C.: World Bank.

Presidential Task Group for a Long Term Vision for Botswana (1997), Vision 2016: A Summary.

Republic of Botswana (1993), *Report of the National Commission on Education*, Gaborone: Government Printer.

Republic of Botswana (2003), *Draft Poverty Reduction Strategy*, Gaborone: Government Printer.

CHAPTER 6

POVERTY PROFILES AND THE EVOLUTION OF POVERTY REDUCTION STRATEGIES IN KENYA

Lineth N. Oyugi

6.1 Introduction

Kenya is located East Africa, with the equator almost bisecting it, and borders on Tanzania to the south, Uganda to the west, Ethiopia and Sudan to the north, Somalia to the northeast and the Indian Ocean to the southeast. The country is divided into eight provinces and 72 districts and occupies a total surface area of 582,646 km², of which 571,466 km² form the land area. Approximately 80% of the land area of the country is arid or semi-arid and only 20% is arable. Kenya is a former British colony that gained independence in 1963 and is made up of 42 ethnic groups, distributed throughout the country. The Kenyan population is estimated to have increased from 10.9 million in 1969 to 28.7 million in 1999 and further to 33.5 million in 2005 (Republic of Kenya 1994; 2001; 2006), with a population growth rate of 2.9% per annum for the period 1989–1999, down from the 3.4% estimated for both the 1969–1979 and 1979–1989 inter-censal periods (Republic of Kenya 2000a).

The Kenyan economy is predominantly agricultural, yet with a comparatively strong industrial base. The performance of the economy since independence has been mixed. During the first decade (1964–1972), the economy grew by 6.6% per annum, a rate attributed to the expansion of the manufacturing sector and an increase in agricultural production. In the 1970s, 1980s and 1990s, the growth rate of the economy progressively reduced to 5.2%, further to 4% and 2.4%, respectively, and to a decline of –0.3% in 2000. The declining growth rates have been attributed to several factors, such as stop-go macroeconomic policies, the slow pace of structural reforms, the freezing of donor budgetary support, high oil prices, low commodity prices, world recession, governance problems, politicisation of development, net outflows of external funding from the public sector, dilapidated infrastructure, natural calamities, and increased appetite for government consumption leading to public investment declining more than overall investment (Republic of Kenya 2001). Over these periods of decline, economic growth was outpaced by population growth, thus worsening the poverty situation in the country. The number of people living in absolute poverty (headcount ratio) in Kenya is estimated to have risen from 11 million in 1990, representing 48% of the population, to 17 million in 1997, representing 52.3% (Republic of Kenya 2001). In addition, it is estimated that the proportion of the people openly unemployed stands at 14.6% of the labour force, with youth accounting for 45% of the total (Republic of Kenya 2003; 2004). However, as a result of the high economic growth rates achieved in 2004 (5.1%), 2005 (5.7%) and 2006 (6.1%), absolute poverty declined to 45.9% of the population in 2006 (Kenya National Bureau of Statistics 2007).

The deteriorating standard of living in Kenya was captured by worsening key social indicators, especially during the 1980s and 1990s. Over this period, illiteracy rates increased as enrolment rates in primary schools declined while life expectancy and child mortality worsened. Though this situation has been reversed following the preparation and implementation of the Poverty Reduction Strategy Paper (PRSP) that articulated deliberate government policies targeted at addressing the poverty situation, not all the indicators have registered positive growth rates. An overview of the performance of the Kenyan economy over the last 3 years and targets for the next 2 years is presented in Table 6.1.

Table 6.1: Overview of the Performance of the Kenyan Economy

Indicator	Baseline value (2003)	2003 /04	2004 /05	2005 /06	2006 /07
		Actual		Targets	
Annual underlying rate of inflation (%)	2.3	3.1	5.8	<5	<5
Stock of Domestic Debt/GDP (%)	25.1	22.2	18.5	22.4	21.5
Public Sector Wage Bill/GDP (%)	9.0	7.9	7.8	7.6	7.3
Revenue/GDP (%) (including Appropriation in Aid)	20.8	21.1	21.3	21.3	22.2
Number of reforms measured by Benchmark Score on Public Expenditure Management and Accountability Action Plan	3	4	6	13	15
Proportion of road network in bad/poor condition (%)	43	38	32	28	20
Rural households covered with power (%)	3.8	4	5	7	8
Rural households with safe and reliable water (%)	50	51	53	56	60
Proportion of urban households with safe and reliable water (%)	73	74	75	80	83
Annual number of fatalities on roads	2676	2100	1700	1,700	1,300
Annual growth rate of tourists (%)	1.5	(20.3)	15.1	9.7	9.7
Growth of volume of exports	14.7	6.2	9.4	5.7	5.7
Fully immunised children as % of less than 1 year population (%)	56	56	57	67	70
Pregnant women aged between 15–24 years attending ANC who are HIV positive (%)	10.1	10.0	10.0	8.4	8.0
Pregnant women attending ANC, at least 4 visits (%)	-	-	42	65	70
Inpatient malaria morbidity as a percentage of total inpatient morbidity (%)	30		26	15	14
Primary net enrolment (%)	80.4 (A) 80.8 (M) 80.0 (F)	79.8 (A) 81.3 (M) 78.3 (F)	82.1 (A) 82.2 (M) 82.0 (F)	83.2 (A) 84.4 (M) 88.2 (F)	84.4 (A) 85.0 (M) 88.3 (F)
Primary net enrolment rate for North Eastern Province (%)	21.2 (A) 26.1 (M) 16.2 (F)	17.6 (A) 23.3 (M) 12.1 (F)	19.6 (A) 23.6 (M) 14.9 (F)	31.5 (A) 36.5 (M) 26.6 (F)	38.5 (A) 43.9 (M) 33.1 (F)
Primary School completion rate (%)	52.0 (A) 54.5 (M) 49.5 (F)	52.0 (A) 54.5 (M) 49.5 (F)	56.0 (A) 57.1 (M) 54.9 (F)	60.0 (A) 60.4 (M) 59.6 (F)	60.3 (A) 60.5 (M) 60.1 (F)
Primary repetition rate (%)	9.8	9.8	9.3	7.4	4.9
Primary to secondary school transition rate (%)	47	47	52	60	60
Agricultural sector growth rate (%)	1.5	2.6	1.4	4	5

Source: Republic of Kenya (2005; 2006)

Table 6.1 indicates that apart from the indicators on the macroeconomic framework that have remained stable and consistent with the set government targets, progress on the other indicators of socio-economic development, such as those on infrastructure, education, health, water and the environment, have remained far below their targets, raising questions as to whether the country's macroeconomic framework is consistent with its sectoral policies and whether it is on the right track to reduce by half the proportion of the people living in poverty and generally be able to meet the Millennium Development Goals.

Following the introduction, this chapter presents an analysis of the poverty profile for Kenya in Section 6.2. Section 6.3 discusses the evolution of the poverty reduction strategies and Section 6.4 concludes the chapter.

6.2 POVERTY PROFILE

Efforts to address poverty can be traced back to the time of Kenya's independence in 1963. *Sessional Paper no. 10 of 1965* identified poverty, disease and ignorance as major constraints to human development that needed to be addressed by the post-independence government (Republic of Kenya 1965). Poverty is widely defined, and most definitions take multidimensional aspects into consideration. According to the World Bank (2000), poverty is a lack of power to command resources and a multidimensional phenomenon. It makes the poor face multiple deprivations due to the interaction of economic, political and social processes. Beyond the lack of income, the multidimensional concept of poverty refers to disadvantages that those afflicted are subjected to when trying to access productive resources such as land, credit and services (e.g. health and education), to vulnerability (to violence, external economic shocks, natural disasters) and powerlessness as well as social exclusion. The poor lack adequate food, shelter, education and health, deprivations that keep them from leading the kind of life valued by everyone. They are also often exposed to ill treatment at institutions when seeking services and are powerless when trying to influence key decisions.

The multidimensional aspect of poverty implies that no uniform standard is available for measuring poverty. Some groups in the population often face a combination of the predicaments associated with poverty – low income, illiteracy, premature death, early marriage, large families, malnutrition, and illness and injury – dimensions that reinforce each other to lock those afflicted into low standards of living. This notwithstanding, poverty has been measured in several ways, predominantly based on household income and expenditure. Nonetheless, multi-indicator measures and surveys are frequently used today, including participatory and community-based monitoring mechanisms. Numbers and percentages of absolute and relative poverty are typically measured against a national poverty (income) line, but with better data and information on nutrition, health and education, the understanding of household and individual poverty is gradually becoming better in Kenya. This has been true in particular since the preparation of the PRSP and the establishment of various institutions to coordinate the operationalisation and implementation of the PRSP throughout the country, such as the Poverty Eradication Commission in the Office of the President and the Poverty Analysis Research Unit (PARU) in the Ministry of Planning and National Development to collect, document, analyse and disseminate poverty data and information.

Kenya has a fairly well developed statistical base on poverty and trends in the distribution of household incomes. The Urban Household Budget Survey 1968–1969 formed the basis of analysis of urban household income distribution by the ILO Mission to Kenya (International Labour Organization 1972). The Central Bureau of Statistics (CBS), later renamed the Kenya National Bureau of Statistics (KNBS), also conducted a household budget survey in Nairobi in 1974, whose results were analysed extensively and used as a proxy for urban income distribution in Kenya by different scholars. The earliest estimates of poverty were for 1976, arising from a series of surveys undertaken within the framework of the Integrated Rural Surveys (IRS) 1 (1974/75), 2 (1976), 3 (1977) and 4 (1978). Data on urban household income were collected in 1974/75. The source of data on rural household income and consumption patterns was IRS-1, as the later IRS cycles did not collect data on income and consumption. The principal analysts of the 1974/75 IRS database (Greer and Thorbecke) pioneered a mode of analysis that represented far-reaching theoretical advancements (Foster et al. 1984), in addition to its application to the poverty assessment of Kenya's smallholder sector (Foster et al. 1984; Greer and Thorbecke 1986a and b).

In the 1980s, the CBS undertook five major surveys of land assets, rural and urban household income and consumption patterns, and nutritional indicators. The surveys were the Rural Household Budget Survey 1981/82, covering 27 strata/32 districts; the Urban Household Budget Survey 1982/83; the Agricultural Production Survey 1986/87, which covered 24 districts, mostly in high and medium potential areas; and two child nutrition surveys – urban (1983) and rural (1987). The first National Welfare Monitoring Survey (WMS I) was conducted during November/December 1992 and summary results were published in the Economic Survey 1993 (Republic of Kenya 1993). The other major output was the Kenya Poverty Profiles 1982–1992, which used the 1982 Rural Household Budget Survey data alongside the WMS I data (Mukui 1993). Finally, WMS II and III were conducted in 1994 and 1997, respectively, and have together provided the basis of poverty analysis for policy-making in Kenya since the mid-1990s.

To complement the statistical studies of poverty in Kenya the government undertook the first Participatory Poverty Assessment (PPA) in the first half of 1994. The purpose of PPA-I was to understand poverty as seen by the poor themselves, as a guide to the design of interventions to alleviate poverty. The PPA covered communities in seven poor rural districts (Busia, Bomet, Kisumu, Kitui, Kwale, Mandera and Nyamira) and Nairobi (the adjacent slums of Mathare Valley and Korogocho). The main poverty-creating factors were inflation; social breakdown (e.g. the emergence of female-headed households); cost-sharing, especially in education and health; and demographic pressure (land fragmentation, breakdown of homes, unemployment, and large family sizes). The report shows the social dynamics that create and sustain mass poverty. For example, the feminisation of poverty was attributed to a lack of property rights such as loss of property in case of divorce, discrimination at the household level in access to education, and the devastating effects of HIV and AIDS. The recommendations were mainly in the areas of access to social services by the poor (mainly education and health), fees payable by the poor for most services (including low-cost water supplies), credit for the poor, and slum upgrading (structures, water and sanitation, road networks, and solid waste management).

The second PPA was carried out during November–December 1996 and covered seven districts (Mombasa, Nakuru, Kisumu, Kajiado, Taita Taveta, Makueni, and Nyeri). One of the important findings of PPA-II was the sharp contrast of view between communities and district-level leaders and decision-makers regarding the causes of poverty, poverty alleviation mechanisms, and escape routes. While communities pointed to a wide range of physical, economic and institutional factors, district-level decision-makers emphasised community characteristics as the major causes of poverty. District-level leaders thought the services provided were leading to poverty reduction while communities thought otherwise. Communities saw credit and institutional support as paths to poverty reduction while the decision-makers saw the removal of socio-cultural obstacles as critical to poverty reduction.

The third PPA was conducted by the African Medical and Research Foundation, Participatory Methodologies Forum in Kenya and the Ministry of Finance and Planning in January–February 2001. The study covered 10 randomly selected districts, namely, Baringo, Busia, Homa Bay, Garissa, Kajiado, Kirinyaga, Kitui, Mombasa, Nairobi, and Nyamira. PPA-III was conducted as a direct input into the PRSP, so that the poor could propose and prioritise suggestions for poverty reduction and thus offer policy recommendations that would have greatest impact in reducing poverty. The key finding of PPA-III was that the poor understood their poverty status and that they also knew how best to address it, if provided with the resources. PPA-III recommended the involvement of the poor in the design and implementation of poverty reduction strategies. The preparation of the district PRSPs involved district-level participation in all districts, and in-depth community participation in the ten districts. The findings at community level and at district consultative forums were triangulated in the preparation of the district PRSP report. The PPAs complemented the welfare monitoring surveys, which collected information on money-metric measures of poverty and on social indicators.

Analysis of data from the various surveys highlighted above is presented in Tables 6.2–6.4. The statistics presented attest to the fact that poverty levels have increased in Kenya over time, poverty varies across regions and though overwhelmingly a rural phenomenon, it is drastically increasing in urban areas. Table 6.2 presents a summary of various studies on poverty and estimates of the levels of poverty by government and scholars.

Table 6.2 below reveals that on average poverty has been on the increase. In the mid-1970s national absolute poverty was around 42% while food poverty was 39% with considerable regional variation (Greer and Thorbecke 1986a and b; Republic of Kenya 1998; Mwabu and Mullei 1998; Mwabu et al. 1999). Absolute poverty rates for 1982, 1992, and 1994 were estimated at 47% while food poverty rates were estimated at 67% in 1982, 72% in 1992, and 47% in 1994 (Republic of Kenya 1998). According to Mwabu and Mullei (1998), this does not imply that absolute poverty remained constant over the years, neither did food poverty drop given that the underlying poverty lines are not comparable and changes in prices between 1982 and 1994 were not accounted for in estimating the rates.

Table 6.2: Summary of Previous Poverty Estimates for Kenya

Author	Reference	Data source	Poverty incidence
FAO (1977)	NA	Food balance sheet, 1972–1974	30% of population
Crawford and Thorbecke (1978)	1974/75, 1976	IRS (1974/75) 1976 Employment Earnings in the Modern Sector, IRS II	38.5% of households 44% of population
Collier and Lal (1980)	1974/75	IRS I Smallholder	34.2% of smallholder population 29% of all population
Vandermoortele (1982)	1976	IRS I 1974/75; Nairobi Household Budget Survey (1974); Social Accounting Matrix	33.1% of smallholders 15.3% of urban households
Crawford and Thorbecke (1980)	1974/75	IRS (1977)	25% of households
Greer and Thorbecke (1986)	1974/75	IRS (1977)	38.6% of smallholder households
Jamal (1981)	1976	NA	32% of population
Bigsten (1987)	1976	National Accounts	40% of population
World Bank (1991)	1981/82	1981/82 Penal survey and complementary statistics	22% of rural population
World Bank (1995), Mukui (1993)	1981/82 1992	1981/82 Penal survey and 1992 WMS I	48% of rural population for 1981/82 46% of rural population for 1992 29.3% of urban population for 1992
Narayan and Nyamwaya (1996)	1994	Participatory Poverty Assessment	Widespread poverty in rural areas, results similar to 1992 WMS above
Republic of Kenya (1998)	1994	1994 WMS I	46.8% rural population 29% urban population 40% national estimates
Mwabu et al. (2000)	1994	1994 WMS II	39.7% rural population 28.9% of urban population 38.8% national population
Government of Kenya (2000)	1997	1997 WMS III	52.9% rural population 49.2% urban population 52.3% national population
Government of Kenya (2003)			56% national population
Kenya National Bureau of Statistics	2005/06	KIHBS	49.1% rural population 33.7% urban population 45.9% national population

Note: NA = not available; urban refers to Nairobi and Mombasa
Source: Republic of Kenya (2000b and c; 2003); KNBS (2007).

As a result of changes in samples during the different survey periods, it has been hard to ascertain whether poverty is increasing or decreasing in different areas. For instance, food poverty has been persistent in Coast and Western Provinces since the mid-1970s. Analysis of the 1974/75 Integrated Rural Household Survey showed that Coast and Western Provinces had the highest food poverty rates of 42% and 45%, respectively. In 1994, the same provinces had the second highest regional poverty rate of 51% and 52%, respectively, with Eastern Province recording the highest poverty rate of around 60%, even though it had the lowest rate in 1975. It appears that the difference in food poverty in Eastern Province between 1975 and 1994 rose mainly from including and excluding certain districts in survey samples in the 2 years, rather than from changes in prices or in the composition of the consumer basket.

Analysis of survey data from the first and second welfare monitoring surveys revealed that 47% of the rural population was food poor in 1994 compared to 72% in 1992 (Republic of Kenya 1998). Absolute poverty was estimated at 47% for 1999 and 1994. In urban areas, food and absolute poverty was estimated at 29%. Absolute and food poverty rates were highest in North Eastern and Eastern Provinces at 56–58% of the population. Central Province had the lowest absolute and food poverty rates of around 32% whereas Kisumu was the poorest of the urban areas with absolute and food poverty rates of 46% and 44%, respectively, and Nairobi had the lowest rates of 27% and 26% for food and absolute poverty, respectively. The districts with the highest levels of food poverty in 1994 were Marsabit (86%), Turkana (81%), Isiolo (81%), Samburu (79%) Tana River (71%), Makueni (70%), Machakos (66%), Kilifi (65%) and Kitui (64%).

It is estimated that of the 56% of the total population that live below the poverty line, about 52.9% are in the rural areas and 49.2% in the urban areas (Republic of Kenya 2003). It is also estimated that about 34.8% of the rural population and 7.6% of the urban live in extreme poverty and therefore cannot meet dietary needs even with their total spending devoted to food.

Poverty estimates have been further disaggregated by region. The geographical dimensions of poverty show that the level of poverty differs across regions. Tables 6.3 and 6.4 indicate that over time, Central Province has always registered lower levels of poverty whereas North Eastern, Nyanza and Coast Provinces have the highest levels of poverty. Even within a province, large variations exist between districts – the poorest being in semi-arid areas largely inhabited by pastoralists.

Overall, Central Province has the lowest level of poverty, estimated at 35.3%, while North Eastern Province has the highest level of poverty at 73.1%. Excluding Nairobi Province, most of the regional indicators of inequality are still in favour of Central Province. These include: low unemployment rate (6.2%); high road density (2.0); high access to water (95.9% of the Central Province population); and high doctor/patient ratio (1:20,715). The data in Table 6.4 portray North Eastern Province as the least developed province with a high unemployment rate (34.7%), low road density (0.1), poor access to water (22.1%), low secondary gross enrolment (4.5%), low doctor/patient ratio (1:120,823), and low life expectancy (51.8 years).

Table 6.3: Provincial Absolute Poverty Trends

Region	1982	1984	1992	1994	1997	2000	2006
Coast	54.60	43.5	43.5	55.6	62.1	69.9	69.7
Eastern	47.73	54.2	42.2	57.8	58.6	65.9	50.9
Central	25.69	35.9	35.9	31.9	31.4	35.3	30.4
Rift Valley	51.05	51.2	51.5	42.9	50.1	56.4	49.0
Nyanza	57.88	54.7	47.4	42.2	63.1	71.0	47.6
Western	53.79	54.8	54.2	53.8	58.8	66.1	52.2
North Eastern	NA	NA	NA	58.0	NA	73.1	73.9
Rural			46.3	46.8	52.9	59.6	49.1
Urban			29.3	28.9	49.2	51.5	33.7
National			46.3	43.8	52.3	56.8	45.9

Note : NA=Not covered during surveys

Sources: Republic of Kenya (2000b), Kimalu et al. (2002) and KNBS (2007).

Table 6.4: Indicators of Provincial Inequalities

Region	Expenditure Gini Coefficient	Unemployment (15–64) (%)	Road Density (Length/km2)	Population with access to water (<15 minutes) (%)	Secondary Gross Enrolment (%)	Doctor/Patient Ratio	Income Poverty 2000 (%)	Life expectancy 1999 (Years)	HIV Prevalence rate (%)
Nairobi	0.565	23.9	3.2	95.9	11.8	-	-	61.6	9.9
Central	0.514	6.2	2.0	70.9	37.7	1:20,715	35.3	63.7	4.9
Coast	0.450	23.4	0.3	63.9	14.4	1:51,155	69.9	52.2	5.8
Eastern	0.545	6.8	0.2	38.7	23.3	1:33,446	65.9	62.8	4.0
North Eastern	0.406	34.7	0.1	22.1	4.5	1:120,823	73.1	51.8	0.0
Nyanza	0.574	12.2	1.4	31.6	23.5	1:28,569	70.9	47.7	15.1
Rift Valley	0.561	12.1	0.4	50.5	18.3	1:36,481	56.4	59.5	5.3
Western	0.558	27.5	1.4	44.6	25.1	1:39,554	66.1	53.5	4.9
Kenya (Av)	0.558	14.6	0.3	53.2	22.2	-	52.6	54.7	-

Source: Society for International Development (2004).

The profiles presented above indicate that in Kenya poverty is widespread across all regions. Nonetheless, the poor have been identified by region and social-economic characteristics. For instance, the majority of the poor are to be found among the subsistence farmers, the illiterate, the landless, female-headed households, large households, widows, polygamous households, pastoralists in drought-prone areas, unskilled and semi-skilled casual labourers, informal sector workers, and households with limited access to markets and social amenities (Greer and Thorbecke 1986a and b; Republic of Kenya 1998; Mwabu and Mullei 1998; Mwabu et al. 1999). Further, 60% of the poor are concentrated in 17 of the 47 districts in the country, indicating that the people most afflicted can be identified by region of residence and by certain social characteristics. This suggests that properly targeted anti-poverty measures can be effective in reducing overall poverty in the country (Mwabu et al. 1999).

6.3 EVOLUTION OF POVERTY REDUCTION STRATEGIES

Since independence, one of the principal goals of Kenya's development efforts has been to reduce poverty. The government has pursued this goal through various development strategies emphasising economic growth, employment creation and provision of basic social services. In the post-independence era (1964–2006), Kenya has transited from a high economic growth path in the 1960s (6.6% average annual growth over 1964–1972) to a declining path (5.2% over 1974–1979, 4.0% over 1980–1989, 2.4% over 1990–2002), and the economy is now on a recovery path, having registered impressive 4.9% and 5.8% growth rates for 2004 and 2005, respectively (Republic of Kenya 2006). Rapid economic growth has been given prominence by the Kenyan government as a means of alleviating poverty and creating employment opportunities. The rapid growth of the economy has been regarded as a key solution not only to poverty, but also to unemployment, poor health, economic exploitation and inequality. For this reason the government's stated economic policy reflected in various Sessional Papers and the 5-year development plans tended to place emphasis on the promotion of rapid economic growth, equality in the sharing of economic growth benefits and the reduction of extreme imbalances and inequalities in the economy as the main goals of economic development.

This policy stance has been maintained throughout the last four decades with slight variations. The first two development plans focused emphasis on rapid growth to alleviate poverty and reduce unemployment. However, in the early years after independence, the two problems of poverty and unemployment persisted and income inequality widened despite the economy achieving high rates of economic growth. Only through sustainable economic growth could the national wealth be created to support measures to alleviate poverty, protect vulnerable groups and raise the standards of living of the people (Republic of Kenya 1994). The government's strategy of promoting growth as a means of poverty alleviation is based on an implicit assumption that a 'trickle down' process would take place to spread the benefits of growth from some of the more dynamic modern sectors to the rest of the economy and sections of the population (Ikiara 1998). This was the basis of 'redistribution with growth', which became a popular slogan with the authorities. However, by the mid-1970s it was realised that the strategy was not producing the desired effects.

Despite the rapid growth of the economy in the first 10 years after independence, the problems associated with a rapidly growing population, unemployment and income disparities were more apparent than they had been in 1963. The failure of economic growth to solve the problems continued to be observed in the 1980s and 1990s. Although economic growth is a necessary condition for meeting basic human wants, it is not in itself sufficient. Fast growth often helps to reduce poverty, but some growth processes may do so more effectively than others. According to the report by the World Bank on attacking poverty (2000), the most valuable asset of the poor is their labour. Thus by shifting resources towards rural and labour-intensive production activities, the government may be able to address poverty. Due to high levels of inequality only a few individuals reaped a disproportionate part of the gains from the high economic growth, while the majority languished in poverty. A report by the Society for International Development (2004) estimates that 10% of the richest households in Kenya control more than 42% of incomes, while the poorest 10% control just 0.76%. That is, for every shilling earned by a poor person, a rich person earns 56 shillings.

Though the government realised the importance of addressing poverty right after independence, attempts to that end started in earnest only in the 1980s. Past government policy initiatives to address poverty articulated in various Sessional Papers and 5-year development plans include the following: land resettlement schemes in the 1960s; provision of basic needs (education and health) in the 1960s; promotion of rapid growth and creation of employment opportunities in the 1960 and 1970s; District Focus for Rural Development in the 1980s; and promotion of the informal economy in the late 1980s with a high potential for alleviating poverty through the creation of employment opportunities. The close relationship between unemployment, poverty and inequality in income distribution has generally been acknowledged by the Kenya government since the mid-1960s, as evidenced by the various polices formulated by the government to address the trio. However, the implicit assumption and belief in the 'trickle down' process proved ineffective. Available data indicate that poverty, unemployment and inequality have worsened over time. Virtually all major indicators of poverty articulated above show that over the last 40 years policies formulated in Kenya to deal with poverty have achieved little in arresting the impoverishment of the Kenya population.

The failure of economic growth to solve the poverty problems necessitated a shift of policy focus to equity and resource distribution. The objectives hitherto pursued by government through the national development plans and national policy frameworks were too lofty and macro to be able to address the meso and, socially contextualised, micro problems of equity, access to economic opportunities and social services for the poor. In an apparent effort by the government to provide for a national policy and institutional framework for urgent action against poverty, the government embarked on the preparation of deliberate policies to address poverty. Prior to the preparation of the PRSPs in Kenya to benefit from debt cancellation offered highly indebted poor countries, Kenya had earlier prepared a poverty eradication plan for the period 1999–2015 that articulated different strategies. The preparation of the PRSP was informed by the necessity to involve the poor in the formulation of strategies to address their poverty problem, not by access to debt cancellation. Though Kenya is poor, it is not a highly indebted country, and thus did not qualify for debt relief under the HIPC initiative. Still, the government went ahead with a major policy formulation exercise to produce a PRSP because the poverty problem remained a serious challenge. The sections below articulate the evolution of the Kenya's poverty reduction strategies, the role of different stakeholders, implementation frameworks, achievements and challenges.

6.3.1. Ownership and comprehensiveness of the PRSP

In 1999, the government prepared the National Poverty Eradication Plan (NPEP) for the period 1999–2015. The plan signalled the government's resolve to address the poverty challenge not only as a political necessity and moral obligation, but also on grounds of sound economic principles that recognised the critical role and potential contribution of the poor to national development. In line with the goals and commitments of the 1995 Copenhagen Summit set out in the declaration of the World Summit for Social Development, the government committed itself to the eradication of poverty, the achievement of universal primary education, various aspects of health for all, and the social integration of disadvantaged people.

The preparation of the NPEP involved extensive consultations with key stakeholders and the document was refined at a number of technical discussions and workshops that involved the government, the private sector, non-governmental organisations and the donor community. Besides, the NPEP also benefited from the findings of two PPAs and the 1994 welfare monitoring survey

The NPEP has three major components: (i) a charter for social integration; (ii) improved access to essential services by low income households that lack basic health, education and safe drinking water; and (iii) a strategy for broad economic growth, with each setting out a framework for further action by government, civil society, the private sector and donor partners. The following specific goals and targets were set by the NPEP:

- reduction of the poor in the total population by 20% by 2004 and by a further 30% by 2010;
- increase of 15% in enrolment rates over the first 6 years of the plan;
- increase in completion rates, especially of girls in the first 6-year period by 19%;
- achieve universal primary education by the year 2015;
- universal access to primary health care to within 5 km of all rural households or within one hour of local transport by 2010;

- increase by 8% each year until 2004 access to safe drinking water by poor households and create universal access to safe water by 2010;
- reduce time spent by women on fuel wood and water collection;
- publish 'best practice' guidelines for rural and urban social development by 2000;
- 20% of communities to draw up action plans by 2004;
- 40% of all extension messages to be relevant to very poor farmers.

As a first phase of implementing the NPEP, the government prepared the Interim Poverty Reduction Strategy Paper (I-PRSP 2000–2003) in 2000 through broad consultations with stakeholders within and outside of government (Republic of Kenya 2000d). The I-PRSP outlined measures to improve economic performance and actions to reduce poverty by deliberately shifting the composition of budgetary expenditures towards priority poverty reduction programmes. The I-PRSP recognised one important element of development, the role of the people and the fact that poverty wastes peoples' potential to work. To empower the poor, the I-PRSP noted the need to provide them with means to help themselves through income-earning opportunities, ready access to means of production, the provision of affordable basic services and the protection of the law. This, it was noted, would only be achieved through a deliberate and long-term policy to facilitate sustained and rapid economic growth, improve governance and security, increase the ability of the poor to raise their incomes, improve the quality of life of the poor, improve infrastructure, and increase equality of opportunity and to ensure that all members have a chance to participate fully in the socio-economic development of Kenya. Though the I-PRSP put forth a broad framework to implement the NPEP, it did not incorporate the voices of the poor. Like the NPEP, the I-PRSP had limited its consultation to the national level.

To mainstream the poor into the development process, the government, through a participatory process, prepared a PRSP for the period (2001–2004). The PRSP is a product of broad-based and inclusive consultations, which took place at the national, regional, district and divisional levels in the country. The process included all stakeholder categories with special attention given to civil society, vulnerable groups (women, youth, pastoralists and people with disabilities) and the private sector. To ensure inclusiveness and broad-based participation, the consultations were organised within a national framework consisting of divisional consultations; district consultative forums; provincial workshops; national consultative and stakeholder forums; thematic groups; and sector working groups. In addition, the preparation of the PRSP also benefited from the PPA studies conducted in ten districts to document the voices of the poor with regard to participation, inclusion and ownership of development programmes and projects and in prioritising activities that directly affect their well-being. The PPA process involved listening to street children, people with disabilities, pastoral communities, unemployed youths, farmers, traders, *jua kali* (informal, open market operations) artisans, the private sector, fishing communities, urban slum dwellers, coastal communities, women, local leaders, professionals, local administrations and government ministries.

The PRSP was at the centre of the long-term vision outlined in the NPEP. Whereas the NPEP proposed a 15-year time horizon to fight poverty, the PRSP put in place a short-term people-centred strategy that sought to implement the NPEP in a series of 3-year plans. By taking into account the voices of the people, it strengthened and gave credibility and ownership to poverty reduction efforts. It played a cardinal role in the development of a pro-poor and pro-growth Medium Term Expenditure Framework (MTEF) budget that linked policy planning and budgeting, thereby ensuring harmonised financing of growth and poverty reduction. Unlike earlier national development planning documents that ignored monitoring and evaluation, the PRSP recognised the need for a feedback mechanism and put in place mechanisms to ensure that poverty-targeted programmes were funded, implemented, monitored and evaluated.

Two years after the preparation of the PRSP, the KANU government that had spearheaded the process was defeated in a multi-party general election that brought the National Rainbow Coalition (NARC) to power. As expected, this necessitated policy shifts and reprioritisation. The NARC government prepared the Economic Recovery Strategy for Wealth and Employment Creation (ERS) 2003–2007, and subsequently its investment programme, which is based on two principles: democracy and empowerment of the people. The preparation of the ERS, like the PRSP, was prepared through a consultative process, though not as extensive as that of the PRSP, and incorporated materials articulated in the PRSP, the government Action Plan, the NARC Manifesto, and the NARC Post-Election Action Plan. The ERS is anchored on the priority to address the endemic menace of poverty and is focused on empowering Kenyans and providing them with a democratic political atmosphere under which all citizens can be free to work hard and engage in productive activities to improve their low standard of living, which is attributed to widespread poor governance, a breakdown in the rule of the law, and lack of respect for democratic practice. Ideally, the ERS articulates the current government's poverty reduction strategies.

The ERS identifies key policy actions necessary to spur the recovery of the Kenyan economy and therefore address poverty as: rapid economic growth; strengthening institutions of governance; rehabilitation and expansion of physical infrastructure; and investment in human capital. To spur economic growth, the government committed itself to the strengthening of the macroeconomic framework, maintenance of a responsible fiscal policy stance and provision of a conducive environment for private sector investment in the productive sectors, especially in the development and maintenance of infrastructure. To reduce poverty, it focuses on the provision of Universal Primary Education, improved access to basic health, development of traditional overlooked arid and semi-arid areas, and upgrading of the living conditions of the urban poor. To enhance the quality of governance, the ERS proposed far-reaching reforms in the judiciary and the strengthening of the rule of law and security, as well as implementation of reforms within the public administration systems that are critical to improving government transparency and accountability. In addition to the general policies geared towards improving the welfare of all Kenyans, the ERS identifies some priority programmes that target poor communities, the poor in Arid and Semi-Arid Lands (ASALs), the urban poor and marginalised groups. These programmes include the establishment of a social action fund, the development of arid and semi-arid areas, the implementation of slum upgrading programmes, and the development of a programme to reduce the vulnerability of marginalised groups.

The ASAL programme is a multi-sectoral programme designed to cater for geographical areas with a high poverty incidence. The strategy for ASALs aims at combining activities in the infrastructural and productive sectors with human resources development, security enhancement and land tenure reform. In the productive sectors, the programme aims at supporting infrastructural development to rehabilitate roads and mobilise community participation in feeder roads maintenance; to implement a broad-based livestock development policy; to facilitate private sector development of fishing infrastructure; and to strengthen community-based eco-tourism. In human resource development, the programme aims at closing the gap with the rest of the country by developing a creative schooling programme for pastoralist children, strengthening community-based health care systems and preventive medicine, and improving food security through the implementation of community-based early warning systems. To implement the ERS, the government prepared an Investment Programme for the Economic Recovery Strategy (IP-ERS) for the period 2003–2007 which provides an implementation framework that details the roles of different stakeholders, enabling activities, targets, costing and timeframes. The IP-ERS also provides for the establishment of an integrated monitoring and evaluation framework.

The preparation and evolution of the poverty reduction strategies have involved representatives of all stakeholders and they are therefore home-grown. The strategies articulated are to a large extent comprehensive as they cover all sectors of the economy. This notwithstanding, the implementation of the various strategies has been constrained by fiscal, institutional and human factors, which have slowed down the realisation of the objectives of the PRSP.

6.3.2 Implementation arrangements

Any strategy is incomplete without a clear-cut framework for implementation. In fact, it is the implementation of the aspirations of a strategy that ultimately prove whether or not it is a worthwhile undertaking.

Milestones and linkages to the budget

Subsequent to the preparation of the NPEP, the Commission for Poverty Eradication was established through a presidential appointment to oversee the implementation of the plan. In addition, a Poverty Eradication Unit was established in the Department of Development Coordination, Office of the President to oversee the implementation of pilot projects.

Specific measures put in place to monitor progress and implementation of the I-PRSP included macroeconomic management, sectoral and governance measures, and consultation to develop a full PRSP. In each of these areas, targets were set and indicators identified to assist in the monitoring and evaluation process (these indicators and targets are presented in Table 6.1). The identification of indicators and setting of targets, like the very preparation of the PRSP, was done through a consultative process.

In the area of macroeconomic management, the government committed itself to the reduction of the budget deficit, domestic debt and interest rates and to maintaining a low and stable inflation regime. Table 6.1 reveals that Kenya has maintained a fairly stable macroeconomic framework. In addition to the macroeconomic framework, the government has implemented various sectoral reforms in efforts to resuscitate growth dynamics and reduce poverty. The latter include increased budget provision to health, education, roads, housing and water in order to support the provision of primary health care, free primary education and bursaries to poor secondary school children, rehabilitation and expansion of roads, slum upgrading and an expanded supply of water and rehabilitation of water projects. Other milestones include cabinet approval of a policy on the coffee sub-sector; reforms to privatise marketing services by the Coffee Board of Kenya; liberalisation of the tea sub-sector by transforming the Kenya Tea Development Authority into the Kenya Tea Development Agency and incorporating it under the Companies Act as an independent and private enterprise owned by small-scale farmers through their respective tea companies; the establishment of the National Environmental Management Authority and the enactment of the Environmental Management and Coordination Act; the preparation of the Kenya Rural Development Strategy, which provides a common vision and framework for rural development; and the establishment of the Micro Finance Unit at the Central Bank of Kenya and cabinet approval of the Micro Finance Bill.

Other achievements include the review of primary and secondary school curricula to reduce the number of examinable subjects and the introduction of free primary education and bursary schemes for poor children in secondary schools to reduce the cost to parents. In addressing HIV and AIDS, the government established the National Aids Control Council (NACC) to strengthen capacity and coordination in responding to this pandemic at all levels. AIDS control committees have been established in all ministries, provinces and constituencies.

With the change of government in 2003, the NARC administration established the National Economic and Social Council (NESC) to provide a forum for partnership, monitoring and evaluation of public policy. NESC provides oversight over the implementation of the poverty reduction strategies and policy advice to cabinet and Ministries of Finance and Planning on national economic and social issues.

In linking poverty reduction to the budgets, in 2003 the government ring-fenced poverty-related expenditures and ministries annually conduct public expenditure reviews and reprioritise their expenditures. Preparation of the poverty maps by the CBS has also greatly informed government allocations on decentralised funds, such that poorer regions get larger allocations in proportion to their poverty indices. In this regard, a number of specially targeted projects have been used in an attempt to achieve poverty alleviation. These include, for instance, the Urban Slums Development Project of Nairobi City, the Street Children's Funds, the Education Bursary Programme to assist bright children from poor families, and the Micro and Small Enterprises Programme, among others. In the last 5 years, for instance, there has been a massive increase in resources devoted to constituency- and community-based development programmes. These include development funds such as the Constituency Development Fund, Community Development Trust Fund, the Roads Fund, the HIV and AIDS Fund and the Constituency Education Bursary Fund. The direct disbursement of funds is intended to improve poverty targeting and project implementation by using local information and encouraging community participation, especially in project identification, implementation and evaluation.

The government's efforts to improve access to health care include at least one government hospital in every district, but with the creation of new districts this is not always the case. In addition, there is one provincial hospital in all provinces and two national referral hospitals. Some of the facilities, however, are in a deplorable state and in dire need of major refurbishment. The initial intention to establish cost-sharing in hospitals has been hampered by people's reluctance to pay fees for prescriptions when there is a lack of drugs. The introduction of cost-sharing in 1989 (and its subsequent abandonment and reintroduction) represented a major shift in policy from the initial period of independence, during which time the government operated a system of 'free' medical services, alongside a subsidised system. To address the plight of the poor, they have continued to receive exemptions from cost-sharing charges in government facilities with respect to a number of diseases. These cost-sharing charges constitute seven percent of the Ministry of Health's recurrent revenue and are reallocated back to the health facilities as an incentive. In addition, the government has always provided free immunisation to all Kenyans through the Kenya Enhanced Programme of Immunisation.

The initial gains after independence in the area of health care are now threatened by the onset of HIV and AIDS, which is taking the lives of the economically active. The costs of prevention, care and support for the infected and affected and the mitigation of its socio-economic impacts have placed a heavy burden on an already hard-pressed economy both at household and national levels. With the declaration of AIDS as a national disaster in late 1999, a lot of resources are being mobilised to fight the pandemic, though the gains cannot be ascertained so far. To address the HIV and AIDS pandemic the government established the NACC, which is the overall coordinating body for all the stakeholders. The NACC has attracted many donors, including the United Nations Programme on HIV and AIDS, the UK Department for International Development, German Technical Cooperation, and the Japan International Cooperation Agency, which are all involved in the areas of reproductive health, research, prevention and many others. The NACC has facilitated campaigns on HIV and AIDS and the formation of associations for those infected and affected by the pandemic.

Education plays an important role in human development by empowering people to improve their well-being through increasing their productivity and potential to achieve higher standards of living. Kenya considers education a basic right and a basic need. To reduce the cost of education to parents, a number of specific interventions have been undertaken. These include grants from the Ministry of Education, Science and Technology to poorer districts and divisions; provision of bursaries to poorer children; revision of the pupil/teacher ratio upwards to allow for more efficient utilisation and a more equitable distribution of teachers; targeting out-of-school children, child workers and AIDS orphans with non-formal education; rationalisation of the curriculum and reduction in the number of schoolbooks to be purchased; and intensification of school feeding programmes in poverty-stricken areas.

Under the project preparation phase for the World Bank-sponsored Strengthening of Primary and Secondary Education Programmes, progress has already been made on reducing to five the number of examinable subjects on the primary syllabus. Efforts have also been made to ensure that there is better teacher management and a more equitable distribution of teachers in the country, and autonomy has been accorded schools and districts in the recruitment of teachers. Further, there has been acceptance of the need to increase the pupil/teacher ratio to 1:34. All of these initiatives will have the effect of reducing the cost to parents in terms of facilities, books, equipment and the hiring of ancillary teachers.

Under the leadership of the World Food Programme Emergency Operations in the drought-affected ASALs there has been an expansion of the school feeding programme. Furthermore, to ensure that bursaries are well targeted and that they benefit the poorest in society, the government has established a constituency bursaries scheme. This has greatly improved the gross enrolment rate to 104% and the net enrolment rate to 84% as of 2004.

PRS monitoring framework

The overarching objective of the M&E system is to facilitate the use of data and information to inform public policy, to measure efficiency in the utilisation of available resources and achievements in poverty reduction, and to provide feedback for policy making, including the MTEF process (Republic of Kenya 2006). The government has put in place a National Integrated Monitoring and Evaluation system to monitor indicators (input and process indicators, output indicators, and income and impact indicators) that measure government efficiency in utilising the available resources and achievements made in the reduction of poverty. In this regard, the government developed a monitorable result-based logical framework matrix, which is consistent with the strategies and priorities of the ERS and the PRSP. The matrix spells out a consistent framework for ERS implementation and identifies key indicators and targets, as well as major constraints and risks. A monitoring and evaluation team comprising the Ministries of Finance and Planning and other stakeholders that include the Poverty Eradication Commission is responsible for the monitoring and evaluation of the PRSP. The Ministry of Planning and National Development spearheaded in 2003 the development of 31 indicators through a consultative process. Though efforts are underway to revise and expand the list of the indicators to take into account the availability of credible data, the 31 indicators were agreed upon by the stakeholders and have been used in the writing of the Annual Progress Reports (APR) on the implementation status of the IP-ERS for the years 20003/04 and 2004/05. The 31 indicators, though acknowledged as not exhaustive, form the M&E baseline data that are regularly collected.

A number of institutions were created to spearhead the implementation of the M&E system for tracking the ERS. These included the NESC, the Monitoring and Evaluation Directorate (MED), the PARU, and the National Stakeholders' Forum. NESC provides oversight of the implementation of the ERS and policy advice to cabinet and the Ministries of Finance and Planning on national and social issues and also liaises with the private sector and civil society organisations on the same. The MED coordinates M&E and stores and disseminates monitoring and evaluation information and data. The CBS is the custodian of data and information. In managing data, Kenya Information (KENIFO), which is Kenya's socio-economic indicators database and provides comprehensive information on the core nationally monitored indicators, has been developed and annually all ministries prepare Public Expenditure Reviews (MPERs). The MPERs articulate the objectives and priorities of ministries and sectors and projects on needed budgetary allocations. Preparation of the APRs on the implementation status of the IP-ERS has also gone a long way in documenting achievements and challenges experienced in the implementation of poverty reduction strategies, in addition to making proposals on what needs to be done to realise the PRSP's objectives.

6.3.3 Role of international partners

Government efforts to address poverty are as old as independent Kenya, motivated by the high levels of illiteracy, poverty and disease that were perpetuated by the colonial masters amongst the indigenous people during the colonial period. Various government development plans and Sessional Papers in various ways articulated diverse strategies to reduce poverty through high economic growth and redistribution. The preparation of the NPEP that preceded the preparation of the PRSP was home-grown after the government had realised that poverty could not be addressed by high growth only. Although Kenya prepared a PRSP, the country is not classified as a highly indebted poor country (HIPC). Consequently, Kenya has not benefited from debt cancellation as a result of the preparation and implementation of its PRS. Besides, for more than two decades the country has not received any budget support due to governance concerns by international development partners over the allocation and utilisation of public resources. The only significant role played by donors in the preparation of the PRSP and indirectly the subsequent ERS was the financing of the consultative process. Nonetheless, the government enjoys programme support from various international development partners, most of which are in support of poverty reduction, through the implementation of projects and programmes especially in the areas of environment, sanitation, health and education. The development partners have also offered technical support for the development of the integrated M&E system and its operationalisation.

6.3.4 Challenges of the PRS

The full realisation of the objectives of the PRS has been constrained by a number of factors. These include the change of government that necessitated the drafting of a new policy document (i.e. the ERS) to capture the priorities of the NARC regime; the implementation of the government policy on retrenchment of staff without adequate compensation and the freezing of employment; the withdrawal of donor budget support and late disbursement of donor programme support due to governance concerns, which has caused delays in the implementation of various projects and programmes; and the lack of an appropriate decentralisation strategy to exploit the abundant potential in communities for the implementation of community-driven development approaches. Other challenges include the lack of harmonised development initiatives by different stakeholders and a dysfunctional delivery system that is characterised by uncoordinated systems, duplication and inefficiencies, asymmetries of information and inadequate transparency and accountability. These challenges have resulted in wastage of resources owing to duplication of effort and have made it hard for targeted poverty programmes to benefit the poor proportionally.

6.4 Conclusion

Poverty reduction is a national challenge. Initially, Kenya hoped to eradicate poverty through economic growth. Poverty was seen as a short-term hardship, which would disappear as the nation developed and grew in economic terms. Poverty is now recognised as a major threat to a very significant proportion of Kenyan households, with worrying knock-on consequences for the security and economic well-being of those with surplus incomes and good services. It is also increasingly recognised that economic growth alone will not be sufficient to reduce poverty and that poverty hampers growth as an independent variable.

In spite of numerous policy interventions and programmes by the government, the poverty profiles presented in this chapter document the fact that poverty is still unacceptably high in many regions of Kenya. This raises concerns regarding the appropriateness and comprehensiveness of the policies adopted to tackle poverty and/or the implementation of the same. Rising poverty is a consequence of poor growth and the lack of efficient mechanisms for the redistribution of growth. Past efforts by the government to address the problem have been inadequate. Current efforts by the government to conduct comprehensive integrated household surveys and measure poverty at constituency levels are commendable. However, the use of these indices as a basis for allocating transfers to local levels needs to be properly weighted, taking into account region-specific needs to avoid widening regional disparities.

There is also need to strengthen institutions of governance to ensure that programmes aimed at improving the welfare of the poor actually reach them, including the education bursary schemes, the resettlement of squatters and affordable health care. The allocation of decentralised funds needs to be in harmony with national objectives and the government needs to put in place systems to monitor and evaluate the performance of programmes. As suggested by the profiles and the evolution of policies presented above, much remains to be done to address the poverty problem in Kenya.

REFERENCES

Foster J., J. Greer, and E. Thorbecke (1984), 'A Class of Decomposable Poverty Measures', *Economica,* Vol. 52.

Greer, J. and E. Thorbecke (1986a), 'Food Poverty Profile Applied to Kenyan Smallholders', *Economic Development and Cultural Change,* Vol. 35, No. 1.

Greer, J. and E. Thorbecke (1986b), 'A Methodology for Measuring Food Poverty Applied to Kenya', *Journal of Development Economics,* Vol. 24.

International Labour Organization (1972), 'Employment, Incomes and Inequality: A Strategy for Increasing Productive Employment in Kenya', Geneva: ILO.

Ikiara, G. K. (1998), 'Economic Restructuring and Poverty in Kenya', in Njuguna N. and W. Owino (eds.), *From Sessional Paper No.10 to Structural Adjustment: Towards Indigenizing the Policy Debate,* Nairobi: Institute of Policy Analysis and Research (IPAR).

Kimalu, P., N. Nafula, D. L. Manda, G. Mwabu, and S. K. Mwangi, (2002), *A Situation Analysis of Poverty in Kenya,* Working Paper No. 6, Kenya Institute for Public Policy Research and Analysis (KIPPRA).

Kenya National Bureau of Statistics (2007), *Basic Report on Well-being in Kenya: Kenya Integrated Household Budget Survey 2005/06,* Nairobi: Government Printer.

Mukui, J. T (1993), *Kenya Poverty Profiles, 1982–1992,* prepared for the Ministry of Planning and National Development, Nairobi.

Mwabu, G., T. Kiriti, G. Ndenge, J. Kirimi, J. Mariara, R. Gesami, W. Masai, P. Kimuyu, M. Chemengich, and F. Munene (1999), *Poverty in Kenya: Identification, Measurement and Profiles,* Nairobi: University of Nairobi, Ministry of Finance and Ministry of Planning and National Development.

Republic of Kenya (1965), *Sessional Paper No. 10 of 1965 on African Socialism and Planning,* Nairobi: Government Printer.

Republic of Kenya (1993), *Economic Survey,* Nairobi: Government Printer.

Republic of Kenya (1994), *Kenya Poverty Profiles, 1982–1992,* Nairobi: Ministry of Planning and National Development.

Republic of Kenya (2000a), *Census Report of 1999,* Nairobi: Government Printer.

Republic of Kenya (2000b), *Second Report on Poverty in Kenya, Volume I: Incidence and Depth of Poverty,* Nairobi: Ministry of Finance and Planning.

Republic of Kenya (2000c), *Second Report on Poverty in Kenya, Volume II: Poverty and Social Indicator',* Nairobi: Ministry of Finance and Planning.

Republic of Kenya (2000d), *The Interim Poverty Reduction Strategy Paper 2000–2003*, Preliminary Draft Paper Prepared by the Government of Kenya.

Republic of Kenya (2001), *Poverty Reduction Strategy Paper for the Period 2001–2004*, Nairobi: Ministry of Finance and Planning.

Republic of Kenya (2003), *Kenya Economic Recovery Strategy for Wealth and Employment Creation (2003 - 2007)*, Nairobi: Ministry of Planning and National Development.

Republic of Kenya (2004), *Investment Programme for the Economic Recovery Strategy for Wealth and Employment Creation 2003–2007*, Nairobi: Ministry of Planning and National Development.

Republic of Kenya (2005), *Annual Progress Reports on the Economic Recovery Strategy for 2003/04*, Nairobi: Monitoring and Evaluation Directorate and Ministry of Planning and National Development.

Republic of Kenya (2006), *Annual Progress Reports on the Economic Recovery Strategy for 2004/05*, Nairobi: Monitoring and Evaluation Directorate and Ministry of Planning and National Development.

Society for International Development (2004), *Pulling Apart: Facts and Figures on Inequality in Kenya*, Nairobi: Society for International Development.

World Bank (2000), *World Development Report 2000/2001: Attacking Poverty*, Washington D.C.: World Bank.

CHAPTER 7

POVERTY PROFILE AND POVERTY REDUCTION STRATEGIES IN NAMIBIA

Klaus Schade

7.1 Introduction

Namibia is located in the south-west of Africa bordering South Africa to the south, Angola and Zambia to the north and Botswana to the east. It is regarded as one of the most arid countries south of the Sahara. Rainfall does not only vary geographically – between 700 mm in the north-east and less than 10 mm on average in the Namib Desert in the west of the country – and within regions, but also from one year to another. Unpredictable rainfall makes rain-fed agriculture a risky undertaking. Furthermore, high solar radiation, low humidity and high temperatures lead to very high evaporation rates; thus only 1% of rainfall ends up replenishing the groundwater aquifers (Ministry of Environment and Tourism, Republic of Namibia 2002: ix). Hence, only 2% of the land is classified as arable land. Namibia shares its few perennial rivers with Angola, Botswana, South Africa and Zambia, while ephemeral rivers in the country carry water only after strong rainfall. Hence, agriculture is characterised by extensive livestock farming – often combined with game farming – in the central and southern regions, while rain-fed crop cultivation is common in the centre-north and north-east. Irrigation schemes are located at perennial rivers and dams. About 41% of the land is state-owned and used for communal farming, 44% is owned by commercial farmers and 13% is in protected areas (Ministry of Environment and Tourism, Republic of Namibia 2002: x).

Namibia covers some 824,000 km², spanning 1,440 km at its widest point and 1,320 at its longest (Office of the President, National Planning Commission 2004). The population grew at 3.1% before 1991, but only by 2.6% in the decade between 1991 and 2001. It is assumed that population growth will decline further, which is attributable mainly to the impact of HIV and AIDS. Despite rural-to-urban migration, two-thirds of the population continue to reside in rural areas (Republic of Namibia 2003). The population density differs substantially between the more fertile north-central and north-eastern regions and the rest of the country. Based on a population estimate of some two million (2007), about 2.5 people live on a square kilometre. The density can, however, reach 100 in the more densely populated areas of the north. The population comprises ten major ethnic groups dominated by the Ovambo, who account for almost 50%, while the population of European origin stands at about 10%.

The country is divided into 13 political regions, where regional councillors are elected every 5 years. General and presidential elections are held at the same interval. Namibia is a multi-party democracy (six political parties are represented in parliament) with a bicameral system. The media and judiciary are independent.

Despite its rich natural resources (minerals, fisheries and landscapes), very good infrastructure and hence a relatively high GDP per capita (classified as a lower middle-income country),

Namibia is characterised by a very skewed income distribution and hence poverty. This is to a large extent the result of a long period of racial segregation under the apartheid regime, which eventually ended with independence in 1990. The government has identified the reduction of poverty and of income inequality as two of its four main national development objectives in its national development plans. However, the government realised that it was necessary to design a more profound strategy to reduce poverty and prepared a Poverty Reduction Strategy (PRS) in 1997 and subsequently a Poverty Reduction Action Programme as well as a Poverty Monitoring Strategy (PMS).

This chapter attempts to describe the approach the government took when it designed its policy responses to the challenge of widespread poverty. Additional sections provide necessary background information and conclusions. Specifically, Section 7.2 provides an overview of trends in economic and social indicators, while Section 7.3 presents a poverty profile. Section 7.4 analyses the policy framework for poverty reduction, and Section 7.5 concludes the chapter.

The analysis presented in this chapter is based on publicly available data and information, primarily from the Central Bureau of Statistics, which forms part of the National Planning Commission Secretariat (NPCS). Namibia has conducted two Household Income and Expenditure Surveys (NHIES), the first in 1993/94 and the second a decade later in 2003/04. These two surveys provide good sources of information on poverty trends. The analysis is further based on information from the Millennium Development Goals report, the National Accounts, the Population Census, sentinel reports and international publications such as the United Nations Development Programme (UNDP) Human Development Reports.

7.2 Overview of socio-economic performance

After sluggish growth during the pre-independence period (averaging 0.9% between 1982 and 1989), Namibia recorded a Gross Domestic Product (GDP) growth rate of 3.5% during the first 8 years after independence. While the economy grew strongly immediately after independence, growth rates declined steadily during the following years. With some major investments in the mining and textile sectors, growth picked up after 2000, reaching on average 4.4%. Table 7.1 provides a summary of growth rates for selected sectors for the past 6 years. Inflation displayed double-digit figures between 1982 and 1992, but dropped to below 10% thereafter with the exception of 2002 (11.4%). Since then, price increases have declined substantially to an annual low of 2.3% in 2005. Owing mainly to increasing oil prices and a slight depreciation of the Namibia Dollar against the US Dollar and other major currencies, inflation picked up again and averaged 5.1% in 2006. The upward trend continued during the first half of 2007, reaching 7.1% in May 2007. The Namibian central bank (Bank of Namibia) follows the inflation-targeting monetary policy of its South African counterpart and has already increased interest rates three times to 9.5% (July 2007) in order to keep price increases within a band of 3–6%.

Table 7.1: Growth Rates of Selected Sectors (Percentages)

Sector	2001	2002	2003	2004	2005	2006
Growth rates of selected sectors (%)						
Agriculture and forestry	-14.9	8.5	3.6	0.9	11	4.3
Diamond mining	-5.1	17.3	-3.5	38.6	-3.4	10.2
Manufacturing	5.5	9.6	5.2	3	2.1	-8.6
Construction	53.1	-13.1	22.9	-0.4	4.4	32.5
Wholesale and retail trade, repairs	2.8	7.4	4.1	7.6	6.2	9.5
Hotel and restaurants	8.4	8.4	4.9	-3.2	0.3	3
Transport and communication	13.9	11.4	3.1	13.5	13.8	10.6
GDP at market prices	2.4	6.7	3.5	6.6	4.7	2.9
Contribution of selected sectors to GDP (%)						
Agriculture and forestry	4.1	5.1	5.4	5.1	6.1	5.7
Mining and quarrying	13.2	13.9	8.8	9.6	8.6	8.3
Diamond mining	10.3	10.4	7.8	8.4	7	5
Manufacturing	9.4	10	11.4	11	10.2	12.6
Wholesale and retail trade, repairs	10.8	10.4	11.8	10.9	10.7	11.6
Real estate and business services	9	8.6	9.3	9.7	9.4	9.1
Producers of government services	21	19.9	20.3	19.5	19.6	18.6
Major export items as share of total exports (%)						
Live animals, animal products and crops, etc.	4.69	6.75	5.47	5.67	6.53	6.37
Diamonds	25.23	27.43	18.48	28.53	27.49	31.07
Metal ores incl. uranium ore	10.68	9.20	8.36	9.34	9.55	9.01
Prepared and preserved fish	19.21	16.39	15.87	15.23	14.38	9.89
Beverages, other food products	7.27	8.08	6.84	4.72	5.18	4.39
Direct purchases in Namibia by non-residents (tourists)	16.95	18.06	15.21	15.89	13.79	13.35
Major import items as share of total imports (%)						
Refined petroleum products	5.80	5.51	5.55	5.88	5.72	7.17
Chemical products, rubber and plastics products	12.64	10.25	9.31	12.29	11.98	11.93
Machinery and equipment	11.71	11.88	10.59	10.46	10.10	12.26
Transport equipment	14.59	14.11	12.55	14.05	18.81	18.16
Food products except beverages	8.85	6.30	6.77	8.19	7.88	7.63
Services (excluding direct purchases abroad by residents)	11.37	9.15	7.68	11.35	9.63	10.88

Source: Republic of Namibia, National Planning Commission, Central Bureau of Statistics (2007).

Gross fixed capital formation hovered around 23% during the period 1996–2005, peaking at 27% in 2005. Because of the narrow economic base, major capital investments such as the development of new mining sites have a major influence on the investment/GDP ratio. Mining companies are leading investors, followed in recent years by manufacturing companies and the real estate sector as well as transport and communication services.

Exports are dominated by diamonds followed by processed and preserved fish and by the direct purchases of foreign tourists in the country. Namibia imports mainly chemicals and machinery as well as transport equipment, foodstuffs and refined petroleum products. These goods account for more than 50% of total imports (see Table 7.1). The import and export structure reflects the picture of a raw-material exporting and finished-products importing country.

The following paragraphs describe the main economic sectors in Namibia in some detail. Agriculture contributes about 5.5% to GDP, of which about 30% is attributable to the subsistence sector (Table 7.1). The contribution of the agricultural sector appears to be low. However, the manufacturing sector (meat processing, food and beverages) depends to a great deal on inputs from agriculture. Secondly, agriculture provides the livelihood of the overwhelming majority of rural people – particularly in the communal areas. According to the latest labour force statistics about 103,000 people are involved in the agricultural sector, of whom probably 70% are employed or self-employed in the subsistence sector (Ministry of Labour and Social Welfare 2006). Investment in new sub-sectors such as grapes and horticultural produce has created additional employment of up to 13,000 jobs in the high season and has resulted in diversification of the sector.

Mining, on the other hand, accounts for between 8 and 13% of GDP but employs only some 7,500 workers. Since this sector is a mature, capital-intensive sector, new mining developments are not expected to contribute significantly to employment. The move from on-shore diamond mining to off-shore mining will result instead in the employment of more technology at the expense of labour. However, the sector contributes significantly to state revenues in the form of diamond royalties and company taxes and ranks as the most important foreign currency earner in the country. Furthermore, the sector produces jobs and income through downstream activities. Diamonds are cut and polished and the new sales agreement between De Beers and the Namibian government will ease the access to Namibian diamonds for domestic polishers and eventually the jewellery industry. Zinc and copper are also processed in the country through a refinery and smelter, respectively.

The fishing industry plays an important role in respect of employment – almost 13,000 people are employed in the sector, and in respect of foreign exchange earnings it ranks second after mining. It provides further employment in the fish processing sector. However, similarly to agriculture the fisheries sector depends on favourable climatic conditions and the availability of fish stocks in Namibian waters. The migration of fish stocks, high oil prices and a strong local currency have put substantial pressure on the sector and resulted in the closure of some businesses. The government regards marine and inland aquaculture as investment opportunities in order to create employment as well as to diversify the industry.

Tourism has emerged as a sector with a great potential for additional jobs, in particular in rural areas. It currently ranks as the third largest contributor to foreign exchange earnings. According to the Tourism Satellite Accounts, the sector accounts directly and indirectly for about 17% of total employment and 16% of GDP (World Travel & Tourism Council 2006).

Overall, the Namibian economy is heavily dependent on its natural resources, both renewable resources dependent on climatic conditions and non-renewable resources. The economy continues to rely on its traditional outputs such as minerals, fish, livestock and crops. However, a diversification process is slowly taking place at the micro level: non-traditional agricultural products such as grapes and horticultural products are produced domestically. New investments have been made in the dairy and pasta industries. Moreover, Namibia succeeded in attracting investment in the textile industry because of preferential access to the US market due to the African Growth and Opportunity Act (AGOA). This investment created about 5,000 jobs, although criticism is mounting because of poor labour relations and low wages.

Despite new investments and stable growth rates of about 4.2% between 1995 and 2005, unemployment remains at high levels. While the unemployment rate in a broad sense dropped slightly towards the end of the 1990s, it increased to 36.7% in 2004 (Ministry of Labour and Social Welfare 2006), whereas the economy grew by 4.0% between the Labour Force Surveys of 2000 and 2004. Despite significant investment in the education sector, the skills level of the workforce often does not meet labour market requirements. Hence, in particular people with no formal or only basic education are hard hit by unemployment while unemployment amongst persons with a tertiary education is almost non-existent.

Since the formal sector offers only limited employment opportunities, the informal economy acts as a last resort for jobseekers. Little is known about the extent of the informal economy and its contribution to GDP is estimated at about 10%. According to the Informal Economy Survey of 2001, about 85,000 informal businesses exist and provide jobs for some 132,000 employees and self-employed entrepreneurs. Two-thirds of informal enterprises are located in rural areas (Republic of Namibia 2004).

The government identified the social sectors as a priority after independence. Education received the largest share of the budget, followed by health during the first 10 years of independence. Increasing public debt and obligations to honour the loan guarantees of parastatals and to a lesser extent private sector businesses resulted in rising statutory expenditure. Since statutory expenditure (public debts, loan guarantees) falls under the Ministry of Finance, its budget increased over time in tandem with increased interest payments and has since 2000 accounted for the second largest share of the national budget. However, increased allocations to the Ministry of Finance as well as the Ministry of Defence has not resulted in declining shares for education and health. About 19.4% of the total national budget is allocated to education, including school hostels. Excluding school hostels, the share stood at 17.5% (Schade and Naimhwaka 2004). Health accounted for about 10% of the national budget (Schade and Ashipala 2004).

New health clinics and health centres were constructed, especially in rural areas to improve access to health facilities, while the number of hospitals was reduced in line with government's emphasis on primary health care rather than the provision of specialised treatment. The 2000 Namibia Demographic and Health Survey depicts the achievements since the 1992 survey. However, the HIV and AIDS epidemic has tainted the positive outcome of investments in the health sector and resulted in a substantial drop in life expectancy (see Table 7.2 overleaf for selected health indicators).

The HIV prevalence rate was on a steady increase until 2002, but dropped in 2004 to 19.7% compared to 22.0% (2002). The Sentinel Survey for 2006 recorded a slight increase in the prevalence rate to 19.9%. The Sentinel Survey is conducted every second year among pregnant women at 24 different sites across Namibia. The government has implemented various programmes to curb the spread of HIV infection, ranging from awareness creation to provision of treatment to prevent the transmission of the virus from mother to child, as well as the provision of anti-retroviral treatment.

Table 7.2: Selected Health Indicators

Indicator	2000 DHS value	1992 DHS value
Mortality Rates		
Infant mortality per 1,000 live births	38	57
Under 5 mortality per 1,000 live births	62	83
Child mortality per 1,000 live births	25	28
Maternal mortality per 100,000 live births	271	225
Immunisation coverage [1]	65	58
Women's tetanus toxoid injections during pregnancy	85	61
Contraceptive prevalence		
All women	37.8	23.3
Married women	43.7	28.9
Antenatal care	91	87
Assistance at delivery		
Nurse or doctor	76	68
Doctor	11	14
Nurse only	65	54
Malnutrition (% of children under 5 years)		
Moderately stunted	24	28
Severely stunted	8	8
Moderately wasted	9	9
Severely wasted	2	2
Moderately underweight	24	26
Severely underweight	5	6
Low birth weight (% of live births)	12	16

[1] Those who have received all of the following injections: BCG, DPT3, polio 3 and measles.

Source: Ministry of Health and Social Services (2003).

Investment in education has resulted in increased literacy and enrolment rates and a drop in the share of people who never attended school. However, there are some worrying signs. Net enrolment rates declined in the late 1990s. Drop-out and repetition rates remain high and subsequently the transition rates from junior secondary to senior secondary and further to tertiary education are low. Compared to the level of knowledge in other countries in the region, Namibian learners perform poorly. According to a test of Grade 6 learners in 13 countries conducted in 1995 and 2000 by the South African Consortium for Monitoring Educational Quality, Namibia ranked 11 out of the 13 countries covered in English reading skills and last in mathematics. In addition, the proportion of Namibian learners that could not read with any level of proficiency increased from 69% to 76% between 1995 and 2000. The private sector has repeatedly expressed concern about the adequacy for the labour market of the skills and knowledge acquired at school. These are challenges the government has to address with the support of international cooperation partners over the next 15 years through its Education and Training Sector Improvement Programme. The first 5-year phase of the programme covers the period 2006/07–2010/11 and is meant to run concurrently with the third National Development Plan (NDP 3).

The government has also invested significantly in the development of infrastructure as a prerequisite for industrial development and private investment. The communal areas were particularly neglected in terms of basic infrastructure during the apartheid era. Hence, the government has focused on providing water, electricity, communications and transport infrastructure to these areas.

Namibia's telecommunications system is backed by fibre optic cables and satellite links. Mobile telephone subscribers have meanwhile outnumbered fixed line subscribers by far. Almost all parts of the country are now covered by the mobile telecommunication network, benefiting in particular the rural areas. The advent of a second private cellphone company during the first quarter of 2007 is expected to increase the use of mobile phones further and reduce costs, which are high compared to neighbouring countries, let alone other regions. Access to a telephone (fixed line as well as cellphones) has increased substantially over the years, in particular in rural areas. While not even a quarter of the rural population had access to a telephone in 2001, the proportion had increased to over 50% in 2003/04. Nationwide, the proportion increased from about 38% in 2001 to about 67% in 2003/04 (Republic of Namibia 2003: 47; Central Bureau of Statistics 2006: 73).

It can be assumed that access to computer and internet services has improved as well, although this is confined to areas with access to electricity. For instance, schools in rural areas are still disadvantaged, despite efforts by government to increase the use of computers in schools.

Likewise, households' access to safe drinking water and toilet facilities has increased over the years as well as access to electricity. The government intends to provide all households with electricity by the year 2010. Based on the progress so far, this appears to be an over-ambitious objective (Table 7.3).

Table 7.3: Various Social Indicators (Percentage)

Indicator	1991[1]	2001[1]	2003/04[2]
Literacy rate	76	81	83.2
Population never attended school	26	15	15.1
Households with safe water	65	87	87.2[3]
Households with no toilet facility	61	54	53.2
Households with electricity	24	32	36.4
Households with access to a radio	59	80	84.5
Households using wood/charcoal for cooking	74	62	59.6

[1]Republic of Namibia (2003: 47); [2] Central Bureau of Statistics (2006: 73); [3]Piped water and boreholes/protected wells.

Economic development is closely linked to the availability of reliable transport infrastructure. Previous gravel roads are being upgraded to tarmac roads, while sandy tracks are being replaced by gravel roads. Most notably, the Trans-Kalahari Highway now links Namibia's deep-sea harbour Walvis Bay to South Africa's industrial hub, the Gauteng Province, while the Trans-Caprivi Highway connects the harbour to Central Africa, namely Zambia, Zimbabwe and further afield to the Democratic Republic of Congo. The construction of a bridge over the Zambezi River in the far north-east of Namibia and of a tarmac road on the Zambian side of the river has contributed to increased shipments from Zambia to Walvis Bay. In addition, Namibia's two harbours were upgraded and deepened to allow for the docking of larger vessels, and provided with modern loading equipment. Airports are being upgraded to facilitate the increase in the number of tourists arriving in the country. Last but not least, the railway line is being extended from the mining town of Tsumeb to the main urban centres in the north-central region – Ondangwa and Oshakati – and further to the Angolan border post of Oshikango. These investments have not only benefited the construction industry and unskilled and semi-skilled labour but are also expected to improve trade with neighbouring countries and attract investment. Hence, the investments are ultimately expected to contribute to poverty alleviation through new employment opportunities and economic growth.

Its natural resources, combined with by and large fiscal discipline and reasonable economic growth, have prevented Namibia from slipping into the debt trap. The fiscal deficit has hardly exceeded 4% of GDP and Namibia managed to achieve a budget surplus in the financial year 2006/07, which it is expected to repeat for the 2007/08 financial year. Total debt stands at 30.4% of GDP, mainly from domestic rather than foreign creditors. Foreign debt accounts for about 19% of total debt, or 6.4% of GDP. Namibia has not borrowed from the Bretton Woods institutions. Its generally sound macroeconomic conditions are acknowledged by an international credit risk rating of A, with a foreign currency rating of BBB-. Namibia features in the same group as, for instance, India with regard to its foreign currency rating.

7.3 THE POVERTY PROFILE

The subsequent sections provide in some detail the poverty profile of Namibia with respect to a number of key indicators.

7.3.1 Income poverty incidence

Namibia's history of colonialism and racial segregation resulted in a dual society and economy and, hence, strikingly divergent standards of living within its population. While Namibia enjoys on average a relatively high GDP per capita – NAD 18,874 (the exchange rate at the time of the study was 1 USD to NAD 6.97), which classifies it as a lower middle-income country – the income distribution is highly skewed. Namibia recorded one of the highest Gini coefficients in the world in 1993/94: 0.7, based on the NHIES. According to the latest data from the NHIES conducted in 2003/04 the Gini coefficient stood at 0.6 and remains one of the highest in the world. The Gini coefficient is only available as a national aggregate; a breakdown to the regional level or in terms of the rural-urban divide does not exist. It can be assumed that the patterns of inequality have not changed much since the 1993/94 NHIES. At that time, the poorest regions with regard to per capita income displayed the lowest Gini coefficient, while the wealthier regions were characterised by a high Gini coefficient.

The definition of poverty is based on the food consumption ratio. Households with a food consumption ratio between 60% and 79% are regarded as being poor, while households with a ratio between 80% and 100% are classified as severely poor. Work is currently ongoing on the construction of a poverty line based on the basic needs of a household. The provisional results suggest that poverty levels do not change much whether the food consumption ratio is applied or the basic needs poverty line. This finding would indicate that both measures are robust. However, a thorough analysis of poverty incidence is needed once a poverty line is approved.

Poverty is predominantly a rural phenomenon in Namibia despite widespread informal settlements in urban areas. About 6.1% and 36% of rural households are classified as severely poor or poor households based on the food consumption ratio, while the levels in urban areas are significantly lower – 0.6% and 6.0%, respectively. Overall, 27.8% of households in the country are poor; 3.9% are severely poor and 23.9% are poor (Central Bureau of Statistics 2006: 121). As is the case with the Gini coefficient, the level of poverty has dropped substantially since the NHIES of 1993/94. However, the two survey results are not comparable since the second survey covered double the number of households (10,920) included in the first (4,752). Besides, the criteria for being a household member changed. While a person was previously qualified as a household member when he/she stayed in the household for one week during a four-week period, this period was raised to two weeks in the 2003/04 survey. Finally, a larger number of expenditure items was included in the last survey (Central Bureau of Statistics 2006).

Poverty is rampant in regions based on subsistence farming or with a large share of subsistence farmers. Some 50% of households in Kavango in the northeast of the country are classified as poor, followed by Omusati and Oshikoto in north-central Namibia with a poverty ratio of 47%. The industrialised and more developed regions, in particular Khomas (with the capital Windhoek), as well as Erongo and Karas, both characterised by mining, fishing and tourism activities, display poverty levels far below average, namely 3.6%, 5.7% and 18.5%, respectively (Central Bureau of Statistics 2006). About 51% of the poor households rely on subsistence farming as the main source of income, followed by salaries and wages (20%) and social pensions (12%). The role of social pensions is more dominant in rural areas where an almost equal share of households relies on these as the main source of income as compared to wages and salaries – 13% compared to 17% (Naimhwaka 2007).

In the gender and poverty literature, it is often reported that poverty has a gender bias. However, in the case of Namibia there is no significant correlation between gender and the incidence of poverty. Furthermore, there is no evidence that households headed by persons younger than 21 years of age are poorer than households with older heads. About 27.7% of persons younger that 21 years of age are classified as poor, which corresponds to the national average (Naimhwaka 2007).

7.3.2 Access to health and education

As described briefly above, the government has prioritised the social sectors and invested substantially in health and education. New facilities have been constructed, particularly in rural and previously disadvantaged areas. However, on average, the poor still have to travel longer distances to education and health facilities than the non-poor (Table 7.4). Health and education are two important ingredients of self-determined living. Being deprived of access to both or facing challenges of accessing education and health facilities often means continued living in poverty. Hence, less favourable access to these facilities by the poor compared to the non-poor could perpetuate poverty for the former.

Table 7.4: Average Distances to Education and Health Services, NHIES 2003/04

	Primary school	High school	Combined school	Hospital
Caprivi	2.6	13.8	5.1	5.8
Erongo	4.2	11.0	31.4	4.7
Hardap	15.0	42.7	146.5	17.0
Karas	12.1	71.8	110.7	16.7
Kavango	3.5	21.3	12.3	6.7
Khomas	4.3	6.8	8.1	5.6
Kunene	16.2	60.0	74.9	30.1
Ohangwena	3.7	24.4	5.4	11.3
Omaheke	26.7	116.7	211.7	33.3
Omusati	3.5	18.3	6.2	8.6
Oshana	2.1	9.3	2.5	4.8
Oshikoto	7.9	23.3	10.5	15.0
Otjozondjupa	16.1	37.2	40.0	20.2
Urban	1.4	5.3	23.1	1.8
Rural	10.9	39.9	37.8	17.7
Non-poor	5.9	22.1	30.1	9.3
Poor	10.1	36.2	36.6	16.46
Namibia	7.1	25.9	31.9	11.2

Source: Naimhwaka (2007: 26).

Similarly, the poor rely to a larger extent than the non-poor on dams, wells or the neighbour's tap for drinking water and have subsequently not only longer distances to travel but also spend more time on fetching water (Table 7.5). This, in turn, reduces the time for other productive, income-generating activities that could contribute to improving the standard of living.

Table 7.5: Access to Water by the Poor (Percentages)

Main source of water	Non-poor	Poor	Total
Piped in dwelling	38.0	3.0	20.5
Dam/pool/stagnant water	1.3	3.4	2.4
Protected well	2.3	4.5	3.4
Unprotected well	4.0	9.3	6.7
Spring	0.1	0.3	0.2
Other	0.3	0.5	0.4
Piped on site	16.0	10.8	13.4
Neighbour's tap	4.7	7.3	6.0
Public tap	22.2	35.3	28.8
Private borehole	2.2	3.0	2.6
Rainwater tank	0.2	0.3	0.2
Water carrier or tanker	0.6	0.9	0.7
Communal bore hole	5.0	12.0	8.5
Flowing water	3.0	9.2	6.1
Mean distance to water sources in km	0.5	1.3	0.9

Source: Naimhwaka (2007: 32).

7.3.3 Impact of the HIV and AIDS pandemic

Namibia is one of the countries most severely affected by the HIV and AIDS pandemic. According to the 2006 Sentinel Survey, 19.9% of the population between the ages of 15 and 49 are HIV positive. The pandemic not only reduces labour productivity due to absence from work because of illness, caring for sick family members or attendance at funerals, but the disease has also resulted in an increasing number of orphans and vulnerable children. It is estimated that

23% of households include one or more orphans. The proportion of households with orphans is more than double in rural areas compared to urban areas – 13 and 30%, respectively (Central Bureau of Statistics 2006: 22); and about 32% of female-headed households comprise orphans compared to 17% of male-headed households. The available data do not allow the poverty status to be linked to the HIV status of individuals. However, the NHIES data reveal that female-headed households are characterised by a higher proportion of orphans. Additional analysis is needed to determine whether these households are more vulnerable and prone to poverty than others.

Based on the Human Development Index (HDI), the UNDP constructed a HPI, which measures the proportion of population that is deprived of certain characteristics. It uses the following indicators: the proportion of the population that does not reach the age of 40 years, the rate of illiteracy amongst adults, and the standard of living. The latter indicator is based on the proportion of the population denied access to clean drinking water and health facilities, as well as the proportion of malnourished under-five children. Contrary to the HDI, a high HPI indicates a high level of deprivation in the society, while a high HDI refers to a high standard of living. As explained above, Namibia has done quite well in most of these indicators. However, the impact of HIV and AIDS has caused a remarkable drop in life expectancy, thereby worsening the HPI gradually over the years. Until 1998, Namibia's HDI was increasing, but thereafter it dropped; while the HPI increased by five percentage points between 1998 and 1999. There are large discrepancies between regions. In the Caprivi region – worst affected by HIV and AIDS – the HPI rose by 15.6 percentage points between 1998 and 2000/01 (Table 7.6). The deterioration can be explained by the impact of HIV and AIDS on life expectancy. While life expectancy improved substantially until the late 1990s, Namibia has since witnessed a dramatic drop. HIV and AIDS has wiped out achievements in other indicators at the aggregate levels expressed by the HDI and the HPI.

Table 7.6: Human Poverty Index by Region between 1998 and 2001 (Percentages)

	1998	1999	2000/01	Percent increase
Caprivi	24.0	32.7	39.6	15.6
Erongo	12.0	16.7	18.7	6.7
Hardap	21.0	25.1	27.5	6.5
Karas	18.0	23.5	26.2	8.2
Kavango	29.0	31.9	32.6	3.6
Khomas	11.0	17.4	19.7	8.7
Kunene	27.0	28.7	29.6	2.6
Ohangwena	35.0	35.8	34.2	-0.8
Omaheke	32.0	32.5	33.4	1.4
Omusati	29.0	30.9	29.7	0.7
Oshana	24.0	26.7	27.5	3.5
Oshikoto	27.0	31.8	32.9	5.9
Otjozondjupa	23.0	27.6	29.3	6.3
Namibia	22.0	25.7	27.1	5.1

Note: HPI-N is used because it includes more up-to-date data (HPI-N stands for the Human Poverty Index calculated with the Namibian formula instead of the global formula).
Source: UNDP (1998; 1999; 2000).

However, there are signs of hope. Government interventions are starting to bear fruit. Besides HIV and AIDS awareness campaigns, the government started a pilot project in two state hospitals to prevent the transmission of HIV from mother to child. The treatment has subsequently been scaled up to include all state hospitals. In addition, all state hospitals provide anti-retroviral therapy for HIV positive patients in need. Presently, more than 20,000 patients are receiving such treatment. The President of the Republic of Namibia recently highlighted further achievements in his 'State of the Nation' address: the proportion of pregnant women visiting antenatal clinics who agree to be tested for HIV has increased from 10% five years ago to 90%. Furthermore, over 75% of women who deliver babies know their HIV status (*The Namibian*, 13 April 2007: 2). This indicates a remarkable change in attitude towards HIV and the stigma attached to it. Furthermore, the Sentinel Survey of 2004 revealed for the first time a drop in the prevalence rate compared to 2002 – from 22.0% to 19.7%. The decline is to some degree attributable to the addition of three new testing sites, of which two had prevalence rates below the average. Excluding these three new sites, the prevalence rate still dropped to 20.3%. According to the Sentinel Survey of 2006, the prevalence rate again increased marginally from 19.7% to 19.9% since the previous survey. Although these fluctuations are within the error margin, the figures could indicate that the pandemic is subsiding. If this is the case and since anti-retroviral therapy prolongs the productive life of HIV positive persons, we can expect not only an improvement in the indices, but an improvement in the real living conditions of people infected and affected by the pandemic.

Table 7.7: Namibia's Progress towards Achieving the MDGs

	1992	2003	2006 target	Progress towards target
1. Eradicate extreme poverty and hunger				
Proportion of households living in relative poverty* (%)	38	28[1]	28	Good[2]
Proportion of households living in extreme poverty* (%)	9	4[1]	4	Good[2]
2. Achieve universal primary education				
Net primary school enrolment (%)	89	92	95	Good
Survival rate for grade 5 (%)	75	94	95	Good
Literacy rate, 15–24 years (%)	89	89	94	Slow
3. Promote gender equality and empower women				
Primary education (girls per 100 boys)	102	100	100	Good
Secondary education (girls per 100 boys)	124	113	100	Good
Tertiary education (girls per 100 boys)	162	111	100	Good
Proportion of seats held by women in National Assembly (%)	9	19	30	Slow
4. Reduce child mortality				
Infant mortality (per 1, 000 live births)	67	52	36	Slow
Under-five mortality rate (per 1,000 live births)	87	71	54	Slow
Proportion of 1-year-old children immunised against measles (%)	63	72	80	Good
Underweight among children under five (%)	26	24	17	Slow
5. Improve maternal health				
Proportion of births attended by trained health personnel (%)	68	75	88	Good
Contraceptive prevalence rate (%)	21	37	50	Good
6. Combat HIV and AIDS, malaria and other diseases				
HIV prevalence among 13–19 year old women (%)	6	11	9	Worsening
HIV prevalence among 20–24 year old women (%)	11	22	15	Worsening
TB treatment success rate (%)	58	69	75	Good
7. Ensure environmental sustainability				
Proportion of rural households with access to safe drinking water (%)	45	80	80	Good
Proportion of rural households with access to basic sanitation (%)	15	21	50	Slow
Freehold land (%)	5	6	8.5	Slow
Registered conservancies (%)	0	5	10.9	Slow
8. Develop a global partnership for development				
Per capita overseas development assistance to Namibia (in USD)	130	60	90	Worsening

Source: Office of the President, National Planning Commission (2004);
[1] Figures included from Republic of Namibia (2006: 32);   [2] Author's own assessment.
Note: Freehold land is commercial land with private property rights as opposed to communal land. A conservancy consists of a group of commercial farms or areas of communal land on which neighbouring landowners or members have pooled resources for the purpose of conserving and using wildlife sustainably (Source: **http://www.met.gov.na/programmes/cbnrm/cons_guide.htm**).

The overall progress towards achieving a better standard of living for all is also reflected in the progress towards achieving the Millennium Development Goals (Table 7.7 above). The Table provides a quick overview of progress on selected targets for each of the eight MDGs. The data are grouped to represent the closest year to 1992, 2003 and the medium-term targets for 2006. The last column assesses progress against the medium-term target. 'Good' means that if the rate of progress since the early 1990s continues the target will be met. 'Slow' means that progress since the early 1990s has been positive but not strong enough to reach the 2006 target. 'Worsening' means that the situation has deteriorated since the early 1990s.

7.4 POLICY RESPONSES

To address the poverty challenges depicted above, the government has adopted a number of policies and taken concrete measures.

7.4.1 Poverty Reduction Strategy

The previous sections clearly show that there is poverty amidst wealth in the country. The government of Namibia was confronted with a dual society at independence in 1990 or as the World Bank put it, 'two Namibias existing within Namibia' (Government of the Republic of Namibia 1995: vii). The well-off segment living in towns and industrial centres in central and southern Namibia enjoy a standard of living not much different from that of other parts of the developed world. The majority, mainly rural population has been deprived of the same benefits. In order to change this pattern, the government identified the following four main national development objectives:

- poverty alleviation,
- reduction of income inequality,
- employment creation,
- sustainable economic growth.

These priorities have not changed throughout the successive 5-year NDP so far, starting with the Transitional National Development Plan, NDP 1 (1995/1996–1999/2000) and NDP 2 (2001/02–2005/06). However, further objectives were added in NDP 2, such as the reduction of regional disparities, the promotion of gender equality, the promotion of economic empowerment, and combating the further spread of HIV and AIDS.

While all ministries had to work towards achieving these goals, the government realised that to alleviate poverty would need a coherent strategy. The government was aware of the assistance offered by the World Bank under the HIPC initiative to formulate PRS papers and therefore sought technical assistance. Since Namibia is not a HIPC country, the government played a larger part in the formulation process. Because of its status as a non-HIPC country Namibia was not bound to a prescribed PRSP format. Namibia received technical assistance from the World Bank and financial assistance from the UNDP for the formulation of the strategy, while the government contributed mainly in kind.

The formulation process of the PRS built on a poverty assessment by external experts. The government emphasised the need to identify short-, medium- and long-term measures. Its interest in long-term measures originated from the initial ideas of a long-term development plan to complement the medium-term NDP. The process of formulating a long-term vision finally commenced in 2000 and resulted in the publication in 2004 of Vision 2030.

The committee that had been set up for the preparation of the Social Summit in 1995 remained in place for the preparation of the PRS. It included government institutions as well as the Namibian Non-Governmental Forum and the Council of Churches of Namibia. Two Namibian research institutions – the University of Namibia and the Namibian Economic Policy Research Unit – worked closely with World Bank experts and government officials in preparing background papers for the strategy. Overall, the active participation of civil society in the formulation of the strategy remained limited except for the research institutions as well as the participation of the regions. The committee was consulted and commented on drafts rather than actively driving the process.

The PRS identified long- and short-term measures to alleviate poverty and pointed out three main issues to be addressed:

- How to foster a more equitable and efficient delivery of public services for poverty reduction countrywide?
- How to accelerate equitable agricultural expansion, including consideration of food security and other crop development options?
- How to promote non-agricultural economic empowerment, including an emphasis on the informal sector and self-employment opportunities (Republic of Namibia 1998: 2).

The long-term vision envisages Namibia as a prosperous nation, a theme eventually picked up by Vision 2030. Two main instruments were identified to achieve this vision: turning Namibia into a transport and manufacturing hub, and investing in the people through education and health. Substantial investment in the transport infrastructure is expected to attract shipments for Southern Africa via Walvis Bay, Namibia's deep-sea harbour. This might also attract investors in a next step to set up local assembly plants, if Namibia offers the right incentives concerning infrastructure, fiscal incentives and last but not least quality of life. Namibia promulgated the Foreign Investment Act in 1990, reinforced by the enactment of the Export Processing Zone Act of 1994. The latter granted tax-free status to manufacturers and exporters. In addition, the Investment Centre was established as a one-stop shop for potential investors. But despite these efforts it is acknowledged that employment creation in the manufacturing sector will be rather modest.

Investment in infrastructure and the creation of a favourable business environment that includes a range of tax incentives as well as the removal of red tape needs to be accompanied by investment in people. The PRS lists a number of shortcomings in the present educational system and suggests three sets of educational reforms:

- continue measures aimed at reducing inter-regional disparities in educational expenditures per student;
- consider options for reorienting the curriculum and promotion criteria for the many who will not complete more than 9 years of basic education;
- in the final years of schooling for adolescents, place increased emphasis on pre-employment vocational education, especially approaches to training which are linked directly to the workplace.

The ministry has tried to address the intra- and inter-regional disparities in expenditure and allocates the same amount per learner for textbooks and educational material to schools. However, not all schools receive the number of textbooks they ordered and, moreover, this formula does not address the existing imbalance in the availability of resources at the school level (Schade and Naimhwaka 2004).

The PRS supports the shift from specialised health services towards primary health care that the government implemented shortly after independence. As with the education sector, it calls for a reduction of inter-regional differences in health expenditure per capita.

While the long-term initiatives will take time to bear fruit, the PRS suggests immediate action, including income-generating activities in the agricultural and tourism sectors as well as through the support of small and medium enterprises (SMEs). The strategy singles out the north of Namibia as an area with a potential for increased agricultural production due to the availability of water and better soil fertility. It builds on increased production of the staple crop, mahangu (millet), but stresses the need for increased funding for agricultural crop research. Improved access of smallholder farmers to extension services could improve productivity further.

Besides agriculture, the PRS identifies tourism as a sector with a high employment potential. Strong emphasis is placed on community-based tourism in the rural and communal areas. However, experience with community-based tourism today is rather mixed.

Finally, SMEs are seen as a vehicle for employment creation and thus poverty reduction. However, the strategy also lists the major challenges SMEs are facing, including a limited experience of non-subsistence production in northern Namibia, the very weak supply of complementary goods and services, and building a critical mass of successful SMEs (Republic of Namibia, National Planning Commission 2002). Access to finance constitutes another major hurdle but could be overcome if landowners obtained land titles that they could use as collateral. The proclamation of towns could support this process, but no initiatives are underway to improve access to credit for communal farmers.

It is acknowledged, however, that even a success in these areas would not be sufficient to alleviate poverty. Hence, it is suggested that the social safety net be strengthened through labour-intensive public works and the strengthening of the existing grant-based transfer programmes. The strategy further acknowledges that the government has reached the limit of additional fiscal resources for its public programmes. The challenge is, therefore, to make the most of the available resources by managing them 'smarter' (Republic of Namibia 1998:20). Hence, it is suggested that there be more debate about what should be publicly financed. Ministries are asked to define some nationally applicable minimum standards of service delivery that are lower than in the richest region, Khomas, in order to be financially sustainable in the short and medium term. Citizens who demand a higher quality of services would be referred to alternative arrangements, for example, private service providers. The number of private schools and health facilities suggests that there is demand for better services and that people are willing to pay for them. Secondly, the PRS supports decentralisation in order to increase the involvement of communities and user groups in the design and implementation of public programmes. Decentralisation would only work, however, if regional administrative capacity is improved. The current slow progress with decentralisation indicates that capacity remains a challenge.

Most of the initiatives included in the PRS are not new. However, they have received added emphasis through the PRS. The only new arrangement is the institutional framework for the implementation of the strategy, consisting of a National Advisory Committee on Poverty Reduction, the National Task Force on Poverty Reduction and in particular a Monitoring and Evaluation Unit within the NPCS, which was upgraded from a sub-division to a division.

The priorities identified in the PRS had received attention in the past, such as transport infrastructure and education and health. International cooperation partners provided financial assistance for investments in new roads, schools and clinics, among other measures, while the national budget allocated substantial financial resources from Namibia's own revenue towards the implementation of such projects. Upgrading airport and seaport infrastructure, the construction of the highways linking Walvis Bay with landlocked countries and the industrial centre of South Africa – Gauteng Province – are just a few examples of how the objective of becoming a transport hub for southern Africa has been pursued. The Southern African Development Community (SADC) provided some funds through its Regional Indicative Strategic Development Plan, notably to agricultural projects.

Namibia is one of the few African countries with a basic social security net. It provides for the payment of a non-contributory old age pension from the age of 60 years, grants for blind people, foster parent grants and a grant for ex-combatants above 50 years of age. Namibia inherited part of the social safety net from the previous apartheid regime. However, at that time the benefits were differentiated by race. Whites received a substantially higher amount than indigenous groups. This discriminatory system was abolished after independence and replaced by one that provided equal amounts to all who are eligible. The grants play an important role in alleviating poverty and in enabling, for instance, grandparents to send their grandchildren to school. The Basic Income Grant Coalition, consisting of a broad range of civil society organisations, including churches, is putting pressure on the government to introduce an even wider social safety net that would grant every Namibian citizen a monthly income of about NAD100. It is proposed to finance the grant through an increase in Value Added Tax and direct taxes. Although the government has rejected the proposal so far, the public debate is ongoing, involving the International Monetary Fund and the United Nations Commission for Social Development.

Cabinet adopted the PRS in 1998 and subsequently took steps to design a National Poverty Reduction Action Programme (NPRAP). The work started in 2000 and was carried out by local consultants with financial and technical assistance from donors. The process included very close consultation with all government agencies that were tasked to identify the impact of their projects and programmes on poverty. The NPRAP specifies actions necessary to implement the PRS and is therefore more detailed than the PRS. The programme ran concurrently with the NDP 2 from 2001 to 2005.

The action programme is based on three broad pillars for implementation, monitoring and evaluation: (a) the role of relevant ministries of the government; (b) regional projects and initiatives; and (c) the role of other stakeholders in poverty reduction (Republic of Namibia 2002: 18). The programme highlighted the importance of regional poverty initiatives because of the variations in the dynamics and types of poverty (Republic of Namibia 2002: 79). Combined with the decentralisation process, this requires regional councils to play a more active role. However, the decentralisation process is progressing at a rather slow pace because of human and financial resource constraints and hence limits on the role of local councils. Despite these limitations, government went ahead with Participatory Poverty Assessments in all the regions. The overall response from the communities was positive although sometimes mixed when politics came into play. Respondents feared victimisation when criticising the government or complaining about lack of resources. Some of these reports have already been published. The NPRAP also suggested the publication of a Namibia Poverty Report every second year and the organisation of a National Poverty Conference in the alternate years between reports. Neither idea has yet materialised. However, a conference is to take place in 2008 once the NDP 3 is finalised, which is planned for the third quarter of 2007, and resources have been released. One agenda item would be to review the PRS, which has been running for almost 10 years, and to include some elements that are not adequately covered in the existing PRS such as land, water and HIV and AIDS.

The NPRAP acknowledges that the co-ordination of activities requires a structure that cuts across all ministries and proposes the establishment of a Poverty Reduction Programme Co-coordinating Committee. The major purposes of the committee are to:

- advise the National Planning Commission on the review and management of the PRS within the context of the overall national development design;
- formulate concrete recommendations to government and implementing agencies on poverty issues;
- brief the government and the public – through the National Planning Commission – on progress in each sector towards implementing its poverty reduction programmes;
- identify and propose annually a priority set of poverty reduction projects for inclusion in the development budget;
- serve as a clearing house for all poverty reduction programmes and ensure that vulnerable groups such as women, children and people with a disability are given priority in poverty reduction programmes and projects (Republic of Namibia 2002: 82/83).

Furthermore, the NPRAP suggests that a Poverty Reduction Secretariat be established within the National Planning Commission. The function of the secretariat would mainly be to direct, co-ordinate and monitor the implementation of the NPRAP as well as to publish reports on its implementation.

Based on the recommendation of the PRS and the NPRAP, the NPCS designed a PMS in close consultation with major stakeholders. It was launched in 2005. Its objective is to ensure that poverty data are collected, analysed and disseminated on a regular basis in order to assess the implementation and effectiveness of the PRS. It is also intended to inform not only policy makers and other stakeholders but the public at large about the progress made in reducing poverty. The PMS will enable assessment of the implementation and impact of the poverty reduction action programme on people's lives. The exercise will provide time-series data since it is continuous in its approach and provides a basis for a thorough analysis over time. The indicators selected are based on the priorities established by the PRS and the NPRAP.

However, the report on the monitoring exercise has yet to be produced. It is not surprising, therefore, that one of its intentions, namely to stimulate a broad debate about poverty issues, has not materialised. Indeed, the PRS and subsequent programmes are not widely known among the population. This can be attributed in part to the lack of roots in the regions and local communities, since most of the activities are centred on the national level. Most of the priority areas identified in the PRS have received priority in the national budget, such as the social sectors and transport infrastructure. However, the financial resources allocated to the sectors do not always yield the expected results. Therefore, there is a greater need to monitor and evaluate poverty indicators on a regular basis in order to improve the efficiency and effectiveness of the strategy.

The government started shortly after independence to produce medium-term development plans. The first 5-year development plan (NDP 1) in 1995 replaced the 3-year Transitional National Development Plan. NDP 1 was formulated through broad-based consultations both inside and outside government (Government of the Republic of Namibia 1995: xi). Ministries drafted sectoral chapters, while the NPCS finalised the chapters in consultation with the respective ministries in order to ensure consistency. The NDPs cover all economic sectors in detail and are large documents published in at least two volumes. In comparison, the PRS is a rather short, concise booklet that focuses on the main issues rather than diving into too many details.

The launch of the NDP 2 coincided with the new millennium, the second decade of independence and the introduction of the 3-year rolling budget in 2001. Since preparatory work for Namibia's long-term development plan – Vision 2030 – had already started by then, NDP 2 was seen as the first medium-term strategy for the implementation of some of the objectives of Vision 2030. NDP 2 contained the following overall targets concerning poverty reduction:

- reduce the proportion of poor households by 5% by 2006;
- reduce the proportion of severely poor households by 5% by 2006;
- reduce the Namibian Poverty Index by a minimum of 10% by 2006;
- reduce the difference in the Poverty Index between the three richest regions and the three poorest regions from 81% to 50% by 2006 (Government of the Republic of Namibia 2001: 564).

The major sector objectives during NDP 2 were in line with the priorities singled out in the PRS, for instance, infrastructure, basic education and health, SMEs, and the social safety net. Again, these priorities received a large chunk of the national budget, although increases in social grants did not always keep pace with inflation. The donor community contributed financially to sector programmes and started channelling funds through the State Revenue Fund rather than transferring funds directly to the implementing agencies. This move increased transparency and accountability and suggested greater trust in the financial management capacity of government. In recent years, some of the partners have moved a step further and are providing direct budget support. After the implementation of the 3-year rolling budget – or the Medium-Term Expenditure Framework – the government took ambitious steps to shift the focus from budgetary inputs to the efficient use of public resources, in other words to outputs. The Performance Efficiency and Management Programme was put in place and most recently Medium-Term Plans and the Integrated Financial Management System. Each ministry has developed a medium-term plan that outlines the programmes within its purview and the objectives each programme is intended to achieve, including indicators to monitor progress. Basically, the Ministry of Finance allocates funds to the programmes and no longer to budget items. It is left, in principle, to the receiving ministry to allocate funds to the various budget lines in order to achieve its programme objectives. It is expected that this move will contribute to greater efficiency and improve targeting. These steps are in line with the PRS, which calls for better use of public resources.

The government conducted mid-term reviews of both development plans to assess progress towards achieving their targets. The reviews involved close consultation with all stakeholders at the national and regional levels. However, the analysis of these consultations and the data collected have usually been available only at the end of the 5-year period and informed the preparation of the next plan. Currently, the formulation of NDP 3 covering the period 2007/08–2011/12 is underway with the financial and technical support of development partners – among others the UNDP. The formulation process is guided and supervised by a broad Guiding Coalition involving public and private institutions and organisations. However, civil society is not involved to a large degree, owing mainly to capacity constraints, but sometimes also to poor communication about meetings, etc. It is not expected that the main development objectives will be changed.

The formulation of Namibia's long-term development – Vision 2030 – was a process that probably involved the broadest range of stakeholders. The process started in early 1998, shortly after the PRS was completed, with the President remarking that Namibia needs to know where we are, where we wish to go and over what time frame (Office of the President 2004: 13). Eight themes were identified and group leaders nominated from the public sector, research community, civil society and private sector. The vision was financed by public funds and contributions from development partners.

The overarching objective of Vision 2030 is to lift Namibia up to the level of an industrialised, developed country by 2030. It is envisaged that Namibia at that time will be a prosperous, harmonious, peaceful and politically stable country; a country that has graduated from a natural resource-dependent economy to a producer of manufactured goods as well as of services. A constituent feature is that poverty would be reduced to a minimum, the existing pattern of income distribution equitable and disparity at a minimum (Office of the President 2004: 104).

Vision 2030 follows the topics identified in the PRS, namely becoming a transport hub for Southern and Central Africa, investing in people to achieve the transition from a resource-based economy to a producer of manufactured goods and services. While this is the long-term goal, expanding the social safety net and supporting income-generating activities through SMEs, tourism and smallholder crop cultivation are the means (Office of the President 2004: 103).

In addition to the areas covered in the PRS, the section on poverty reduction in Vision 2030 sets targets for access to water, sanitation, housing and the integration of people living with disabilities that should be reached by 2030. In order to achieve poverty alleviation the following strategies need to be pursued, among others:

- ensure there is equitable distribution of income;
- ensure all people enjoy equitable access to services and resources, with limitations and barriers removed;
- ensure sustained economic growth and intensification of employment creation opportunities;
- create minimum standards for service delivery;
- implement HIV and AIDS reduction strategies; and
- implement the Millennium Development Goals in the country.

Vision 2030 sets a very ambitious goal. While the latest results of the NHIES suggest some achievements in poverty alleviation, much faster, employment-creating growth is needed.

Although economic growth increased during NDP 2 period compared to NDP 1 period (4.7% compared to 3.6%), it would by no way be sufficient to catapult Namibia to the level of industrialised countries. Tentative results from modelling exercises indicate that growth rates of more than 10% per annum would be necessary to fulfil the expectations of Vision 2030. Additionally, growth alone would not be sufficient to reduce poverty. In a country with a high rate of unemployment (36.7% in 2004), growth has to generate jobs. Furthermore, higher growth rates need to be translated into a redistribution of wealth to create a more equal society and equal local purchasing power in order to increase the contribution of local demand to economic growth. Presently, Namibia's economic performance hinges largely on the performance of the world economy and in particular the demand for primary commodities. This is certainly not in line with the development objective of increased and sustainable growth.

7.4.3 Millennium Development Goals

Namibia's Prime Minister served as President of the UN General Assembly during the Millennium Summit in New York in 2000 while Namibia's President co-chaired the Millennium Summit with the President of Finland. Therefore, the country might feel a special commitment towards achieving the Millennium Development Goals. The launch of the first report on progress towards the MDGs coincided with the launch of Vision 2030 in 2004. Vision 2030 regards the implementation of the MDGs as one component in achieving the sub-vision of poverty reduction.

The MDGs are: eradicate extreme poverty and hunger; achieve universal primary education; promote gender equality and empower women; reduce child mortality; improve maternal health; combat HIV and AIDS, malaria and other diseases; ensure environmental sustainability; and develop a global partnership for development (Office of the President, National Planning Commission 2004: 1). These goals are supported by time-bound targets and indicators in order to assist the monitoring of progress towards their achievement. These targets and indicators are clearly linked to the milestones of the NDPs and in particular to Vision 2030. Hence, monitoring the progress towards achieving these targets is not only an international commitment but probably even more so, a domestic exercise in the pursuit of Vision 2030. It is intended to inform the debate about the challenges and opportunities in realising Vision 2030.

Table 7.7 indicates that Namibia has made progress towards achieving some of the goals, notwithstanding considerable remaining challenges. It is a surprising coincidence that according to the NHIES data Namibia achieved what it was supposed to achieve, namely to cut relative poverty by 10 percentage points and severe poverty by 5 percentage points. However, economic growth rates have fallen far short of the required minimum of 7.7% per annum over the period 2001–2015 for achieving the first Millennium Development Goal of halving poverty by 2015. The most severe challenge facing Namibia is bringing down the HIV and AIDS prevalence rate. The latest figures based on the Sentinel Survey 2006 suggest that it is an uphill struggle. The pandemic is most likely contributing to the slow progress in achieving the child mortality targets, since children infected with the virus at birth often die before the age of 5 years. However, this might change and lower the child mortality rates since the government is providing treatment for the prevention of mother-to-child transmission as well as anti-retroviral drugs. The availability of treatment in all state hospitals for the prevention of mother-to-child transmission of HIV could contribute to achieving these targets. As noted above, the government is responding to the poor outcome of its investment in education through the Education and Training Sector Improvement Programme. It is expected that the implementation of the programme will have positive impacts on literacy rates as well.

7.5 THE ROLE OF REGIONAL ORGANISATIONS

Namibia is a member of various regional groupings that support trade facilitation and regional integration. It is member of a customs union, the Southern Africa Customs Union (SACU), which has a common external tariff. Customs and excise duties collected by member countries are transferred to the common revenue pool and divided among member countries according to a revenue sharing formula. The formula consists of three components, including a development component that benefits the poorer member states. Namibia receives about 33% of total revenue from the pool. These transfers contribute greatly to Namibia's 'investment in the people', for example, by funding health and education expenditure. It can be assumed that the transfers from SACU exceed the revenue from customs and excise duties Namibia would have collected if it were not part of SACU.

Namibia is, moreover, a member of SADC that aims, among other objectives, at creating a free trade area by 2008 and a single currency by 2016. The guiding document for SADC is the Regional Indicative Strategic Development Plan that was prepared in 2001. It lists poverty eradication as one of its priorities. Poverty alleviation is identified as a cross-cutting issue to be taken into account in policy interventions in trade, economic liberalisation and development; infrastructure for regional integration; combating the HIV and AIDS pandemic; and in human and social development (SADC not dated). SADC's objective is to halve the proportion of the population that lives on less than USD 1 per day by 2015. However, the SADC Secretariat does not provide financial support to any interventions geared towards achieving this objective. It is the task of member states to provide the financial resources.

Namibia benefits from the AGOA, which provides duty-free access to the US market. This preferential treatment has spurred investment in the textile industry and contributed to the direct creation of 5,000–6,000 jobs. However, there is much criticism concerning the environmental impact of the production process as well as labour relations and wage levels. Namibia is also a member of the African, Caribbean and Pacific countries that enjoy preferential access to the EU market. Although there are indications that Namibia could not increase its EU market share despite preferential treatment, it still benefits from often higher prices on the EU market than on other markets and hence generates a higher income than otherwise.

In a nutshell, it is only SADC's strategic plan that states poverty alleviation and ultimately eradication as an explicit objective. The SADC Secretariat, through the Formative Process Research on Integration in Southern Africa, is conducting a study on the implementation capacity for poverty-reducing policies in selected member countries in order to support them. However, the Secretariat does not provide financial support for programmes and projects aiming at reducing poverty.

7.6. THE ROLE OF INTERNATIONAL PARTNERS

As stated above, as a non-HIPC country Namibia does not qualify for debt relief under the HIPC initiative, nor is it bound to a particular format of its PRS. However, Namibia did receive technical and financial assistance from various multi- and bilateral agencies in designing its PRS, NDPs and other government policies. But the donor community did not play a dominant role in those endeavours. Namibia is also not a donor-dependent country. The government envisages Official Development Assistance (ODA) of roughly USD 90 per person, which is below the average of the first decade of independence but higher than per capita ODA in 2001 (USD 60 per person) (Office of the President, National Planning Commission 2004). ODA would account for about 10% of the total national budget if the country were to receive USD 90 per capita. However, national budget documents refer to much lower amounts that translate into a contribution of around 0.5% (Ministry of Finance 2006). The difference can in part be explained by the fact that not all ODA is channelled through the State Revenue Fund but is often channelled directly to receiving institutions.

7.7 CONCLUSION

The PRS for Namibia was formulated with financial and technical assistance from donors, but with the involvement of local stakeholders from government institutions and academia. Subsequent documents, such as the Poverty Reduction Action Programme and the Monitoring Strategy, were to a much greater degree produced locally, although with some guidance by international consultants and some external financial support. The same holds for the formulation of the medium- and long-term development plans that are increasingly prepared by Namibians. These documents are not discrete policy declarations, but interlinked. Vision 2030 refers explicitly to the PRS but identifies additional targets that were not included in the PRS. Progress towards the MDGs is seen as a monitoring instrument that reflects on progress with the implementation of strategies to achieve Vision 2030, and NDP 3 is part of the implementation of Vision 2030 and hence the PRS. In addition, the PMS will provide policy makers with information on progress towards poverty alleviation, but has not yet taken off. The PMS would be strengthened if the government conducted NHIESs every 5 years instead of every 10. The next NHIES would then be due in 2008/09. Since the PRS will turn 10 years shortly, the envisaged poverty conference in 2008 could provide an opportunity to review the strategy and, if necessary, amend and refine it. While the PRS does not refer to a specific time frame, the NPRAP covered the period of NDP 2, namely 2001–2005, implying that it needs to be revised.

The PRS's priorities are by and large reflected in the national budget. However, as the outcomes in the education and health sectors indicate, large amounts of funds allocated to a particular sector are not a sufficient condition for achieving the expected results. The government has acknowledged this and has shifted the focus from financial inputs to the efficient use of public resources and to outputs, as proposed in the PRS.

The PRS, as well as other policy documents, builds on a two-pronged approach. First, the policy package is designed to create an environment conducive for economic growth and employment generation through investment in infrastructure and the productive sectors as well as in education and health. Second, the government has also acknowledged that the first prong alone would not benefit all citizens and has therefore expanded the coverage of the social safety net, in particular through the inclusion of orphans and vulnerable children. The art is to strike the right balance between the two prongs as well as to avoid overstretching the government's financial resources, which continue to a large extent to depend on the export sector and revenue from the SACU pool.

Despite the achievements to date, the existing incidence of poverty suggests that there are still large population groups that do not benefit from the social safety net, or that the net is not always strong enough to prevent people from falling through it into poverty and that economic growth has not created adequate jobs to lift more people out of poverty. It will require a more thorough analysis of the latest NHIES data to identify the root causes of poverty as well as the characteristics of the poor. Such an analysis would ideally inform the poverty conference in 2008 and the review of the PRS.

REFERENCES

Central Bureau of Statistics (2006), *Namibia Household Income and Expenditure Survey – Main Report*, Windhoek: Central Bureau of Statistics.

Government of the Republic of Namibia (1995), *First National Development Plan (NDP1) 1995/1996– 1999/2000*, Windhoek: National Planning Commission.

Government of the Republic of Namibia (2001), *Second National Development Plan (NDP2) 2001/2002–2005/2006*, Windhoek: National Planning Commission.

Ministry of Environment and Tourism, Republic of Namibia (2002), *Namibia Initial National Communication to the United Nations Framework Convention on Climate Change*, Windhoek: Ministry of Environment and Tourism.

Ministry of Finance (2006), *Medium Term Expenditure Framework 2006/07–2008/09*, Windhoek: Ministry of Finance.

Ministry of Health and Social Services (2003), *Namibia Demographic and Health Survey 2000*, Windhoek: Ministry of Health and Social Services.

Ministry of Labour and Social Welfare (2006), *Namibia Labour Force Survey 2004, Report of Analysis*, Windhoek:

Naimhwaka, E. (2007), *Poverty and Inequality in Namibia*, Final Unpublished Draft, Windhoek

Office of the President (2004), *Namibia Vision 2030: Policy Framework for Long-term National Development*, Windhoek: Office of the President.

Office of the President, National Planning Commission (2004), *Namibia 2004 Millennium Development Goals*, Windhoek: Office of the President, National Planning Commission.

Republic of Namibia (1998), *Poverty Reduction Strategy for Namibia*, Windhoek: National Planning Commission.

Republic of Namibia (2002), *National Poverty Reduction Action Programme 2001–2005*, Windhoek: National Planning Commission.

Republic of Namibia (2003), *2001 Population and Housing Census, National Report, Basic Analysis with Highlights*, Windhoek: Central Bureau of Statistics and National Planning Commission.

Republic of Namibia (2004), *The Namibia Informal Economy Survey 2001*, Report of Analysis, Windhoek: Ministry of Labour.

Republic of Namibia (2006), *Preliminary Report: Namibia Household Income and Expenditure Survey 2003/04*, Windhoek: National Planning Commission and Central Bureau of Statistics.

Republic of Namibia, National Planning Commission, Central Bureau of Statistics (2007), *Preliminary National Accounts 2006*, Windhoek: Central Bureau of Statistics.

Schade, K. and E. Naimhwaka (2004), *Public Expenditure Tracking Survey (PETS) and Quantitative Service Delivery Survey (QSDS) – The Education Sector*, Windhoek: Office of the Auditor General.

Schade, K. and J. Ashipala (2004), *Public Expenditure Tracking Survey (PETS) and Quantitative Service Delivery Survey (QSDS) – The Health Sector*, Windhoek: Office of the Auditor General.

Southern African Development Community (not dated), *Regional Indicative Strategic Development Plan*, Gaborone: SADC.

The Namibian, 13 April 2007, The State of the Nation.

United Nations Development Programme (1998), *Namibia Human Development Report 1998*, New York: UNDP.

United Nations Development Programme (1999), *Namibia: Human Development Report 1999*, New York: UNDP.

United Nations Development Programme (2000), *Namibia: Human Development Report 2000/2001*, New York: UNDP.

World Travel and Tourism Council (2006), *Namibia: The Impact of Travel and Tourism on Jobs and the Economy*, London: World Travel and Tourism Council.

CHAPTER 8

COMPARING POVERTY REDUCTION STRATEGIES IN EASTERN AND SOUTHERN AFRICA

Flora Kessy and Arne Tostensen

8.1 INTRODUCTION

The preceding chapters have detailed the poverty profiles of six country cases, and recounted the process leading up to the poverty reduction strategies currently in place. Three of the country cases (Tanzania, Uganda and Zambia) are classified as HIPC countries and, as a result, their poverty reduction strategies have been charted under the guidance and auspices of the Bretton Woods institutions. The remaining three country cases (Botswana, Kenya and Namibia) do not fall under the HIPC umbrella. Consequently, they have formulated poverty reduction strategies of their own volition, largely without direct external influence in the form of conditionalities, i.e. their strategies can be characterised as home-grown.

This concluding chapter provides a comparison of the various country cases along a set of key dimensions. It starts with a section on fundamental differences and similarities, including poverty levels, economic growth performance, inequality trends and unemployment. It goes on to consider two aspects of the respective poverty reduction strategies: substance and process. In terms of substance, the macro-economic regime, including pro-poor growth, is considered, as well as sectoral emphases. In terms of process, the chapter discusses participation and ownership; institutionalisation and implementation arrangements; alignment with budgets; the time perspective and sequencing of interventions; and the role of donors and regional groupings. The conclusion summarises the findings.

8.2 SOME FUNDAMENTALS

From a careful reading of the country case studies it emerges that regardless of their classification as HIPC and non-HIPC, they differ fundamentally only in terms of GDP per capita and level of indebtedness. Although they are not equally poor, all six countries have considerable poverty problems to address within their borders. Their respective poverty headcount ratios are depicted in Table 8.1:

Table 8.1: Poverty Headcount (Percent)

Country	Poverty Headcount
Botswana (non-HIPC)	30 (2005/06)
Kenya (non-HIPC)	46 (2006)
Namibia (non-HIPC)	28 (2005)
Tanzania (HIPC)	36 (2000/01)
Uganda (HIPC)	31 (2005/06)
Zambia (HIPC)	70 (2000)

The table above shows that poverty is a major challenge for all countries. This applies to Botswana as a middle income country with a GDP per capita of USD 3,671 and Namibia as a lower middle income country with a GDP per capita of USD 2,035 as much as it applies to the remaining four countries, whose GDP per capita ranges from USD 427 to 262. With the exception of particularly high poverty rates in Zambia (70 percent) and Kenya (46 percent), the poverty headcount hovers in the 28–36 percent range. It should be noted, however, that the definitions of poverty and the attendant cut-off points vary between the countries. Besides, the data stem from different points in time. Therefore, the figures are strictly speaking not comparable.

In addition to differences in GDP per capita, what sets them apart is the degree of indebtedness.[16] Only three of them are both poor and indebted enough to qualify for HIPC debt relief: Tanzania, Uganda and Zambia. The other three – Botswana, Kenya and Namibia – are perhaps poor or are confronting considerable poverty problems but are not deeply indebted. Indeed, Botswana is a net creditor to the Bretton Woods institutions while Namibia has not borrowed from those institutions at all. Kenya has a debt burden of some magnitude but it is serviceable. The less burdensome debt servicing of the non-HIPC countries presumably means that they have a wider scope of manoeuvrability and are less financially constrained when trying to chart their strategies to redress poverty. By contrast, the HIPCs are experiencing severe financial constraints. In order to benefit from debt relief under the HIPC Initiative they are required to formulate Poverty Reduction Strategy Papers (PRSPs) along the lines suggested by the Bretton Woods institutions and subject to their approval. This chapter is intended to assess the degree to which the diverging constraints have affected the nature and direction of the respective poverty reduction strategies.

The six countries differ in population size. Botswana and Namibia have small populations of only 1.7 and 2 million respectively. At the other end of the spectrum are Tanzania and Kenya with 35 and 34 million, while Zambia and Uganda occupy the middle positions with 12 and 28 million. The small Botswanan population has gone through rapid urbanisation and is currently 60 percent urban, whereas the populations of the other countries are still predominantly rural with Zambia at 67 percent rural, Namibia 67 percent, Tanzania 80 percent, Kenya 60 percent and Uganda 73 percent.

8.3 KEY INDICATORS

The sub-sections below describe developments in key indicators and bring out differences and similarities among the six cases under comparison.

8.3.1 Economic growth

With few exceptions, all six countries have in common fairly high and stable economic growth rates, in some cases over long periods. At one extreme is Botswana, which has enjoyed an annual economic growth rate averaging 6 percent over the four decades since independence

---

[16] The level of indebtedness keeps changing. When reaching the HIPC completion point some countries, e.g. Zambia, have benefited from considerable debt relief, which has eased the burden and made it serviceable in the short term.

in 1966. As such, it is one of the fastest growing economies in the world, certainly in Africa. During the same period, GDP per capita increased tenfold. A fair share of that growth derives from mineral rent and windfall from high diamond prices. But it also stems from prudent management of the economy by the political leadership.

Uganda is also a good performer in terms of economic growth. The economy grew by 6.5 percent annually during the 1990s but has slowed to an average of 5.5 percent per annum since 2000. Sluggish and erratic agricultural growth has kept the overall growth rate down.

In recent years the economic growth rate of Zambia has picked up and averaged 3.9 percent per annum during the 1998–2004 period, and in 2003 and 2004 it climbed to more than 6 percent. Still, agricultural growth has been lagging behind with growth of only 2.6 percent during the 1998–2004 period.

Tanzania has also seen growth rates picking up in recent years. During the period 1996–2000 the economy grew by 4.1 percent annually, and from 2000 until 2006 by 6.2 percent with a peak of 6.8 percent in 2005. The growth rate of agriculture was somewhat lower at 5.1 percent (2001–2005).

Trends in economic growth rates in Kenya started at a high level after independence but fell back until 2000 when a decline of -0.3 percent was recorded. The growth rate picked up after 2002 and has since been on the increase. Agricultural growth has fluctuated over time, partly owing to weather conditions and the movement of world market prices for key export crops such as coffee and tea.

In Namibia the economic growth rate averaged 3.8 percent per year in the 1990–1998 period, increasing to 4.4 percent after 2000. Similarly to Botswana, the mining sector is a major source of growth in the Namibian economy.

8.3.2 Inequality

While economic growth may have resulted in a reduction of poverty, it has also been accompanied by a highly skewed distribution of income. Most of the six countries have registered high Gini coefficients, as shown in Table 8.2 below:

Table 8.2: Inequality: Gini Coefficients

Country	Gini Coefficient
Botswana	0.6 (2005)
Kenya	0.558 (2004)
Namibia	0.7 (1993/94)
Tanzania	0.35 (2000/01)
Uganda	0.428 (2002/03)
Zambia	0.42 (2005)

In Namibia, the skewed income distribution is largely a legacy of the apartheid era before independence, which continues to linger. Botswana's high Gini coefficient means that the poorest 40 percent of the population received 12 percent of the national income, the middle 20 percent earned 29 percent and the richest 20 percent earned 59 percent. In Kenya the high Gini coefficient means that the richest 10 percent of households control more than 42 percent of national income, while the poorest 10 percent control just 0.76 percent. In other words, for every shilling received by a poor person, a rich person gets 56 shillings. Uganda saw its Gini coefficient increase somewhat from 0.365 in 1992/93 to 0.428 in 2002/03. Tanzania experienced a slight rise in income inequality as measured by the Gini coefficient, from 0.34 in 1991/92 to 0.35 in 2000/01. Zambia's economy is still characterised by extreme dualism between rich and poor. Even though inequality has fallen over the past few decades, it still remains well above that of many other low-income countries.

8.3.3 Unemployment

Fairly high economic growth rates have not been accompanied by job generation to the extent one would have expected. The number of new entrants to the labour force far exceeds the number of jobs created in the formal and informal sectors. Although unemployment figures are fraught with methodological problems and prone to error, they nevertheless provide a useful indicator. The unemployment rate in Tanzania was estimated at 12.9 percent in 2003, covering both rural and urban areas, but this is likely to have been an underestimate. Like Tanzania's, the economy of Uganda is predominantly agrarian. Revival of the agricultural sector is therefore the key to employment generation. However, agricultural sector growth in Uganda has been lagging behind other sectors. The same applies to Zambia, where agricultural employment generation has been sluggish.

Botswana faces a serious unemployment problem. Increasing since 2002, unemployment stood at 23.8 percent in 2006, while at the same time there are skill shortages. The problem is above all prevalent among youth in the 15–24 age bracket. Unemployment remains at a high level in Namibia, estimated at 36.7 percent in 2004. Yet, the skills of the workforce do not match labour market requirements. Hence, the informal economy is a last resort for jobseekers. In Kenya, the regional disparities in unemployment rates are considerable, ranging from 6.2 percent in Central Province to 34.7 percent in North Eastern Province.

8.4 DIMENSIONS AND PARAMETERS OF COMPARISON

The countries under comparison find themselves at different stages on the road to poverty reduction and have gone through various revisions of their plans and strategies for achieving this overriding objective. By way of introduction, therefore, it would be helpful to give a tabular overview of the trajectories of the countries concerned as far as document preparation is concerned.

Table 8.3: Overview of Poverty Reduction Strategies and Plans

Country	Major Pre-PRSP Poverty Reduction Plans and Strategies	Post-PRSP Poverty Reduction Plans and Strategies
HIPC Countries		
Tanzania	Vision 2025 (1997); National Poverty Eradication Strategy (1998), surpassed by PRSP in 2001	Poverty Reduction Strategy Paper (PRSP) (2001); revised in 2004 to form the National Strategy for Growth and Reduction of Poverty (2006-2010)
Uganda	Poverty Eradication Action Plan (PEAP), (1997)	PEAP was revised in 2000 to form the Poverty Reduction Strategy Paper for Uganda; PEAP revised again in 2004 to form second generation PRSP in Uganda
Zambia	Rolling National Development Plans, the current one being the Fifth National Development Plan (FNDP) (2006-2010)	Poverty Reduction Strategy Paper (2002). Superseded by the FNDP, which is the current PRS
Non-HIPC Countries		
Botswana	National Development Plans since 1966, Vision 2016, National Policy on Rural Development revised in 2002	Botswana National Poverty Reduction Strategy (BNPRS) 2003. National Development Plan IX (2003–2009)
Kenya	National Poverty Eradication Plan (NPEP) (1999–2015)	Poverty Reduction Strategy Paper (2001–2004) revised in 2003 to form Economic Recovery Strategy for Wealth and Employment Creation (2003–2007)
Namibia	Five-year National Development Plans (NDP), starting with the Transitional National Development Plan, NDP 1 (1995/96 to 1999/2000).	Poverty Reduction Strategy (1998); National Development Plan II (2001/02 to 2005/06), National Poverty Reduction Action Programme (NPRAP); formulation of Vision 2030 in 2005 to complement the NDPs

From the above table we see that among the HIPC countries Uganda made an early start by preparing a PRS already in 1997, before the HIPC initiative was launched. In many ways it is justified to claim that Uganda thereby pre-empted the Bretton Woods institutions and, in effect, provided a 'model' document for poverty reduction that inspired the subsequent PRSPs. Gradually, all HIPC countries moved towards the prescribed PRSP formats. Among the non-HIPC countries Kenya made an early start, even though it was ineligible for HIPC debt relief. Botswana has generally used its national development plans as the reference documents for poverty reduction policies, both before and after the launch of the HIPC initiative. The same applied to Namibia in the pre-HIPC era but afterwards a specific PRS was elaborated.

Mechanisms for the monitoring and periodic review of poverty reduction strategies have been put in place for HIPC and non-HIPC countries alike. The HIPC countries are, in fact, required to submit periodic reviews to the Bretton Woods institutions. Such reviews have led to amendments, such as the incorporation of new elements, some reordering of priorities and the reinforcement of some points. As PRSs have been reviewed, they have been improved upon and become more comprehensive. It is also noteworthy that the review processes have been fairly participatory in nature, albeit variably so.

The review of the first generation PRSP in Tanzania was concluded in 2004, leading in 2005 to a second generation PRSP renamed the National Strategy for Growth and Reduction of Poverty (NSGRP), popularly known under its Kiswahili acronym MKUKUTA. It runs until 2010. The first generation PRSP focused on priority sectors that were likely to have strong poverty reduction impacts while MKUKUTA adopted an outcome-based approach, the underlying idea being that for broad-based success to be achieved, linkages across sectors had to be fostered to ensure a common contribution to the overall objective of reduced outcome poverty. The three expected MKUKUTA outcomes are economic growth and reduction of income poverty; improved quality of life and social wellbeing; and good governance and accountability. However, both generations of strategy have given considerable weight to cross-cutting issues such as HIV and AIDS, gender, environmental protection and conservation, and the role of good governance and accountability.

The second modification of the Ugandan PEAP was made in 2004 to include findings from the latest research studies, second community PPAs and fresh consultations with stakeholders. This second PEAP was organised under five pillars: economic management; production, competitiveness and incomes; security, conflict resolution and disaster management; good governance; and human development. In addition, security and conflict resolution and cross-cutting issues such as HIV and AIDS, environment and gender were added.

The Zambian PRSP was reviewed when a new president came to power in 2002. A Transitional National Development Plan (TNDP) was developed to absorb some elements that had been abolished under the previous incumbent. Signed by the president in October 2002, the TNDP explicitly absorbed the PRSP into its broader framework, with some modifications. The TNDP was linked to the PRSP in three significant ways. First, it shared the overriding poverty reduction theme with the PRSP. Second, it drew heavily on the work of the PRSP working groups by converting the PRSP's chapters into the TNDP format. Third, it encompassed areas not adequately covered by the PRSP, i.e. the consolidated TNDP incorporated the PRSP as a core aspect and added other sectors that had not been included previously.

Botswana's overall reference policy documents as far as poverty reduction is concerned have always been successive National Development Plans, which have served as the framework within which other specific poverty reduction programmes have been designed. The targeted programmes have been many over the years and each of them has been reviewed periodically. But there does not seem to have been an overall review mechanism, except the considerations going into the design of new development plans. It is difficult to ascertain, therefore, in which ways monitoring and review have led to the modification of poverty reduction strategies.

Two years after the preparation of the Kenyan PRSP, the change of government in early 2003 led to policy shifts and a reordering of priorities. The new government prepared the Economic Recovery Strategy for Wealth and Employment Creation (ERS) 2003–2007. The ERS incorporated elements articulated in the PRSP, the government's Action Plan, and in the National Rainbow Coalition (NARC) Election Manifesto. The ERS emphasised economic growth and job creation while at the same time empowering Kenyans through a democratic political atmosphere (good governance) in which all citizens would be free to work hard and engage in productive activities to improve their standard of living.

Namibia has produced successive five-year National Development Plans (NDP) that have been reviewed to include new issues as they arise. For instance, the Second National Development Plan (2001/02 to 2005/06) added objectives not included in its predecessor, such as the reduction of regional disparities, promotion of gender equality, promotion of economic empowerment and combating the further spread of HIV and AIDS. Furthermore, the government has emphasised the need to identify long-term measures to complement the medium-term NDP, from which emerged in 2005 a long-term strategy: Vision 2030.

When comparing poverty reduction strategies it is useful to distinguish between dimensions and parameters that have to do with the *substance and orientation* of strategies, and those that relate to the *process* of formulating and implementing them. While the substantive orientation of the strategies is paramount in terms of policies and priorities, the process aspects are also important because they are instrumental and bear significantly on commitment and implementation so as to avoid slippage and to encourage the recipients to take greater responsibility. We start with a discussion of the substantive elements. Subsequent sections will deal with process aspects.

8.5 MACRO-ECONOMIC FRAMEWORK AND PRO-POOR ECONOMIC GROWTH

It has become a truism that economic growth is a necessary precondition for poverty reduction to be feasible. Moreover, economic growth rates need to be sustained at a consistently high level over a long period of time for a significant dent to be made in the poverty problem. When charting their anti-poverty strategies, most countries have started with economic growth as an overriding goal and have largely succeeded in that endeavour. Annual growth rates in the 6–7 percent bracket have been common in most of the six countries under study. To achieve such high rates they have all striven to get the macro-economic fundamentals right by reducing budget deficits, managing the exchange rate, controlling the money supply, and keeping the inflation rate at single-digit levels. This macro-economic framework – widely known as the 'Washington consensus'– has long been a contentious matter because it was seen as a form of conditionality imposed by the Bretton Woods institutions on the HIPC countries.

The non-HIPC countries were not bound by the same conditionality, which, in theory, gave them scope for alternative frameworks, if not in the fundamentals then at least in the less central elements. As it were, however, the macro-economic framework as reflected in the 'Washington consensus'has proved to be conducive to economic growth when coupled with real sector investments. Furthermore, it appears that the macro-economic frameworks were basically the same in the two groups of countries, thus providing grounds for inferring that the views of the political and economic policy-making elites of the non-HIPC countries had converged with those of the HIPC countries.

Most proponents of economic growth as a priority seem to bank on the 'trickle-down' mechanism to reduce poverty, i.e. that the benefits of economic growth tend to spread throughout society more or less automatically through job creation and rising incomes. Others doubt the effectiveness of the 'trickle-down' mechanism and express concern about the distributional effects of economic growth unless deliberate state interventions are made to ensure a 'fairer' distribution. While not denying that some benefits do accrue to poor people from economic growth, they tend to be meagre and slow in trickling down. Arguments are advanced, therefore, in favour of so-called 'pro-poor growth'.

The discussion about making economic growth pro-poor acknowledges that long-term per capita economic growth is a *necessary* precondition for sustainable poverty reduction.

However, economic growth is not a *sufficient* precondition for poverty reduction. In fact, high rates of economic growth can have differential impacts on income and consumption poverty under different conditions, varying in time and space. Whereas aggregate economic growth over the long term may pull a number of poor people out of poverty through the 'trickle-down' effect, more and more attention is drawn to the pattern and distribution of economic growth among social groups, including the poor. It is increasingly acknowledged that the distributional effects of growth are critical to poverty reduction. That is why the adjective 'pro-poor' is now almost invariably attached to the 'growth' noun in policy debates on poverty reduction. Growth can be defined as being pro-poor if poor households increase their income (or consumption) proportionally more than the non-poor, i.e. the households above the poverty line. Conversely, if growth is negative, the effect is pro-poor (perversely so) if the income or consumption decreases proportionally less for poor households than for the non-poor (Son and Kakwani 2006).

What factors determine the growth patterns – whether they are positive or negative, and whether they are pro-poor or anti-poor? From a pro-poor growth perspective, the key question is whether poor people are able to participate in economic growth processes, or otherwise benefit from them. This may be achieved through direct participation in productive activities, for example through increased real wages, new employment opportunities or increased returns from self-employment. The poor may also benefit indirectly from increased public spending on education, health care, water supplies, etc. or from private transfers made possible by increased revenues from growth. There is also a highly significant inverse statistical relationship between inflation and pro-poor growth. In other words, low inflation is associated with pro-poor growth because high inflation is effectively a tax on the poor.

Empirical findings suggest that inequality affects the pro-poor impact of growth. Rising inequality may cancel out poverty reduction gains stemming from growth in fast-growing countries. In other words, economic growth *per se*, although extremely important, does not explain variations in poverty reduction. Initial inequality and changes in inequality over a growth period are also important factors which may restrict the access by the poor to the growth benefits.

Although the specific policies pursued may differ and exogenous factors affecting growth may vary, there appear to be some robust strategic features. A successful sustainable growth strategy needs, as its foundation, macro-economic stability, well-defined property rights, trade openness, a good investment climate, an attractive incentive framework, well-functioning factor markets, and broad access to infrastructure and education. In addition, policies need to be designed to enable the poor to participate in and benefit from growth. Since labour is the most abundant asset of the poor, it is hardly surprising that the most successful experiences with poverty reduction have occurred where policy has supported the creation of attractive jobs that are accessible to poor households. Given the concentration of poor households in agriculture, making agricultural activities more productive is a key success factor. Improved access to markets and technology, strengthened property rights, and better methods of risk management each have a role to play. A complementary measure is to enable the rural poor to engage in productive off-farm activities and to take advantage of urban employment.

Overall, three pillars seem essential in facilitating private initiative and investment among the non-poor and poor alike: (i) good macro-economic and structural economic policies,

(ii) political stability, and (iii) public investment in physical and human capital (Thorbecke and Mwabu 2006). More specifically, four key elements may be singled out for inclusion in a pro-poor growth strategy: (1) discontinuation of discriminatory policies against rural and agricultural development because most African populations still live in the countryside and derive an income from agriculture, notwithstanding rapid urbanisation; (2) investment in human capital, i.e. education, health, including nutrition, water supplies and sanitation, in order to contribute directly to human welfare and a productive workforce; (3) making markets and public infrastructure accessible for the poor; (4) facilitating the creation of job opportunities for the unskilled poor and investing in enhancing the skills of the unemployed.

Analyses of economic growth processes have produced considerable knowledge about the interface between growth and poverty reduction. Recent theoretical strides based on empirical findings and insights have provided good analyses and *ex post* explanations of the growth–poverty reduction nexus, i.e. why different growth trajectories are more or less poverty reducing. The challenge, however, is to use those theoretical insights to design prescriptive *ex ante* policies that can facilitate economic growth *and* at the same time contribute to poverty reduction in a major way (Gore 2007).

This challenge is formidable because it is not confined to the sphere of analysts and policy-makers. Not only is the task complex in itself, but its challenging nature also arises because poverty reducing policies which entail empowerment of the poor may clash with entrenched power structures and forces whose material interests are threatened. Even if a disinterested poverty reduction policy package were available in a sound technical sense, its adoption and implementation would most likely be resisted by entrenched political and economic elites.

Notwithstanding broad agreement that sustained high rates of economic growth are a prerequisite for making significant progress in poverty reduction, there has been less agreement on the relative emphasis put on economic growth as opposed to expenditure in the social sectors. The latter address the immediate concerns of poor people, whereas endeavours to reinvigorate the economy have a longer gestation period. On the other hand, it has been argued that while social sector spending will no doubt alleviate poverty in the short term, it is unlikely to be sustainable over time without a concomitant upturn in the economy to buttress public expenditure through increased revenue generation. In the absence of economic growth and increased revenue, any country would remain dependent on foreign aid for the implementation of anti-poverty programmes. Social sector spending also runs the risk of creating dependency on handouts and of diverting attention from measures to enable the poor to become self-reliant and fend for themselves.

Before turning to the question of sector emphasis, it is warranted to ask whether the PRS documents of the six studied countries have in fact embraced pro-poor growth policies. Yes, they have to some extent and to varying degrees. Not all strategies are explicit in this regard but implicitly they contain a range of pro-poor growth elements as mentioned above. For example, the heavy emphasis on agricultural growth in all countries is a clear indication that the plight of smallholders is at the centre of attention, assuming that a large share of agricultural investment accrues to smallholders. If concomitant investments are made in infrastructure to facilitate access to markets, e.g. rural access roads, agricultural growth is likely to receive an added boost. Most PRSs also talk about job generation, although it is rarely specified how it is to be achieved. Complementary investment in social sectors such as education, health and water supply also serves to buttress pro-poor growth processes, albeit in a longer-term perspective. That said, none of the PRS documents specifies in any detail policy packages that are designed to promote pro-poor growth. It is rather assumed that pro-poor effects will ensue if the various interventions are implemented.

8.6 SECTOR-SPECIFIC EMPHASES

Poverty reduction strategies are by nature comprehensive in scope and coverage, cutting across the full gamut of sectors and spanning many levels of intervention. It is probably helpful, therefore, to investigate whether certain sectors receive special emphasis and how these sectoral emphases are justified in terms of the expected poverty reduction impact. In the economic growth domain, rejuvenating agriculture presents itself as a sensible priority in all documents with a palpable pro-poor slant. The same applies to infrastructure, especially the type that facilitates agricultural growth, and to labour-intensive tourism that creates new jobs. Capital-intensive mining, on the other hand, will probably not generate pro-poor growth in the short run, even though it could generate revenue to be applied to social spending, as the case of Botswana illustrates. However, the pro-poor growth potential of the productive sectors is often juxtaposed with that of the social sectors. A PRS with a 'welfarist' orientation would be inclined to stress social sectors such as education, health, water supply and sanitation.

Certain sectoral priorities are discernible in the six PRS documents. An overview in tabular form is provided in Table 8.4 below. Although economic growth has been underscored as a pre-requisite for poverty reduction in any poverty reduction strategy, it is evident that the social sectors have received much attention in most strategies. The reason is probably twofold. First, expenditure in the social sectors (education, health, water supply and sanitation) is usually pro-poor and produces direct and immediate benefits for the poor segments of the population. Second, the political need to produce tangible results tends to tempt politicians into social spending which is easily visible and popular among the voters, i.e. there is a populist aspect to such expenditures. Thus, by being held accountable to the voters the political establishment at the same time addresses the challenge of growth distribution.

The relative emphasis on growth and the real sectors of the economy versus the social sectors seems to tilt somewhat in favour of the former in Botswana, Kenya, and Zambia. The poverty reduction strategy in Botswana has three pillars, one being stimulation of economic growth in an environment of macro-economic stability through economic diversification, job creation, income generation, economic empowerment and entrepreneurship. In Kenya, rapid economic growth has been given prominence as the principal means of alleviating poverty and creating employment. The Zambian PRSP emphasised economic growth but its operationalisation was based on a growth promotion analysis that paid scant attention to how policies and investment priorities would create a pro-poor distribution of growth. Livelihood strategies were absent in the PRSP. It was largely assumed that no additional intervention was needed beyond investment in farming, infrastructure and education. Lacking a pro-poor analysis, the informal sector was largely ignored as an important source of new jobs and income for the poor. As a result, the distributional effects of growth were less noticeable than expected. Above all, it did nothing to even out the differential levels of poverty between regions.

Table 8.4: Sectoral Emphases in HIPC and Non-HIPC Countries

Country	Productive Sectors	Social Sectors	Cross-cutting Issues
HIPC Countries			
Tanzania	Agriculture, rural roads	Primary education, health, water, legal and judicial system	Environment, gender HIV and AIDS, good governance
Uganda	Agriculture, roads, environment (land and wetlands)	Education, health, water, justice, law and order)	HIV and AIDS, environment and gender
Zambia	Agriculture, industry, mining, tourism, transport, communication, roads, energy	Education and training, health and nutrition, water and sanitation	Environment, gender and HIV and AIDS, good governance
Non-HIPC Countries			
Botswana	Agriculture, energy, infrastructure	Education, health	HIV and AIDS, gender, environment, and technology (IT)
Kenya	Physical infrastructure (roads, railways and telecommunications, energy), manufacturing (including SMEs), agriculture, tourism and trade	Education, health, water	Environment, water and sanitation, land, information and communications technology, science and technology (HIV and AIDS features under health)
Namibia	Agriculture, tourism, transport, industry – in particular Small and Medium Enterprises (SMEs)	Education, health	

Notwithstanding the above points of departure, in implementing their poverty reduction strategies all countries have made heavy investments in the social sectors and most indicators for reporting progress were developed for the social sectors that could generate immediate benefits for the poor. It may be argued that investment in the productive sectors (agriculture, infrastructure, etc.) is the means whereas the social sector interventions produce the tangible ends of poverty reduction efforts, even though the picture is not as unambiguous in reality. Although the emphasis on economic sectors differs slightly by country, agriculture features in all countries (HIPC and non-HIPC) as a priority sector in predominantly agrarian economies. After all, an overwhelming majority of the population derive their income from agricultural pursuits, even if the contribution of agriculture to overall GDP may compare unfavourably with other sectors. Concomitantly, infrastructure was an item high on the priority list, especially roads.

The emphasis on education, health, water supply and sanitation was notable in all countries. These basic social services are fundamental to the functioning of all households, whether rural or urban. Apart from the justification for allocating major resources to these social sectors, there are secondary effects that, in turn, feed into the productive system and serve to reinforce it in the longer term. Investment in education equips the population with skills and capabilities that can be put to productive use if the economy is able to absorb this labour into productive activities. Similarly, investment in health is not only an end in itself; it is also a means to creating a healthy labour force which, in turn, could provide an input into further growth. In the same vein, water and sanitation are critical in at least two ways. First, the drudgery and time spent on fetching water is reduced so as to free labour for other purposes. Second, clean drinking water and good sanitation contribute to reducing health hazards and preventing disease in order to keep the population healthy.

Social safety nets to assist the extremely poor, the destitute and particularly vulnerable groups were only adopted in Botswana and Namibia. In Namibia, labour-intensive public works were seen as the main safety net, complemented by the strengthening of the existing grant-based transfer programmes. In Botswana, a number of social safety nets have been in operation, including social allowance and assistance programmes involving support in cash and kind, as well as the Destitutes Policy as revised in 2002.

Environment, gender, and HIV and AIDS featured in all countries as cross-cutting issues. Information and communications technology features as a cross-cutting concern only in the Botswanan and Kenyan strategies.

Are PRSs with pro-poor growth and 'welfarist' emphases, respectively, contradictory in nature? Not necessarily. Owing to political pressures the social sectors are often given some prominence. As long as public budgets are sustainable by collected revenues stemming from high growth rates and a broad revenue base, investment in the social sectors may in fact be reinforcing the growth processes and underpinning the legitimacy of the PRS in question. It may even be justified to use aid money to finance social sector spending in an interim period as a bridging operation. The problem that might arise and exacerbate the underlying tension between growth and 'welfarist' emphases to the point of creating contradiction is threefold. First, public revenues may be insufficient to sustain social sector spending over a long time. Second, social sector expenditure may unintentionally create dependency among the poorest on handouts and subsidies. Third, the magnitude of social expenditure may be too large compared to investment in directly productive activities and thus undermine long-term sustainable growth, pro-poor or not.

As mentioned above, the process aspects are not only an explicit conditionality within the HIPC framework, they are considered instrumental in creating ownership at the recipient end. In the subsequent sections various process aspects will be discussed in some detail.

8.7 OWNERSHIP AND PARTICIPATION

In order to promote ownership and the effective implementation and monitoring of poverty reduction strategies, extensive consultation involving a wide range of stakeholders from the national to community levels is crucial. In this regard, it is worth noting that participation can range from token consultation through genuine expression of opinion to deep involvement with real influence on the outcome. The analysis of the consultative process in the HIPC countries revealed mixed results, with Zambia and Uganda engaging in a wider consultative process compared to Tanzania. In Zambia, the consultation seemed extensive, involving the full gamut of stakeholders: the cabinet, the legislature, government bodies, the private sector, academia, donors, civil society organisations (CSOs) and the provinces. In Tanzania, on the other hand, little or no involvement of some of these bodies was noted. The process was rushed, and consultations were limited to a small group of donors, internationally linked NGOs and government technocrats – a group labelled the 'iron triangle' (see chapter two). During the formulation of the full PRSP some community-based organisations were invited to participate in the process, but it is difficult to ascertain to what extent the views and concerns of the people consulted outside the 'iron triangle' were included in the final PRSP document.

What is apparent from the Zambian and Tanzanian processes (notwithstanding the extensive consultations in Zambia) is that the voices of the poor were not echoed in the resulting PRSP documents. Even when the consultations occurred at the provincial/regional level, the participants were drawn from the provincial/regional leadership, district administrators, a few sector experts in agriculture, education and health, and representatives of CSOs, with limited effective participation of community leaders and community-based organisations. In Uganda, although the formulation of the original PEAP in 1997 had limited community involvement, the revised PEAP (2000) which was submitted to the World Bank and the IMF as the PRSP document included the voices of the poor through consultations with communities when undertaking the first Participatory Poverty Assessment (PPA). The PPA in Tanzania was done after the inception of PRSP.

The involvement of CSOs has been characterised as vivid and vibrant in Zambia compared to Uganda and Tanzania. The formation of an umbrella organisation – Civil Society for Poverty Reduction (CSPR) – and of PRSP working groups composed of CSOs in Zambia epitomised heavy CSO involvement in contrast to the other two HIPC countries. Nevertheless, even when CSOs were engaged, their involvement might have been reactive rather than proactive with limited chances of real influence on the substantive policy issues at stake.

With the exception of CSOs in Botswana and Namibia, overall participation by civil society stakeholders in the PRS processes of non-HIPC countries is also noteworthy. The Kenyan PRSP was the product of broad-based and inclusive consultations, which took place at the national, regional, district and divisional levels throughout the country. The process included all stakeholder categories with special attention being paid to civil society, vulnerable groups (women, youth, pastoralists, and people with disabilities) and the private sector. In addition, the preparation of the PRSP also benefited from the PPA studies conducted in ten districts to document the voices of the poor with regard to participation, inclusion and ownership of development programmes and projects and in prioritising activities directly affecting their well-being. Notably, the voices of street children, people with disabilities, pastoral communities, unemployed youth, farmers, traders, *jua kali* (informal) artisans, the private sector, fishing communities, urban slum dwellers, coastal communities, women, local leaders, professionals, local administration and government ministries were echoed in the PPAs.

According to a survey conducted by the Botswana Institute for Development Policy Analysis (BIDPA) in 2005, three-quarters of the respondents indicated that the BNPRS was really participatory when it was formulated, as house-to-house surveys were conducted by social workers to profile the poor. However, the same study showed that most non-state agents, especially civil society organisations, were not involved. The involvement by civil society organisations was perceived not as having been 'genuinely participatory' but rather as 'reactively consultative'. In Namibia, the formulation of the PRS was built on a poverty assessment by external experts and a committee set up for the preparation of the Copenhagen Social Summit in 1995. The committee included government institutions as well as the Namibian Non-Governmental Forum, the Council of Churches of Namibia and two Namibian research institutions (University of Namibia and the Namibian Economic Policy Research Unit). The team preparing the PRS also worked closely with World Bank experts and government officials in producing background papers for the strategy. The committee was consulted and commented on drafts rather than actively driving the process. Overall, the active participation of civil society in the formulation of the poverty reduction strategies in Botswana and Namibia remained limited except for the research institutions.

Albeit to varying degrees, it may be concluded that participation in and ownership of the process leading to the formulation of poverty reduction strategies were unprecedented in HIPC and non-HIPC countries alike. Of the six country cases, Kenya showed the highest level of participation in the preparation of its PRSP and the meticulous inclusion of the voices of vulnerable groups in the process. It is also in the Kenyan PRSP and to a lesser extent in Tanzania's that private sector participation was notable. Generally, it can be assumed that the broader and deeper the participation, the stronger the legitimacy of and support for the PRS document amongst the population at large.

8.8 INSTITUTIONALISATION AND IMPLEMENTATION

Poverty reduction is a major challenge that requires a long time horizon to be successful. Therefore, the efforts towards reaching that objective need to be institutionalised. Furthermore, the PRS documents that spell out the policies to be pursued and the actions to be taken need to be implemented and carefully monitored with a view to documenting results. Such institutionalisation means grounding the endeavour within the government machinery, i.e. in government departments in line ministries up to those dealing with economic affairs and planning, and further up to higher echelons such as the President's or Vice President's Office to provide political clout and priority. In Tanzania, the Poverty Eradication Department in the Vice President's Office was mandated to oversee the implementation of PRSP activities and produce and disseminate annual progress reports covering progress in priority sectors and on cross-cutting issues. In Uganda, the Ministry of Finance, Planning and Economic Development oversees the implementation of PEAP and the monitoring and evaluation of PEAP is the responsibility of the National Integrated M&E Strategy (NIMES) in the Prime Minister's office. In the third HIPC country, Zambia, the Ministry of Finance and National Planning (MoFNP) coordinated the preparation of the PRSP through a specially established unit headed by a consultant coordinator. The unit was subsequently absorbed into the Planning and Economic Management Department (PEMD) of the MoFNP. The PEMD coordinated and monitored the implementation of the PRSP and also managed the preparation of the Fifth National Development Plan, which in 2006 superseded the previous PRSP.

A Multi-Sectoral Committee on Poverty Reduction, comprising representation from within and outside government, was established in Botswana to oversee the preparation and implementation process and to ensure its continuity. In addition, early in 2005 a Poverty Reduction Programme Advisor was attached to the Ministry of Finance and Development Planning to work with other ministries and stakeholders to help them sharpen the anti-poverty components of their programmes. In Kenya, a Commission for Poverty Eradication was established through a presidential appointment to oversee the implementation of the plan. In addition, the Poverty Eradication Unit was established in the Department of Development Coordination, Office of the President to oversee the implementation of pilot projects. After the 2002 elections a new government took over and launched the Economic Recovery Strategy for Wealth and Employment Creation (ERS) 2003–2007 and put the Ministry of Planning and National Development in charge of implementation. To oversee the implementation of Namibia's National Poverty Reduction Action Programme (NPRAP) and publish reports on its implementation, a Poverty Reduction Secretariat was established within the National Planning Commission.

Based on an appropriate institutional placement, monitoring and evaluation plans were developed and put in place in order to ensure that the implementation of PRS policies was kept on course and the desired results well documented. This was noted for all six countries under study. Monitoring involved the tracking of key indicators over time and space with a view to recording what changes had taken place in terms of the selected indicators. The purpose was to assess the impact on poverty of the policies and interventions laid down in PRS documents. Thus, the monitoring system was expected to provide the basic input data for evaluating the PRS as a whole or its constituent programme components and policies.

When drafting the PRSPs for HIPC countries, thorough poverty analyses were expected to underpin them and to serve as baselines from which to measure progress. However, dedicated surveys were not always undertaken for the specific purposes of PRS formulation. Instead, one often had to rely on existing data sources such household budget surveys, population censuses, and demographic and health surveys to set baselines, progress indicators and targets. In most cases these data were not collected at the desirable time and did not conform to the specific needs of a PRS, especially non-income poverty indicators. For instance, most Household Budget Survey data have a 5–10 year time span, whereas most PRSs had a duration of three years. This data deficiency or inadequacy was also apparent in non-HIPC countries. It is worth noting, however, that apart from the use of the mentioned large data sets, the poverty analyses also drew on country poverty assessments by the World Bank (Zambia), PPAs in Kenya and Uganda and other location-specific studies.

Working groups were convened to ensure public participation in the formulation process but they have also been used for monitoring and evaluation purposes. This is clearly evident in the three HIPC country experiences. In Zambia, there were eight working groups, each addressing a specific sector. In Tanzania the working groups were organised by theme: the Routine Data Group under the President's Office; Regional Administration and Local Governments; the Survey and Census Groups under the National Bureau of Statistics; the Research and Analysis Working Group overseen by the President's Office; Planning and Privatisation, in collaboration with an independent research outfit, Research on Poverty Alleviation (REPOA); and the Dissemination Group under the Vice President's Office. In Uganda, the National Integrated M&E Strategy (NIMES) has a National Coordination Committee (NCC) accountable to the Technical Implementation Coordination Committee, which comprises three working groups: spatial/geographical information systems, district information systems, and research and evaluation. Sector working groups have also been formed in Kenya but no such working groups exist in Botswana and Namibia.

Linkage with the MDGs has been apparent in Botswana and Namibia through these countries' Vision documents. The MDGs are integrated into two Botswanan strategies – Vision 2016 and the current National Development Plan, although Vision 2016 is more ambitious than the MDGs. The Namibian Vision 2030 from 2005 regards the implementation of the MDGs as one strategy for achieving the sub-vision of poverty reduction. For Tanzania, Uganda and Zambia, linking the poverty reduction strategies with the MDGs has been done thoroughly in the second generation of PRSPs. Kenya's Vision 2030, launched in late 2006, makes a superficial reference to the MDGs but the economic and social pillars implicitly seek to achieve these goals.

8.9 ALIGNMENT WITH BUDGETS

A critical feature in the implementation of poverty reduction strategies is their alignment with annual national budgets. In the HIPC countries, an improvement in this regard was notable from the second year of implementation. By then, these countries had introduced financial management and accountability tools such Medium-Term Expenditure Frameworks (MTEF) and Activity-Based Budget (ABB) systems. In countries such as Zambia, the goals in the PRSP were clearly linked to budgetary resource availability. In preparing provincial and sectoral budgets, planning officers were expected to refer to the PRSP for broad policy goals, programmes and targets. For capital expenditure, reference would be made to the Public Investment Programme (PIP). Expenditure ceilings were established that broadly reflect priorities and available resources in the medium term.

In Tanzania, the alignment of budgets/resources with PRSP milestones was ensured in the priority sectors, and Public Expenditure Reviews (PER) of the priority sectors have been conducted. However, given the capacity constraints and the short time frame for implementation, there were concerns that already existing social poverty programmes without adequate analytical underpinning might be selected just to show some measurable targets. The introduction of the Poverty Action Fund (PAF) in 1997 in Uganda and its subsequent implementation plan is a best practice that incorporates sector planning and allocations, thereby increasing the effectiveness of pro-poor spending. The PAF is regarded as a 'virtual fund' because it is part and parcel of the national budget and designed to contribute directly to poverty reduction. This part of the budget is given special treatment in that its share of the total budget has been rising, it is protected from within-year budget cuts, and it is subjected to much stricter reporting and monitoring requirements than other parts of the budget. PAF has been challenged, however, due to the perceived distortion of budget allocations towards specific social sectors which are favoured by donors, reduced flexibility in the budgeting process, and the concentrated deployment of scarce monitoring resources at the expense of other components of the national budget.

In the three HIPC countries, increased external aid inflows are in evidence. The formulation of a PRSP not only released debt relief from the HIPC facility of the World Bank and the IMF. It also provided a stamp of policy approval that prompted other donors to contribute towards PRSP implementation. However, despite increased volumes of external aid inflows, aid management has been weak, thereby adversely affecting effectiveness. Key weaknesses include lack of capacity to implement PRSPs; unclear procedures regarding how best to mobilise, receive, plan/budget and manage external resources; inappropriate systems of monitoring programme/project implementation and consequently inability to determine the level of impact; and weak coordination between government departments in aid management. Nevertheless, as the PRSP implementation processes unfolded, efforts were made to rectify some of the weaknesses. The Paris Declaration of 2005 led to new efforts to harmonise and align aid modalities with the systems of recipients. Agreed principles of development partnership were set out in the Tanzania Assistance Strategy (TAS) and the TAS Action Plan, the Independent Monitoring Group (IMG), and later a new Joint Assistance Strategy for Tanzania (JAST). With the adoption of cluster-based implementation of the second generation PRSP (NSGRP) in Tanzania, the government budget has been realigned so that it is consistent with the NSGRP clusters. This is being done through cluster-based expenditure programming and a rolling Strategic Budget Allocation System (SBAS) for the local government level in addition to government ministries, departments and agencies. Under this arrangement, direct interventions for NSGRP implementation are assured a certain amount of resources in the budget which for 2006 was estimated at 48 percent.

Similar joint assistance strategies have been elaborated for Zambia and Uganda, the Uganda Joint Assistance Strategy (UJAS) in 2005 and the Joint Assistance Strategy for Zambia (JASZ) in early 2007, both with a view to enhancing aid effectiveness, strengthening accountability and building mutual trust, and eventually to reducing dependency.

Alignment of poverty reduction strategies with national budgets was also noted in non-HIPC countries. Kenya earmarked considerable proportions of the budget for poorer regions. In 2003, the government of Kenya ring-fenced poverty-related expenditures and ministries are required to conduct annual public expenditure reviews and reprioritise their expenditures with the poor in mind. The poverty maps prepared by the Central Bureau of Statistics have also greatly informed government allocations of devolved funds, so that poorer regions get larger allocations that are more in proportion to poverty indices.

Overall, the studied poverty reduction strategies could be seen essentially as a medium-term mechanism for funding priority areas and sectors that have the highest impact on poverty reduction. A notable difference is seen in Botswana, where its poverty reduction strategy is rather the successive general development plans. The current expenditure framework is the Ninth National Development Plan.

8.10 Time perspective and sequencing of interventions

Timeliness and the appropriate sequencing of interventions are essential for the effective implementation of PRSPs. The findings from the country case studies are mixed in this regard, even though the time that has elapsed in all HIPC countries has been too short (only three years) for achieving and measuring results in terms of indicators. Many indicators were focused mainly on input and output rather than outcome and impact. Furthermore, there were delays in implementing the PRSPs, in some countries (Kenya and Zambia) due to changes in political leadership. In Zambia, the PRSP was to last from 2002–2003. However, in January 2002, President Mwanawasa instructed the Ministry of Finance to develop a Transitional National Development Plan (TNDP) (2002–2005) as a temporary measure pending the completion of a new five-year plan. The TNDP was adopted in late 2002, and explicitly absorbed the PRSP into its broader framework, with some modifications.

Only the Botswana National Poverty Reduction Strategy is reported not to be time bound as it only provides a framework within which an array of poverty reduction programmes are implemented. The NDP is a framework for sequencing and prioritising poverty reduction interventions.

8.11 International funding and the role of regional groupings

The role of international partnership in the PRS processes can be looked at from two different angles. On the one hand, the PRSP processes were driven by the Bretton Woods institutions and thus the donors had an inherent stake in their formulation. On the other hand, the budget processes of the majority of countries that qualify for HIPC debt relief are donor driven. Thus, the involvement of the donors from the outset in PRSP formulation is clear, given their expected funding contributions. It was observed in Zambia, for example, that in the initial years of PRSP implementation it was widely acknowledged in government circles that the USD 1.2 billion PRSP budget could not be funded from domestic sources and that this amount would largely be funded by donors. The PRSP document was quite explicit about this: 'most of the existing domestic revenue will remain committed to running government, with hardly any room left for spending on PRSP programmes beyond those that are already running'.

Donor dependency has also been high in Tanzania and Uganda, despite significant commitment by the government. The Tanzanian PRSP document indicated the financial envelope to be 70 percent domestic and 30 percent international. However, since alignment and harmonisation of government and donors with PRSP milestones was not fully achieved, capturing that planned percentage from the partners has been difficult. Nonetheless, huge support from development partners is evident in the development budgets compared to the recurrent budgets, as indicated in various sector Public Expenditure Reviews. The Ugandan government's commitment is apparent in the establishment and operation of PAF. However, several caveats warrant mention with regard to donor dependence: (i) donor commitment to PRSP-related expenditure might cause neglect of non-PRSP activities in the medium term; (ii) the unpredictable nature of aid flows might lead to PRSP budgets running short of expected funds; and (iii) donor interests may not be fully in line with PRSP milestones and may have a disruptive effect.

Botswana is one of the few African countries that never subscribed to a World Bank Structural Adjustment Programme (SAP), and is actually one of the only two African countries that are net creditors of the Bretton Woods institutions. Hence, external assistance is playing a very limited role in the development efforts of Botswana. In this sense, Botswana's poverty reduction strategy is home grown without submission to the conditionalities of the World Bank and the IMF. In Namibia, budget allocations have largely reflected the priorities set out in the PRS, with social sectors (education and health) and transport and infrastructure receiving a major chunk of the budget. The PRS acknowledges that the financial resources of government are limited while poverty reduction requires additional resources. The strategy, therefore, emphasised smarter spending as an approach to achieving better outcomes with the same resources.

In Kenya, the preparation of the NPEP that preceded the preparation of the PRSP was home grown, after the government's realisation that poverty could not just be addressed by high growth. Although Kenya prepared a PRSP, it is not classified as a HIPC country. Consequently, no debt cancellation resulted from Kenya's preparation of a PRSP. Besides, for more than two decades the country has not been receiving any budgetary support owing to the governance concerns of the donor community over the allocation and utilisation of public resources. Still, the donors did contribute to the preparation of the PRSP by financing the consultative process. Notwithstanding donor reservations about governance, Kenya continues to enjoy support from various international sources, most of which support poverty reduction through the implementation of targeted projects and programmes.

The countries under study are members of multiple regional groupings. Notable is the Southern African Development Community (SADC), of which all six countries are members except Kenya. The East African Community (EAC) comprises Kenya, Tanzania and Uganda. Other regional groupings include the Common Market for Eastern and Southern Africa (COMESA) (Kenya, Uganda, Zambia); the Southern African Customs Union (Botswana and Namibia); the Cross Border Trade Initiative (Kenya, Namibia, Tanzania, Uganda, Zambia); the Indian Ocean Rim Association for Regional Cooperation (Kenya and Tanzania); and the Intergovernmental Authority on Development (IGAD) (Kenya and Uganda). It has sometimes been argued that such regional groupings could play a role in poverty reduction. There is no doubt a case for regional initiatives on poverty reduction, but only indirectly. The subsidiarity principle should be applied, meaning that activities should be carried out at the level where they stand the best chance of being most effective. Regional ventures can contribute to facilitating economic growth in a variety of ways that transcend national borders. Building physical infrastructure linking states through grids of transport and energy is vital. Regional groupings are also instrumental in dismantling tariff and non-tariff barriers and establishing trade regimes conducive to growth and regional integration, and to poverty reduction as a spin-off. Policy environments at the member state level can be harmonised to a certain extent through regional consultation but at the end of the day member states are sovereign in determining what policy packages are best tailored to their national circumstances.

8.12 Conclusion

The comparison of poverty reduction strategies in HIPC and non-HIPC countries has revealed that there are more commonalities than differences. The HIPC countries have been subjected to certain conditionalities by the Bretton Woods institutions on account of their vulnerable situation of indebtedness, which gave them little choice but to succumb. It seems, however, that the non-HIPC countries that elaborated strategies of their own volition have adopted perspectives very similar to those in the HIPC category. It can be argued, therefore, that a convergence is discernible between HIPC and non-HIPC countries with regard to both substance and approach when producing PRS documents. The macro-economic frameworks of both categories conform largely to the so-called 'Washington consensus', notwithstanding some nuances. It might even be justified to argue that an epistemic community has emerged internationally and in the Eastern and Southern African regions with regard to the economic fundamentals that need to be put in place for poverty reduction to be feasible.

There are also similarities with regard to sector emphasis. In the interest of pro-poor growth the agricultural sector has been singled out for special attention, combined with infrastructural investment to buttress access to markets for agricultural produce. Even in Botswana and Namibia, where agriculture is less significant in the economy, agriculture – including animal husbandry – is given priority, mainly because a sizeable proportion of the population derives an income from such pursuits. The labour-intensive tourism sector is also of great importance, albeit variably so. Mining is particularly important in Botswana and Namibia (and to some extent in Tanzania and Zambia), not as a vehicle for direct poverty reduction but rather as a source of state revenue to fund social sector investment.

Notwithstanding an emphasis on economic growth as a precondition for poverty reduction, all countries – whether HIPC or non-HIPC – have made massive investments in the social sectors. While this 'welfarist' inclination is partly driven by political considerations of a populist brand, it responds directly to the needs of the poor. Social spending also makes economic sense and will reinforce efforts to promote growth in the longer term because an educated and healthy workforce is a key factor to achieving further growth. Perhaps with the exception of Botswana, where a significant proportion of its small population has been receiving transfers from the state for a long time, the expenditures on the social sectors appear not to be uncomfortably burdensome as long as economic growth rates are maintained at a high level. However, there will always be tension between different expenditure priorities.

All six countries are also similar in respect of the process criteria, although ranging from genuinely participatory (Kenya) to token consultative (Botswana). In this regard it is interesting to note that these two extremes are found within the non-HIPC category. The three HIPC countries generally underwent a participatory PRSP formulation process. It is believed that these processes have produced indigenous ownership of and commitment to the implementation of the respective strategies. Broad participation has created initial legitimacy among the population. Whether this legitimacy will wane or remain ultimately depends on the implementation of the strategies. If the poor fail to see tangible improvements in their daily lives the legitimacy will dwindle, regardless of the status at inception.

REFERENCES

Gore, C. (2007), 'Which Growth Theory is Good for the Poor?' *European Journal of Development Research*, Vol. 19, No. 1, pp. 30–48.

Son, H.H. and N. Kakwani (2006), *Global Estimates of Pro-Poor Growth*, Brasilia: UNDP International Poverty Centre, Working Paper No. 31.

Thorbecke, E. and G. Mwabu (2006), *Research Contributions of the AERC Poverty Project*, Nairobi: African Economic Research Consortium (AERC) Research News.

INDEX

LaVergne, TN USA
19 August 2009
155111LV00001B/115/P

9 789987 080069